"In *Mesa of Sorrows* one of our most subtle and daring borderlands historians plumbs an old story swollen with mystery and pain. Ingeniously pivoting back and forth across different centuries, James Brooks braids together insights from wildly different perspectives in order to fathom a cold morning in 1700 when Hopis massacred Hopis. An unsettling and deeply illuminating meditation on violence, belonging, and the porous boundary between present and past."

—Brian DeLay, author of *War of a Thousand Deserts:*
Indian Raids and the U.S.–Mexican War

MESA OF SORROWS

ALSO BY JAMES F. BROOKS

*Captives and Cousins: Slavery, Kinship, and
Community in the Southwest Borderlands*

*Confounding the Color Line:
The Indian-Black Experience in North America*

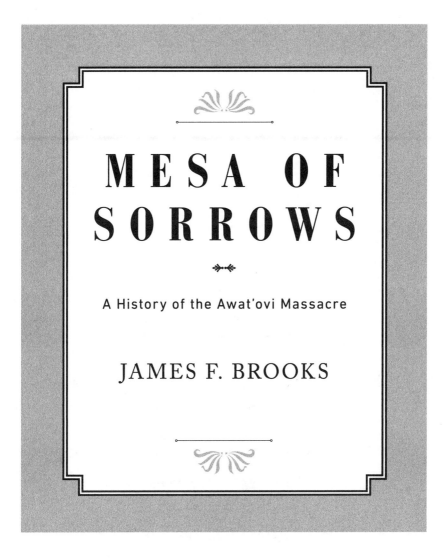

MESA OF SORROWS

A History of the Awat'ovi Massacre

JAMES F. BROOKS

W. W. NORTON & COMPANY

Independent Publishers Since 1923

New York • London

For information about permission to reproduce selections from this book,
write to Permissions, W. W. Norton & Company, Inc.,
500 Fifth Avenue, New York, NY 10110

For information about special discounts for bulk purchases, please contact
W. W. Norton Special Sales at specialsales@wwnorton.com or 800-233-4830

Manufacturing by Berryville Graphics
Book design by Ellen Cipriano
Production manager: Anna Oler

ISBN 978-0-393-06125-3

W. W. Norton & Company, Inc.
500 Fifth Avenue, New York, N.Y. 10110
www.wwnorton.com

W. W. Norton & Company Ltd.
Castle House, 75/76 Wells Street, London W1T 3QT

1 2 3 4 5 6 7 8 9 0

For those who survived. For those who did not.
For those who bear the weight.

CONTENTS

1.

2.

3.

4.

5.

6.

CONTENTS

MESA OF
SORROWS

*. . . the woes that come on men whose city is taken; men slain
and city wasted by fire, their children and low-girdled women
taken into captivity.*

—*THE ILIAD*, BOOK IX, 592–594

The past is never dead. It's not even past.

—WILLIAM FAULKNER, *REQUIEM FOR A NUN*

1

A Gate Unguarded

---

*The women and maidens you take; the men and
old women you may kill.*

—TA'POLO, CHIEF OF AWAT'OVI, 1700

I had thought about the bodies, but not about the bones. They weren't a lot, but they drew the eye. One could hardly take a step without the crunch of a ceramic sherd underfoot, but now I stepped even more carefully. Bleached white with exposure to sun and wind, just a few lay scattered on the sage-covered mounds of the ruins, a splinter of ulna here, what seemed a fragment of cranium a few steps farther along. Until the site had been fenced, sheep grazed the run of Antelope Mesa. Maybe these were sheep. If not, it seemed ironic that so many people's remains rested in tidy curatorial boxes in the Peabody Museum at Harvard University, while these, perhaps their own brothers and sisters, mothers and fathers, were strewn across fallen walls and houses of the High Place of the Bow Clan.

As my guide and I walked the site, we discussed how, although descendants of the victims might today wish to see their distant relatives repatriated from Cambridge and reburied in their former home, the larger, diverse Hopi community harbored doubts. Their proper handling posed an unexplored challenge. The Hopi Cultural Preservation Office bears responsibility for balancing the past with the present, the wishes of the remnant surviving clans, and the cultural integrity of the Hopi nation. As recently as the 1990s, the tribe had contemplated opening the ancient pueblo and its seventeenth-century Franciscan mission for public visitation and interpretation. That would provide an opportunity for Hopis to render their history in a location under tribal control and relieve the burden of tourist visitation on living Hopi towns. But when the prospectus, prepared in consultation with archaeologists from Arizona State University, came up for public comment, objections from descendants of those who died at Awat'ovi foreclosed further consideration. For them it remained an open wound of memory and sorrow, of an event distant in time while still immediate in meaning.

After several hours in the winds that leapt over the rimrock from the Jeddito Valley, we snaked our way back through the sagebrush and cholla and barbwire livestock trap and returned to the dusty SUV. We had walked each precinct of the site, the ancient Western Mound, the two plazas, the Eastern (and later, Colonial) Mounds, the tumbled stone walls of Mission San Bernardo de Aguatubi and its convento, and the mysterious kiva depressions. Its twenty-five rolling acres seemed stunning in their expanse—certainly the largest town in the Southwest when Spaniards stumbled upon it in 1540—and yet terribly intimate in their closer details. Vaguely traced by remaining lines of sandstone masonry, these were storage rooms and milling rooms and cooking rooms and living rooms, and subterranean places of worship. Nearly five centuries of history lay beneath these low rises, some twenty

San Bernardo Polychrome Sherd.

to thirty feet of human striving and loving, hunger and want, sex and death. A trained eye would see the sweep of the Hopi ceramics sequence lying scattered on the surface—from the earliest Kayenta Black-on-Whites through the local Jeddito and Awatovi Black-on-Yellows to the splendid artistry of Sikyatki Polychromes, and finally the more crudely fashioned San Bernardo Polychrome, the style attendant to the sixty-one years (1629–1680) when the Franciscan Order held sway on the mesa. A half-millennium of history and artistry in the glance of an eye.

This much I knew. Fortress Awat'ovi, the easternmost pueblo village on Antelope Mesa, Arizona, had stood for centuries as the eastern gateway to the whole Hopi landscape. Long renowned for its martial strength, in the autumn of 1700 it fell easily to an early dawn assault, not by traditional enemies like the nomadic Utes or Navajos, but to a combined force of Hopis from neighboring villages. Its assailants apparently gained entrance under cover of darkness through an unguarded gate in the fortified masonry wall that encompassed the village. They encountered little resistance, for most of the people of Awat'ovi had spent the night in their kivas practicing traditional, yet perhaps unorthodox, rituals. Trapped therein, their attackers rained crushed red peppers, flaming torches, and arrows upon the victims. Those who were spared were taken captive and marched westward toward the other Hopi pueblos. At a place later known as "Mas'tcomo-mo" (Ghost Mound) many were tortured and slain; some few women and children survived to be married or adopted into their attackers' villages. Balance had been restored, according to most Hopi accounts.

Yet the enigma remains—what provoked such gruesome internecine violence? How could the massacre have "restored balance?" Why were some allowed to live? Who collaborated in leaving the gate unguarded? What role did the recent return of Franciscan missionaries to the village play in the catastrophe? Why does this account resonate with even more ancient tales of violence in the pre-Columbian era? Why do Hopis, archaeologists, historians, and anthropologists each contend to know and explain the significance of that moment in the late autumn of 1700? What do the event, the place, and the people involved have to tell us about communal violence in the past, and in today's world? Does a species of hope exist somewhere amid the rubble and lost lives of Awat'ovi Pueblo?

To an outsider attuned to the Western classical tradition, the annihilation of Awat'ovi evokes the destruction of another ancient city, Priam's great and windy Ilium, "strong-built Troy." That city's fall in the twelfth century B.C. provided the foundation for the Western humanistic tradition. No less has the fall of Awat'ovi formed one substance of Hopi, and perhaps by extension, Puebloan, worldviews. The legendary anthropologist Ruth Benedict, writing in the 1930s, borrowed from the Classics in describing Puebloan peoples as "Apollonian," in their values of order, control of the senses, and humility in self and behavior. The crisis at Awat'ovi sculpted the very core of these values, as the epic of Troy provided the rootstock for Western ideas about honor, shame, and the ruinous consequences of pride.

While the destruction of an entire city— its residents either slain or in bondage—in retribution for Paris's abduction of Helen, seems barbarous and extreme today, Paris's violation of the sacred laws of hospitality would have made perfect sense to Homer's audience. Honor between men served as the bond that held life together and prevented "society from flying apart into lawlessness and savagery." So, too, did the sense of *koyaanisqatsi* (chaos, or moral corruption) emerging at Awat'ovi offer only one solution: regeneration of an ideal social order through obliterating violence.

Tuhu'osti, autumn, brought a swirling cold wind across Antelope Mesa that night. The mesa's sandstone escarpment loomed for several miles above the sandy bottoms of Jeddito Wash in what would become Arizona, and its few scrubs of sagebrush and stunted junipers did little to break the course of the cold front. A new moon cast dim light, catching the wisps of smoke as they were torn from the rooftops of Awat'ovi Pueblo. Looming three masonry stories in height, and home to several hundred people, it had been founded centuries before by members of the powerful Aawatngyam (Bow Clan).

Once, six other villages had crowned this mesa's eastern rim, frontier outposts in an ancient Pueblo Indian world that spoke many languages while sharing some ceremonial and cultural customs and contesting others. Five centuries had passed since the grand experiment at Chaco Canyon, Yupköyvi (the Place Beyond the Horizon) in the Hopi tongue, drew to a close and the *hisat'sinom* (those who lived long ago) had journeyed in search of Tuuwanasavi, "the earth-center." These migrations had themselves taken centuries, leaving their traces in many places, until gradually the clans came together again at Situqui (Flower Butte), the four mesas of the Hopi world. Each clan brought new ideas, new ceremonies, new artistic expressions, and new villages had again been built of stone and adobe on mesa tops and sheltering slopes.

Now only Awat'ovi remained on Antelope Mesa. From the valley below, the village seemed to sleep. But an owl perched on the parapets of the Franciscan mission church at Awat'ovi would have seen signs of life.

From subterranean ceremonial chambers known as kivas there extended tall pine ladders, vaguely lit by the flicker of hearth fires within. Late autumn was the season of the *wuwutcim wimi* ceremonies, wherein the Tao (Singers), Ahl (Horns), Kwan (Agaves), and Wuwutcim societies initiated adolescent boys into tribal knowledge and manhood. Even more than the matrilineal clans, these four kiva societies were a man's primary allegiance. Lasting more than two weeks and including collective rabbit hunts, shrine visits, dances, feasts, and nightlong singing in the kivas, the *wuwutcim wimi* had, for centuries, ensured the transfer of sacred knowledge across generations of men.

This night was, perhaps, that known as *totokya*, the climax of the ritual. Seven arduous dance performances by the scores of initiates had filled the day, dawn to dusk, young men painted in yellow pigments, kilted, with fox-skin pendants and feathers of parrots and eagles. Hundreds of villagers had turned out to view the dances, at times grave and at times bawdy, with women of the Mamzrau society occasionally taunting and tossing water or urine on the boys. The rhythm of drums had filled Awat'ovi's plazas, pounded now to fine dust by the naked feet of the dancers. As dusk fell, the initiates returned once again to their kivas to resume their training. At the top of each kiva ladder remained one senior man to receive bowls and baskets of food—mutton stew, dried peaches, sliced squash, rolls of paper-thin blue corn piki bread—prepared by the women of the Pueblo in honor of their young men. Feasting would be followed by exhausted sleep.

But this night would—in fierce and enduring trauma—create questions that remain unanswered. Just what transpired in those kivas that night is one of the ghosts that haunt the story of Awat'ovi.

Even the wisps of smoke and firelight could not be seen by the encamped warriors below the mesa's cliffs, tucked as they were below the eyesight of any *a'losaka* patrols who maintained order and security during such rituals. Young men and seasoned fighters composed the raiding throng, it is said, and "their number was incredibly large." They had gathered beneath the mesa at sundown, while the people of Awat'ovi focused their attention on the culminating dance. All night they had lain low, awaiting a signal. To pass the hours, "some sharpened the points on their arrows, others the blades of their stone axes." Preparing for the fight ahead, "they painted their faces, putting red ocher along their eyes above their nose." They slashed vertical lines down their cheeks with black hematite. White eagle plumes adorned their hair, which allowed them "to run with great speed in pursuit of the enemy." Each had with him a bundle of finely shredded juniper bark and greasewood kindling. Silent, they waited through the long and cold night.

They had come from Oraibi. From Walpi. From Mishongnovi. Hopi villages to the west.

At the very "moment of the yellow dawn" the signal came. From atop one kiva, out of sight from below, they heard a sharp crack, the snap of a blanket in the chill air. Rising up, they filed swiftly up stairstep stones to the unguarded western gate in Awat'ovi's defensive wall. Fanning out through the village, the attackers followed their orders. Running from kiva to kiva, one group of the strongest men yanked the ladders out and hurled them aside. Those inside had no chance of escape. Dipping their juniper bark into the still-hot embers of the women's cooking fires, the attackers hurled the burning torches and kindling into the kivas. Grabbing firewood and strings of dried red chiles from nearby house walls, they thrust this new fuel through the small kiva entrances. Arrows followed. "There was crying, screaming, coughing." As the heavy roof beams of the kivas caught fire, they began to sag and collapse, one after another.

Another group of warriors raced through the village with their own orders, storming into the sleeping houses. "Wherever they came across a man, young or old, they killed him." Some they seized and cast into the kivas, some suffered crushed skulls from stone axes, and some were thrown off the cliffs. Old women died too. Younger women and girls were seized and herded together along the western wall, under guard, while the attackers set fire to the village itself. Firewood stacks prepared for winter now became bonfires. Stores of corn flared as well. "Awat'ovi presented a terrible sight. It had been turned into a ruin."

Forcing scores of captives before them, the attackers descended

Antelope Mesa and journeyed toward their home villages. Crossing a small wash that locally dwelling Navajos called Tallahogan (Singing House)—a reference to the Catholic hymns they had heard emanating from the mission church in earlier years—the warriors began to debate among themselves the division of their spoils. The men from Oraibi claimed they were to have first choice among the captives, after which the Mishongnovi men were to have their selection. The Walpis would have rights to the planting fields of Awat'ovi, no women. If any women were left after the Oraibis chose theirs, the men from the other villages might have them. Yet the Mishongnovis and Walpis recalled no such agreement. They had already selected the women they wanted. "These are ours. We won't give them back to you!"

While they argued, a small contingent of surviving Awat'ovi men and boys overtook them and attempted a rescue. They were quickly defeated, and the victors severed their heads and piled them in a cairn. Turning again to the dispute, since the Mishongnovis and Walpis would not give up their captives, the Oraibis shouted, "In that case no one will have them. Let's get rid of them. If we kill them all, nobody can have them."

Slaughter ensued. Several dozen women and girls died in the carnage, stabbed, beaten, or pierced with arrows. Pleas for mercy only enraged the men further. Some women suffered mutilation before death, arms or legs amputated, their breasts slashed. Finally, one woman cried: "Some of us are initiates of a society. We know how to make rain. We'll teach you the art of rainmaking if you spare us and take us along." A handful of Mamzrau (Rain) and Lakon (Basket) society members found safety in this way and were divided equally among the three villages. These few, made anew as Oraibis, Mishongnovis, or Walpis, were warned "never to show any longing" for Awat'ovi, "never to think of returning to it."

Recently, Eric Polingyouma of Shungopovi Village has explained that since its destruction Awat'ovi "has been considered an evil place. No one at Hopi claims it." It now stands as a caution to future generations.

❧·❧

Like the winds on that fateful night, Awat'ovi swirls with stories. Seldom do they align precisely; even less often do they resolve into consensus. Different forms of evidence and differing genres of recounting history—that of traditional Hopi oral narratives, that of Franciscan missionaries, that of the archaeologist's trowel, that of the ethnographer's notebook, to name but a few—produce diverse and refracting voices through which we hear the mystery. A tension that is an enduring attribute of the past. What follows is but one history of Awat'ovi, *a* history, not *the* history, one author's journey into a distant time and enigmatic event. The swirl of stories recounted here reminds us that we may think we are done with the past, but the past may not be done with us.

Early in the year 1881, for instance, "a mysterious and self-styled ethnographer" named Alexander McGregor Stephen arrived at Keams Canyon, a trading post and stagecoach stop just beneath the northwest slope of Antelope Mesa. Born in Scotland in 1845, perhaps educated at the University of Edinburgh, by 1862 he was in the United States and enlisted as a private in the Union Army, 92nd New York Infantry. He probably saw combat at the siege of Petersburg and the battle at Little Sailor's Creek, Virginia. Mustering out in 1866, he headed for the West and prospected for gold and silver in Nevada and Utah, practicing metallurgy to keep himself in cash. At Keams Canyon he hooked up with Thomas Keam, who ran the Tusayán Trading Post there.

Whatever Stephen's education, he had an exceptional facility for languages, and after marrying a Navajo woman, he quickly picked up that language and soon was fluent in Hopi as well. Well equipped to serve as guide and interpreter for the sudden arrival of anthropologists yearning to study the ancient denizens of the Southwest, Stephen would give us one of the earliest Hopi accounts of Awat'ovi's demise.

In 1892, just two years before his death, Stephen transcribed and translated the Awat'ovi story from Sáliko, a woman of Walpi Village and, by virtue of her descent from a captive survivor of the Awat'ovi destruction, the hereditary chief of the women's Mamzrau Society ceremonials at Walpi. Certain key details enter the narrative with Sáliko, the only woman to provide an account in what is today more than a century of Hopi versions of the event.

A large village with many inhabitants, said Sáliko, Awat'ovi lay under the leadership of a man named Ta'polo, who was "not at peace with his people and there was quarreling and trouble." Because of the internal strife, little rain had fallen, although the spring-fed gardens below Awat'ovi remained fertile. Despite this, the men of Awat'ovi were thuggish with their neighbors; "they went in small bands among the fields of other villagers and cudgeled any solitary workers they found. If they overtook any woman they ravished her, and they waylaid hunting parties, taking the game, after beating and sometimes killing the hunters."

Ta'polo believed the source of this behavior to lie in sorcery, "his people had all become *powáko* (sorcerers), and hence should all be destroyed." It was Ta'polo who approached Oraibi and Walpi for aid; recruiting warriors to lay waste his own village. It was Ta'polo who left the gate in the massive wall unbarred, and even he who swung it wide as the attackers made their entrance. It was he who pointed out the large kiva called Püvyüñobi, "the sorcerers' kiva," wherein the massacre commenced. On Ta'polo's fate Sáliko was silent.

Of the captives she offered more detail. Sáliko's ancestor was recognized during the carnage at Mas'ki (Death House) as the *maumzrau'mongwi* (chief of the Mamzrau Society) by one of the men from
Walpi, who asked "whether she would be willing to initiate the women
of Walpi in the rites of the Mamzrau." Thus she survived, and the ritual
too stayed alive in a new home. Other of the women who "knew how to
bring rain" and were willing to teach the songs were spared. The Oraibi
men, she said, even saved "a man who knew how to make the peach
grow, and that is why Oraibi has such an abundance of peaches now."
The Mishongnovis saved a prisoner who knew "how to make the sweet
small corn grow." Any woman who had "song-prayers" and was willing
to teach them also survived, and "no children were designedly killed, but
distributed among the villages"—although most went to Mishongnovi.
The remainder "were tortured and dismembered and left to die on the
sand hills, where their bones were to be found at "Mas'tcomo-mo."

Thus intervillage conflict, rape, political struggles, sorcery, revenge,
and annihilation have inflected the story for over a century. As have
rescue, redemption, the persistence of sacred ceremonies, song-prayers,
sweet corn, and peaches. Even as new historical forces swept across the
Hopi mesas, the narrative retains, discards, and leaves unknown many
elements. And beneath this century of stories lay different tales, buried
deep within the fallen stones and drifting sands of Awat'ovi.

⇒·⇐

Today, the mysteries we seek to resolve involve a larger story, that
of the Awat'ovi ruins, the Hopi people, and the tortured relationship between America's indigenous communities and our fascination
with their archaeological heritage. Hopis, Navajos, Native American

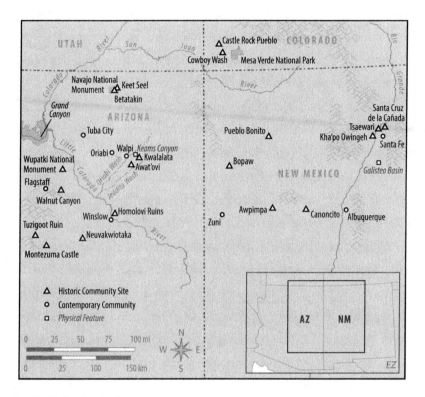

Awat'ovi in the Greater Southwest.

activists, archaeologists, ethnographers, physical anthropologists, historians, museum curators, the Catholic Church, even U.S. Bureau of Indian Affairs agents each have a stake in how the story is rendered. Combined, their claims become a cacophony of stories.

Mutilated bodies, wizards, sorcerers, Indians, and archaeologists—this is the stuff of popular fiction and adventure films. But much more lies within this vignette; in fact, the enigma of Awat'ovi and its many contested meanings are matters of intense urgency. In its essence, "Awat'ovi" now serves as a lightning rod for questions of vital significance: how does one narrate the meaning of an event that many of the descendants of both its perpetrators and its victims might rather forget? Yet it remains intensely alive for them. How do communities learn from the past, and what are the consequences of avoiding painful memories? What might be gained, and lost, in retelling the story?

It seems ironic that in American popular culture and in much tribal tradition itself the term "Hopi" is synonymous with "peace," for Awat'ovi was not the first Hopi village to experience prophetic violence in the interest of cultural purification. Hopi oral histories recount similar "tales of destruction" across several centuries, some lodged in mythic pasts, others clearly identifiable in place and time. These prophetic histories stress cycles of corruption and renewal, tales that oppose *koyaanisqatsi,* or disorder and transgressions of the sacred, against *suyanisqatsi*—lives lived according to principles of communitarian harmony and balance. In each case the narrative pattern resonates across time: spiritual corruption requires violent cleansing. In what now appears a timeless trope, in 1938 the Hopi man Byron Adams declared to representatives of the BIA that at Awat'ovi "the other villages got together and decided to destroy it because evil things were done there. There was no decency. It was agreed that it should never be touched again."

2

The Sorcerer's Kiva

*. . . there has been a lot of interest in the village from the
scientific community, who want to investigate it and learn
who lived there and how they lived before it was destroyed.*

—ERIC POLINGYOUMA, 2008

*Observing the anxiety of the Hopi workmen, I abandoned
excavations in the po-wa'-ko kib-va . . . for I did not wish the
report to be circulated among their people that I desired to find
the skeletons of wizards, as it might prejudice them against me.*

—JESSE WALTER FEWKES, 1893

But for the cloven hoofs of grazing sheep and the soft tread of
shepherds, Antelope Mesa's dune grass and juniper groves lay
untouched for nearly two hundred years. Yet across the century thereafter it witnessed some of the most vigorous and culturally intrusive
archaeological investigations in the American Southwest, especially
through the archaeologists' convention of employing Hopis as dig-

gers and sifters of the remnants of their own ancestral homes. In these early expeditions, the questions that adventurers-cum-academics sought to answer, along with naïve curiosity, often led them to impinge upon aspects of Hopi (and other Pueblo peoples') culture in ways that produced discomfort and dismay. This, initially a matter of cross-cultural confusion, would intensify in time toward outright and mutual discord.

We might dismiss this as the legacy of an earlier, imperial approach to studying "primitives," the seedbed from which anthropology itself arose in the nineteenth century as Great Britain, France, Germany, Japan, and the United States extended their economic and military presence into the homelands of "exotic indigenes." Yet some of these questions, especially those that suggested that the pre-Columbian history of the Southwest might not have been so peaceful, self-sublimating, and communitarian as popular imagination wished, have in the twenty-first century emerged as central to social scientists' thinking about the region's past. Thus the very human inclination that people be stewards of their own history—especially indigenous people who have experienced prolonged surveillance by non-Indian fetishists—runs smack into the equally human curiosity to "know what happened." Sorcery—the practice of maleficent arts on neighbors—figures prominently among these questions, and the study of those dark talents has become something of a cottage industry among anthropologists. Whether it be a fascination with familiar cases, like that of the witchcraft outbreak at Salem, Massachusetts, in 1692, or the much less familiar phenomenon of witchcraft among America's Indian nations, anthropologists have long offered interpretations that stress sorcery's role in explaining human misfortune and in regulating communal conflicts in small-scale societies.

❧·❧

Alexander Stephen solicited Sáliko's story about the "Sorcerer's Kiva" at the behest of Jesse Walter Fewkes. Like Stephen, Fewkes would become a member of the charter generation of southwestern anthropologists. Little in Fewkes's background would have suggested this trajectory, however. Born in Newton, Massachusetts, in 1850 and educated at Harvard, he took a Ph.D. in zoology with an emphasis in marine biology, further refined by a two-year postdoctoral position at the University of Leipzig. Returning to Cambridge in 1879, he obtained a position at Harvard's Museum of Comparative Zoology.

A decade later Fewkes's life took a dramatic turn. In 1887 a summer field season studying California medusae (jellyfish) included a visit from Harvard classmate Augustus Hemenway's family, who were undertaking a grand tour of the continent. The Hemenways, Bostonians with enormous wealth from the shipping industry, were passionately interested in southwestern Indians and archaeology, having been introduced to both by Frank Hamilton Cushing during the summer of 1885. Fewkes, Cushing, and the Hemenways would, over a weekend in Carmel, begin one of the seminal (and strained) triangular partnerships in southwestern archaeology.

Soon to be Fewkes's mentor, Frank Cushing had pioneered American anthropology, "the first professional anthropologist to 'go to the field' and function as a 'participant observer,'" according to historian of anthropology Don D. Fowler, and shaped what would become standard rites of passage for graduate students hoping to gain entrance to the new discipline. Born in upstate New York in 1857, a lonely and often sickly child who turned to the woods and "playing Indian" to satisfy his imagination, Cushing read the seminal works

From the top of Zuni, looking east, by John K. Zillers, 1879.

of Lewis Henry Morgan on the Iroquois and human social organization as a teenager, and at age seventeen had successfully published an essay on his local archaeology with the Smithsonian Institution.

Cushing left Cornell University in his freshman year to take work at the National Museum in Washington, D.C., concentrating on exhibits for display by the Smithsonian at the 1876 Philadelphia Exposition. Just three years later, he found himself appointed as "ethnologist" to John Wesley's Powell's Smithsonian-sponsored "collecting party" under orders to "find out all you can about some typical tribe of Pueblo Indians. Make your own choice of field, and use your own methods; only, *get the information*," were his orders.

Cushing chose as his subjects the people of Zuni Pueblo, distant neighbors to the Hopis across the New Mexico line among the red cliffs and green pines of the Zuni Mountains and some one hundred miles southeast of Antelope Mesa. Although under orders to "get the information" within three months, Cushing would stay among the Zunis for more than four years. He insisted on making sketches of ceremonials at the Zuni Pueblo of Halona, poked into secret ritual areas, and earned the resentment of many of his hosts. Yet an alliance with Patricio Piño (Palowahtiwa), the pueblo's governor, protected him, and he proved remarkably adept at learning the Zuni language (an "isolate" unrelated to any other indigenous language in the Americas). Within two years he gained initiation into the Bow Priest Society, one requirement of which was to take an enemy scalp, which Cushing claimed to have done on an Apache battlefield; others believed it to have been mailed from his father and colleagues at the Army Medical Museum. Within a year, he earned the Zuni name Tenatsali, or Medicine Flower. In his enthusiasm to "become Indian" he fashioned himself a costume that earned him the perhaps less honorable name of "Many Buttons."

Despite what might seem a caricature of the anthropologist "gone Native," as the four years progressed, Cushing played an important role in furthering Zuni diplomacy in Washington, in preventing white ranchers from encroaching on Zuni lands, and in resisting Mormon and Presbyterian evangelizing efforts at the pueblo in New Mexico. Even as his frail health continued to limit his aspirations, he accompanied the delegation of Zuni elders and Governor Piño to a meeting with President Chester A. Arthur in 1882, and took Zuni legal battles into the halls of Congress.

On one such trip, Cushing brought three Zuni guests to the Hemenway house at Manchester-by-the Sea, and spent long eve-

"Many Buttons" (Frank Hamilton Cushing) in Zuni costume, ca. 1880–1881.

Frank Hamilton Cushing with Laiyuahtsailunkya, Naiyutchi, Palowahtiwa, Kiasiwa, and Nanake (detail), 1882.

nings translating their "legends and folk tales" for his enchanted hosts. With these trips would come the links to Jesse Fewkes and the latter's role as heir apparent to Medicine Flower.

By 1886, Mrs. Hemenway decided to sponsor the Cushing-led Hemenway Expedition to trace Zuni and Hopi migrations through archaeological field research. But Cushing's fragile health and often-quixotic theories (he had decided that the Zunis descended from Mexico's Toltecs) led to his removal in 1889. Fewkes, of all people, found himself appointed director of the expedition. His decision to accept the job was doubtless reinforced by the fact that his position at the zoology museum had not been renewed. It seems a pattern of plagiarism had been discovered in his research and writing. His new focus on archaeology would not correct that tendency.

Fewkes endorsed Cushing's research agenda, if not his interpretations. As journalists, photographers, and railroad tourism opened the Southwest to American readers and travelers, the discovery of ancient civilizations inspired popular fascination. While these ruins might not resonate with European cultural traditions like those of the classical Mediterranean, their massive masonry walls and wide windblown plazas offered something in addition to lost cities and cliff dwellings—living Puebloan neighbors who claimed direct lineal descent from the builders of those archaeological enigmas.

Unlike Europe, the Mediterranean, or the Tigris-Euphrates Valley, the American Southwest allowed the curious to imagine that in the exotic ceremonies they witnessed at pueblos like Acoma, Zuni, Taos, and Walpi—renowned for its Snake Dance, wherein Snake Society priests danced with live rattlesnakes clenched in their teeth—they might be experiencing millennium-old rituals firsthand. "Living ancients" inhabited the desert Southwest, and the founding members of the American archaeological profession saw it as their duty to make the connections between the wind-swept plazas of abandoned pueblos and the dancing throngs and thundering drums of similar plazas in thriving, if "timeless," modern Indian villages.

This imperative gave birth to what would be called the "direct-historical" method. Avid amateurs with aspirations to scientific legitimization like Cushing, Fewkes, Adolph Bandelier, and Edgar Lee Hewett sought to use the information contained in Indian "legends and folk tales," as well as contemporary study of ritual and social organization gleaned through the new field of ethnology (literally, the knowledge of culture), to inform scholarly and public understanding of the ancient denizens of the Southwest. Using analogy and homology, they proposed to "read backward" their ethnology and assess that against archaeological materials discovered in their excavations to test the hypotheses that clear links across vast sweeps of time might exist.

Fresh to his new position directing the Hemenway Expedition, Fewkes employed his scientific training in zoology to shape his research agenda. In contrast with the charismatic and highly emotional Cushing, who absorbed languages and lifeways by full immersion (some would say by the romance of conquest), Fewkes sought detachment and distance in his data collection. But he was not above pillaging his predecessor's field notes for insights that he happily published as his own. Shortly before his death, Cushing would write a friend, "Not only does Dr. Fewkes pre-empt my field, or rather, jump my claim, but he makes use of my material . . . without even quotation marks when my own words are used." Fewkes would become a master at utilizing others' hard work for his own professional advancement. As old southwestern hand Washington Matthews would write to Cushing, "Our Boston friend [Fewkes], while in Zuni never spoke a word of Zuni and didn't know a word of Spanish . . . yet he learned all about them in two months. What a pity we have not a few more such brilliant lights in Ethnography!"

Doubtless Cushing and Matthews were right to criticize Fewkes's peripatetic and superficial ethnography, but the latter's research agenda pointed to a development in the discipline that would come to dominate the field in later decades: a comparative approach that emphasized the generation of theoretical advances about human cultural evolution alongside the collection and inventory of clay vessels, grinding stones, projectile points, and ancient textiles preserved in the dry desert air.

Zuni and Hopi begged for comparison, since of the pueblos west of the Rio Grande Valley they were unquestionably the "least tainted" by contact with Euro-Americans. Although each spoke mutually unintelligible languages, and would come to be understood as quite different in many aspects, their similar aggregated pueblo settlements, clan-based social organization, and ceremonial calendars suggested membership in a broader Puebloan worldview. Like the Hopi's search for Tuuwanasavi, "the earth-center," Zuni migration stories organized around a quest for *Itiwana*, "the exact center point of the universe," wherein they would locate at the village of Halona. They shared the Katsina religion, and many secret societies. From his vantage point at Zuni, the Hopi mesas beckoned to Fewkes, who saw there the possibility of crafting a regional understanding of Southwestern prehistory.

In 1891, Fewkes moved the headquarters of the Hemenway Expedition from Cushing's old house at Zuni Pueblo to the Hopi mesas. In well over his head, uncertain of himself, and given to bouts of insecurity, he found a savior in Alexander Stephen. Deeply engaged in his language and culture studies of the Hopi, and living on First Mesa with his Navajo wife, Stephen seemed not to aspire to an academic life, but very much wished to see his knowledge of the Hopis available to the wider world. Stephen provided Fewkes introductions and access to Hopi people and ritual life that Fewkes could never have obtained on his own. For $115 per month from 1892 to 1894, Stephen served as a researcher and ambassador for Fewkes, who regularly published "Stephen's intimate knowledge of Hopi dances and ceremonies as his own."

In the summer of 1892, Fewkes decided to test his scientific methods against Hopi oral tradition by exploring the destruction of Awat'ovi. He first directed Stephen to collect as many forms of the narrative as possible, while he himself looked into the writings of predecessors like Bandelier and John Bourke. Bandelier had gleaned some few references to the event from his study of Spanish colonial archival documents—the earliest a 1701 mention by Juan Domingo de Mendoza of the "annihilation of the converted Indians of Aguatubi."

In addition to Sáliko, Stephen spoke to Wi'ki, chief of the Antelope Society, and Si'mo, chief of the Flute society, both from Walpi. Sáliko's version proved richest, however, and dominated Fewkes's essay in the *American Anthropologist* in 1893. Fewkes cautioned in his article that while folk tales were capable of scientific treatment, "they are not mathematically exact," suggesting that his archaeology would prove more empirically reliable. His purpose, he would write, was to "demonstrate by archaeological evidence the truth of a Tusayán [Hopi] legend" about how the site came to be "tragically destroyed." He neglected to mention that he had never conducted excavations before.

Fewkes sketched the site in anticipation of adding excavation detail as he progressed. Among the largest of such ruined towns in the ancient Southwest, spectacularly situated on the high natural ramparts of Antelope Mesa, the site divided roughly between the west—where the massive mound of the main pueblo rose several stories high—and the east, where the Franciscan church still showed standing walls and a mound of rooms suggesting an Indian residential block in close association with the Spanish mission. Based on the accumulated masonry rubble and the presence of early ceramic sherds, the Western Mound seemed "to be the older" of the two habitation areas.

Employing Hopi men as his field crew, Fewkes sunk a series of eight test pits in locations within and around the ruins. Soon he could report that "in almost every room evidences of a fire or a great

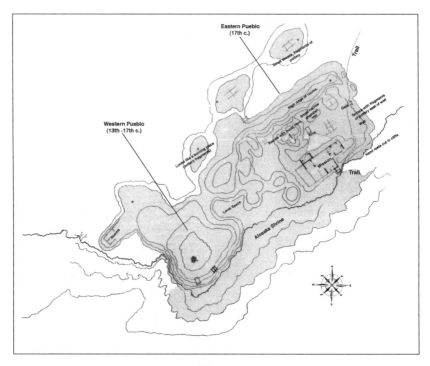

Jesse Walter Fewkes's site map of Awat'ovi, 1892, rendered by Jessica Calzada.

conflagration were brought to light." Charred beams had collapsed and rarely did they find "a room without finding the beams and burnt fragments of wood upon the floor." Storage rooms featured great piles of stacked corn, so many that "bushels of charred fragments were taken out." Many rooms preserved items of daily life still in place. "Mealing troughs . . . and cooking pots and vessels of both smooth and coiled ware" were found in both the western and eastern precincts of the ruin. No looting had attended the end of Awat'ovi.

He drilled in on one location, however, drawn by the presence of a shallow depression in a plaza area midway between the mission church complex and the Indian residential room-block to its north-west, which "the Indians employed in the excavation called . . . a kib-va. . . . The fact that the men were in the kib-va at the time of the destruction and that many were killed there" made him "anxious to identify this room." His workmen sunk a trench "several feet in width, from corner to corner," and then another in the center of the room "dug down to the floor," which "was covered with flat stones." Measuring fourteen feet by twenty-eight feet, the large room lay some five feet below the plaza's surface.

Charred wood and ashes abounded in the fill his workmen removed. But most important was the discovery of "a human skull and other bones . . . four feet six inches below the surface in the middle of the chamber, directly under the place where the old sky-hole formerly opened, through which the relentless Hopi may have thrown down burning faggots and dried chiles upon their helpless victims." The Hopi workmen refused to touch the bones with their hands, and that night, one of them, related by marriage to the Kat-sina chief at Walpi, returned to that pueblo ten miles distant. The next day, having received advice from Walpi, the workman laid sev-eral na-kwa'-ko-ci, "strings with feathers attached" in the trenches "as propitiatory offerings to Ma'sau'wuh, the Death God. . . ."

Even in his excitement at this discovery, Fewkes observed "the anxiety of the Hopi workmen" and decided to abandon the excava-tion, for he did not "wish the report to be circulated that I desired to find the skeletons of wizards, as it might prejudice them against me." Noting that only "new excavations" could resolve whether additional bodies lay buried in the chamber, which was "great enough to cover many more," he believed that he had indeed excavated the sorcerer's kiva. As did his Hopi workmen.

Almost as an afterthought, Fewkes noted that a cemetery existed at Awat'ovi in "the sand-dunes somewhat back from the mesa and to the west of the ruin . . . and from it has been taken some of the best pottery found in Tusayán." As sandstorms swept over the dunes, "skeletons of the dead and fragments of food vessels" were brought into view, but "many unbroken bowls" had "also been found there. The dead were buried in a sitting posture, the knees drawn up to the breast." When, in 1895, Fewkes returned to dig more of these formal burials in hopes of obtaining additional perfect bowls, he was forced to "discontinue work" when his crew of Hopi laborers revolted and walked off the site.

Not all the bodies at Awat'ovi were buried with such attention to proper Hopi ritual. Some were not buried at all. Others found a quite different form of interment. But Fewkes is only a portion of that story. His "wizards and sorcerers" are themselves an enigma.

※·※

Accusations of witchcraft and sorcery are commonplace across human societies, past and present, especially in small communities when misfortune arrives from unseen sources. Medieval European witch-burnings, the antiheresy witch hunts of the Spanish Inquisition, and the Salem Witch Trials are familiar cases, but wizardry, sorcery, and the summoning of maleficent forces also appeared in the indigenous Americas. The "dark arts" have a deep history in the Puebloan Southwest.

Evidence for violence and community conflict in the ancient Puebloan world erupted in popular accounts in just the last decade. Long idealized as "classless" societies where so little opportunity (or desire) to acquire wealth existed that the rise of social elites was impossible, ancient Puebloan people were revered as symbols of a better, simpler way of organizing human affairs. At the dawn of the twentieth century scores of young (often wealthy) white women from New York and Boston relocated to New Mexico Territory in search of another imagined model: the existence among the Pueblos of societies in which women wielded real social power. With everyday life indistinguishable from the colorful and moving ritual dramas of the Pueblo ceremonial calendar, white Americans saw the Indians of the Southwest as living antidotes to the frightening transformations of industrialization and untrammeled modernization. The "peaceful Pueblos" stood as opposites to warlike tendencies in so many of their neighbors, the fearsome Apaches, Comanches, and Navajos.

Yet major archaeological salvage projects associated with modern coal-fired energy and southwestern utilities development in the twentieth century brought startling new evidence to light that the past millennium in the region featured moments of widespread and terrifying warfare, in which whole communities vanished in conflagrations of brutality and fire. To be sure, evidence also exists for truly remarkable swaths of time when virtually no violence swept the land—especially during the heyday of the Chaco Phenomenon (A.D. 900–1150)—but when that experiment came to an end, and when the great drought of the late thirteenth century withered regional crops, neighbors turned on neighbors with undeniable viciousness. As one archaeologist describes it, the period after 1250 became one of universal "crisis and catastrophe." Dramatic population losses and consolidation of refugees into new aggregated villages crafted the landscape that early Spanish conquistadors would see, at a wishful and mistaken distance, as the "Seven Cities of Cibola" or the "Kingdom of Gran Teguayo."

A good deal of the public furor about this new evidence circulates around various assertions of cannibalism as a central aspect of these conflagrations. While the jury remains out on these highly provocative charges, equally important questions have lain below the glare of the anthropophagic spotlights. What fear or loathing, we ask, could inspire people—who had for generations lived quiet lives and invested what surpluses they could muster toward community well-being—to suddenly take up hunting weapons and farming tools and wield them against nearby villages wherein slept in-laws and trading partners? How could these raiders—relatively unpracticed in the arts of war—obliterate victim villages in a matter of a day? And what of cases where it seems that no distant enemies brought destruction upon the villages, but instead that neighbor slew neighbor in astonishing displays of brutality?

Such questions would not seem so startling without the counter example that did so much to shape scholarly and popular conceptions about the ancient Puebloan world—the extraordinary centuries-long success of the Chacoan cultural system centered in the nine-mile-long canyon that bears its name in western New Mexico. A landscape today almost harrowing in its austerity, in its heyday across the eleventh and early twelfth centuries it bloomed with a cultural vitality never seen in the region before or since. The canyon was home to massive masonry "Great Houses" counting hundreds of rooms, expansive ceremonial spaces and platforms, ancillary residential villages, and sophisticated astronomical devices used to forecast planting and harvesting cycles. Beyond the canyon itself, the Chaco Phenomenon reached as far as Utah, Colorado, New Mexico, Chihuahua, and Arizona in the form of distant colonies or communities that emulated Chaco architecture and ceremonials. Massive seasonal pilgrimages from these "outliers" would fill Chaco Canyon itself, not unlike Mecca, with peoples of differing languages and local identities who shared a devotion to the power, perhaps priestly, that expressed itself in the ceremonial theater that was Chaco Canyon.

Far-traveling pilgrims seem also to have gathered at Chaco to build the Great Houses themselves. During the height of their construction between 1050 and 1125, hundreds of thousands of hours were dedicated to shaping stone, raising walls, transporting pine roof timbers from as far distant as the Chuska Mountains, sixty miles away, and the finer work of plastering and whitewashing the massive monuments to Chacoan cosmology.

Feeding and housing these willing—or perhaps unwilling— migrants proved yet another challenge to social organization. Opportunities for conflict, whether among migratory laborers of vastly different languages and identities, or between the small elite corps

Artist's reconstruction of Pueblo Bonito at Chaco, the largest Great House in the canyon, 1895.

who controlled the canyon and the pilgrims, seem obvious, yet virtually no evidence of violence exists in the canyon (or throughout the regional southwestern community) during its peak. Just what kept "Pax Chaco" working so successfully for more than two centuries will provide gist for debate long into our own century. So too will the cruel and sudden collapse of that peace.

When the complex social and ceremonial world of Chaco Canyon unraveled, swiftly and mysteriously, in the mid-twelfth century, violence erupted both within the stunning center-place and in its distant hinterlands. Archaeologists working at the canyon's Great Houses like Pueblo Bonito or Chetro Ketl discovered few burials therein, nor did inhumations in the more modest residential hamlets throughout the canyon suggest major population at any time. Since the great canyon complex was often nearly empty of residents, filling with masses of pilgrims only during regional ceremonies conducted around the celestially driven agricultural calendar, the absence of cemeteries in the canyon is not surprising.

However few, some of the burials imply that Chaco's end was not an easy one. Only two truly "high-status" burials have ever been found at Pueblo Bonito (the "capital" of the canyon), both entombed deep inside much earlier room construction, and beneath many additional bodies that one expert has called "retainers." Rich burial goods of turquoise beads, pottery, prayer sticks, and exotic shells from the Pacific coast accompanied both men.

One man, however, exhibited signs of a violent end. Crippled first by a slash to his left leg, he died from blows that crushed both sides of his skull. Perhaps this is the end carried now in the memory of elders at Laguna Pueblo: "in our history we talk of things that occurred a long time ago [at Chaco], of people who wielded enormous amounts of power: spiritual power and power over people. . . . These people were causing changes that were never meant to occur."

Harnessing spiritual power through ritual performance combines the invisible and supernatural with everyday political outcomes. One year, those who practice these arts may be revered as priests, bringers of rain and good harvests; the next year they might be viewed as bringers of flood, drought, or famine. Efficaciousness, either for a community's well being or toward its degradation, represented the two faces of sorcery (*powaqa* in Hopi). Respect and awe might be replaced with fear, suspicion, and campaigns of persecution. Certainly, the decades after 1125—marked by deep declines in rainfall and signs of popular disaffection with the Chacoan ritual complex—hint that the high priests of Pueblo Bonito may have fallen suddenly from favor.

More than just a few ruling priests died during the fall of Chaco, however. Throughout the thousands of square miles of the Chacoan world lies evidence that the organizing power of "Pax Chaco"

Aerial view of Pueblo Bonito today.

had begun to unravel. Beginning with isolated cases of household violence, and expanding over time to encompass whole valleys and regions—so much so that once-populous towns were emptied seemingly overnight—the strong sinews that had once bound the people of the Chacoan phenomenon together were severed.

Some one hundred miles northwest of the Chaco Canyon center, in what is now the Four Corners region of Utah, Colorado, New Mexico and Arizona, lay a disturbing illustration. Amid the sagebrush and cholla cactus along today's southern piedmont of Sleeping Ute Mountain, a scattering of farming households suffered a catastrophic end around 1150. The members of four households, each comprising perhaps an extended family, were slaughtered and systemically mutilated in concentrated acts of violence that required real investment of time and effort by their perpetrators. At least twenty-four people from an estimated population of thirty-five died that day, both sexes and all ages, ranging from those newly born to the elderly. Many of the dead were butchered—limbs separated from limbs, flesh separated from bones—and in some cases it seems that the butchered portions were roasted over hearths in the pit-house dwellings. Genetic testing of one coprolite—feces—deposited in one hearth suggests that it was human and contained proteins from another human. The effort devoted to this climactic end suggests more than a swift and ephemeral raid by neighbors or wandering nomads. Something inspired the attackers to linger and systematically abuse the dead.

The piedmont community around Cowboy Wash would be abandoned that day, with dozens of valuable tools, ceramics, items of clothing, foodstuffs, and ceremonial objects left where they lay. Those who did not die—whether led away as captives or stealing away as perpetrators—left behind all material connections to their past. Among those were a noteworthy collection of "foreign" ceramics—a style associated with the Chuska Mountains along today's New Mexico–Arizona border, evidence of either an immigrant community or one with more intimate ties to distant peoples in the Chuskas than with those closer to home. Whatever their origins, their material culture may have marked them as "outsiders." Those who did not walk away from the massacre, voluntarily or otherwise, were literally stripped of their humanness, rendered animal prey in their last moments.

At Chaco Canyon, a high priest was slain, yet buried with ceremony deep in the architectural wonder he once ruled. Far distant in southwestern Colorado, a humble farming community was wiped out in a manner appalling for its balance of systematic killing process and brutal passion. In either case, we wonder about the identities of the kinsmen, neighbors, visitors, or raiders who either wreaked this violence or watched in horror as the events unfolded.

In other instances, women were sometimes singled out as victims. Even before the emptying of the Four Corners region, a fortified community of some 75 to 150 residents, known today as Castle Rock Pueblo, suffered total destruction in 1274. Men of fighting age comprised only 3 of the 41 bodies found during excavations of the site. Many of these skeletons exhibit perimortem violence (wounds delivered at the time of death, or shortly thereafter) visited upon their remains. Limbs were slashed from bodies, heads from torsos, and parts scattered or thrown into burned rooms. Castle Rock suffered a level of passion in the attack not unlike what would take place at Awat'ovi. Were annihilation of a community the sole aim, once the inhabitants were slain, we would expect the attackers to pillage stored corn granaries and move on to new targets. To linger and des-

Castle Rock Pueblo, 1874, William Henry Jackson.

ecrate the remains indicates an effort, like those in known witch-craft cases, to permanently incapacitate even the spirits of the dead. In other cases of even larger villages thus destroyed in the region, archaeologist Kristen Kuckelman noted "the remains of few men in their prime were found . . . the deaths of primarily women, children, the ill and incapacitated suggests that the able-bodied men were absent from the villages during the attacks." Might the village men have been themselves perpetrators of the massacre?

A final example lies closer in time and location to Antelope Mesa. Along the Little Colorado River just north of Winslow, Arizona, is a chain of seven large towns closely associated with the migration tales of modern Hopi peoples. Dating from the thirteenth and fourteenth centuries, the largest (some numbering more than 1,000 rooms) are organized in a settlement cluster known as the Homol'ovi (The Place of Small Buttes) Ruins. At the town known today as Homol'ovi II (dating from 1330 to 1400) archaeologists found a sequence of ritualized "kiva closures" that hint at combinations of both the Chaco and Cowboy Wash stories.

At least seven of the forty kivas in the enormous plazas of Homol'ovi II had been carefully and ceremoniously decommissioned at various times during the settlement's history. At first glance, the burned and collapsed roofing suggested the trauma of warfare, but as archaeologists worked through the strata of debris, they realized a longer-term, systematic pattern was at work. In most cases, beneath the windblown sand that covered the depositions, careful sealing of ventilator shafts, positioning of unbroken ceramic vessels, and placing of ritual objects preceded the fires that burned the roofs—roofs which had seen their huge primary beams removed before the torches did their work. Almost certainly the work of the town's residents rather than enemy outsiders, the site's investigators puzzled over the find.

Until they dug deeper into two of the kivas. More than ritual artifacts lay on these two floors. In one were found the skeletons of three people—an adult woman, an adolescent boy, and a child. The woman's jaw had been broken before death, and her left femur crudely severed above the knee. The boy and child had probably died of soft-tissue wounds. In the second kiva an adult man's remains lay on the floor, with two projectile points recovered from the area of his abdominal cavity. It seemed that he had been shot with arrows and the kiva burned down over him—and perhaps the arrows had not finished the job, since his head lay inside the ventilator shaft, as if reaching for air. Again, preplanning seems evident, for two whole pots had been placed on the burning roof beams as they slowly collapsed upon the victim. William Walker, an archaeologist associated with the project, surmised "what appears to have happened is not a battle or series of accidents, but a carefully planned ritual burning and burial of the ceremonial structures at different times and for different reasons. In two cases these rituals included the disposal of victims of ritual violence," likely a situation in which "witches, violently 'set apart' from other burials at the site" were "emplaced in ritual contexts."

Everyday people, or so it seems, killed by neighbors (or so it seems), and thrown (dead or alive) into revered ceremonial places— kivas were modeled as reminders of earlier centuries when people lived in pit-houses—after which the kivas were "closed" by deposits of sand and sealed by fire. In one case a lone man, in another what might have been a family.

The Homol'ovi towns grew up during a period of religious transformation in the Southwest. In the thirteenth century we see the earliest evidence of the arrivals of the *katsinam*, sacred beings who walked as lightning, wind, or rain clouds and held power over the seasons. The arrival of the Katsina religion in the region was an astonishing process of culture-wide conversion, and some scholars believe that the proto-Hopi settlements along the Little Colorado River played a role in its genesis. The Katsina societies would allow diverse and linguistically disparate peoples to transcend divisions of kinship, sodality, and residence to create larger communities that provided social and spiritual comfort in troublous times.

But the Katsina conversion would not come without cost— throughout the Southwest an explosion of violent iconography—war shields, Venus stars-of-war, warrior figures, and gruesome monsters suddenly decorate pottery, wall murals, and rock surfaces. Surely some families and individuals who held earlier forms of power resisted the conversion, and paid the price. Or traveling evangelicals who brought the "good news" of the Katsina religion met fates familiar to those proselytizers attempting to spread Christianity into new regions of Asia and Africa at the same time. In either case— and perhaps in that of the Chaco priest and the inhabitants of Cowboy Wash—it seems likely that the motivation toward violence was born of a profound fear of unseen and little understood power. Those whose power lay in hidden knowledge, like the Chaco priest, in signs of cultural difference like the Cowboy Wash community, or in supernatural struggles between old and new religions as at Homol'ovi, may have been marked for death. Thus was the fate of sorcerers, wizards, and witches in the Southwest. And not only in eras shrouded by the fog of time.

❖

When Frank Cushing first insinuated himself at Zuni Pueblo in 1879, he took quick note of accusations of witchcraft that swirled around that village—some of which were aimed at him, since the Zunis had good reason to believe he wished to gain access to secret knowledge. Combining a deft touch with the Zuni language and subtle coercion as a nominal representative of the U.S. government, Cushing would defend himself successfully against charges of sorcery and by 1881 find himself initiated into the Zuni Bow Priesthood. From his increasingly prominent role in Zuni affairs he would have perhaps the most intimate experience with Puebloan witchcraft of any early American anthropologist.

Zuni Indians Torturing a Sorcerer, by Henry François Farny, 1882.

As a member of the Bow Priesthood—specifically charged with trying and punishing sorcerers and wizards—Cushing had a ringside seat for some dozen witchcraft trials at the pueblo between 1879 and 1885. In some cases he intervened to stop the proceedings, yet in others he remained a silent participant in seeking justice. At least nine who were accused died during the period, in one case a family of eight who were clubbed to death and their bodies left to rot. The crimes examined in Bow Priesthood kivas included the bringing of drought, drying winds, murder by invisible means, bewitchment causing illness, fire, crop destruction, grave robbery, and heresy. If not sentenced to die, the convicted might be ordered to join a kiva society or sacred order, suffer ostracism, be beaten, forced to perform public confession, or hanged just short of death.

Cushing's public statements about witchcraft at Zuni were noteworthy in their sympathy for the accusers, while also attempting to withhold full endorsement of their beliefs. "Absurd as it may seem," he wrote in the *Washington Evening News* in 1892, "there is no question of the existence of a certain guild of at least would-be sorcerers or wizards among Zuni Indians. Nor do they owe their reputation, either imputed or self-constituted powers, wholly to superstitious beliefs." A kind of "hypnotic power" lay within witches, and Cushing felt them fully capable of wreaking havoc on individuals or communities, empowered if nothing else by Zunis' widespread belief in their efficacy.

Cushing illustrated a sorcerer's work in crafting an arrow from a stick of mountain laurel, blackened by charcoal to the color of death, fletched with owl feathers (the bird of darkness), and tipped with black obsidian bound to the shaft by feathers of nighthawk, "the swiftest and most silent bird of the night." Thus armed, the sorcerer will place the object somewhere that the quarry might casually encounter it, "so without further operations on the part of the sorcerer" the knowledge of his bewitchment "prays upon the mind of the victim . . . until he rapidly sinks under its spell."

Cushing confessed his own naïveté in the judicial process, explaining that when he "first witnessed the trial of a sorcerer, in a most foolhardy manner I attempted by even violent means to protect him. I did not understand the full intents and purposes of these so-called sorcerers at that time." He cautioned his readers that "while the peculiar beliefs and principles of the Pueblo Indians in regard to sorcery have sometimes the most direful consequences, leading to divisions of the tribe and ultimate separation," it must also be understood that "it can be seen that their only civil method of eliminating from the native population the undesirable element has been through trial, condemnation, and execution."

⇒•⇐

What if a whole community, hundreds of men, women, and children, somehow composed that "undesirable element?" What forces, malevolent or otherwise, might they have had the power to invoke? Could the intracommunity conflict among the Hopi in 1700 hint that the sorcery practiced among the residents of Awat'ovi might demonstrate connections to the *powaqa* at work among the Zuni two centuries later? What of a later crisis at Hopi itself, which suggests that a *powaqa* could sometimes embody very different—and perhaps benevolent—qualities of vision and hope for a better future, albeit at the expense of tradition, mean to the story of Awat'ovi Pueblo? The Oraibi crisis of 1906, in which the suspicion of sorcery seems inextricably mingled with historical and social forces that beset the Hopi mesas at the dawn of the twentieth century, provides a more recent reverberation of these questions. Yet three centuries earlier, with the arrival of Franciscan missionaries in the Hopi Mesas, numinous forces from afar stoked fears of metaphysical threats, of evangelical religion, and intensified an ancient anxiety.

3

The Singing House

I wonder if you would be willing to place the body of the padre
found under the altar at Awat'ovi in the care of the Bishop
of Tucson. I believe it right that all the numerous martyrs—
soldiers, colonists, and friars—of the Pueblo Revolt be declared
saints, and the placement of the body with the Bishop would
assure authenticity of the relic.

—THE REV. VICTOR R. STONER TO J. O. BREW, 1938

The people of Antelope Mesa met Spaniards in 1540 in the same manner they had greeted strangers for centuries—with a practiced diplomacy that blended guarded hostility with overtures of hospitality. In the spring of that year, conquistador Francisco de Coronado detailed Don Pedro de Tovar to explore the regions west of the Rio Grande, so with seventeen horsemen, a handful of foot soldiers, and Franciscan friar Juan de Padilla, the small column passed through the Cibola (Zuni) territory and entered Tusayán, where "the villages [were] high and the people warlike."

The massive sandstone cliffs of Antelope Mesa gave Tovar pause, and after a night spent concealed under the ledges and eavesdropping on the whispered conversations above (he had brought an interpreter from Zuni), he arrayed his group on the sands of Jeddito Wash, where a belligerent detachment of armed Hopis met them. Those men forbade entry to Antelope Mesa, etching a symbolic boundary line in the earth. One restless horseman challenged the line and his horse suffered a club blow to the head, in turn triggering a brief fight, the Spaniards chasing the Hopis back to the mesa. The situation calmed when "the people of the village [came] out with presents, asking for peace."

Laying cotton cloth, dressed and tanned skins, cornmeal, pine nuts, "birds of the country," and turquoise ("but not much") before Tovar's men, the residents of Awat'ovi invited the Spaniards "to visit, buy, sell, and barter with them." From conflict to commerce with barely a shrug. The governing assembly of "the oldest men" grudgingly allowed Tovar to make camp near the village, and used the next few days to take the measure of the visitors' power—military, economic, and spiritual—the same qualities that they judged in considering new clans for acceptance into the Hopi world. Friar Padilla doubtless strove to deliver his message of salvation to the people of Awat'ovi and neighboring villages, but nothing in the expedition's reports suggests much interest in matters spiritual.

Having "received the submission of the whole province," Tovar returned to Coronado's camp along the Rio Grande with news of an even greater river to the west. By late summer of 1540, Coronado had dispatched don García López de Cárdenas back to Tusayán to explore this possible route to the "South Sea," the Colorado. Well received at Tusayán and "entertained by the natives," López enjoyed the services of Hopi guides to the river, who managed to avoid revealing the location of their ancient trails down from the rim.

The people at Tusayán experienced glancing Spanish visits over the next seventy years. In 1583, Antonio de Espejo arrived on the mesa and was later reported to have been astonished by the generous reception offered his small group of ten men. Hardly had they pitched camp when "about one thousand Indians came laden with maize, ears of green corn, piñole, tamales, firewood, and they offered it all, together with six hundred widths of blankets small and large, white and painted, so that it was a pleasant sight to behold." So, too, did the Hopis provide "venison and dried rabbits" to the Spaniards, a bountiful and hospitable welcome that in Indian custom had long served to establish an expectation of reciprocal grace and generosity. An expectation that too often the strangers failed to meet.

Tamales, tortillas, venison, cotton mantas, and dried rabbit did not form the wealth that had drawn Spanish adventurers northward, however. The decades after Juan de Oñate's establishment of an outpost at San Gabriel del Yunque at the junction of the Rio Grande and Chama River featured disappointment after disappointment in their quest for wealth like that of the Aztecs and Incas. So severe was the operating deficit of the early colony that by 1608, the Council of the Indies recommended abandonment of the settlements, to which the crown gave serious consideration. Yet the regular orders of the Catholic Church held the balance of power in Madrid and the fragile, underfunded colony persisted with the goal of harvesting souls from the clutches of the devil, who tried "in all possible ways to impede and obstruct the promulgation of the divine law." The arrival in New Mexico of thirty new Franciscan missionaries in 1629 permitted the Church to look westward again at the province of Tusayán.

On August 20 of that year, Padres Cristóbal de la Concepción, Andrés Gutiérrez, and Francisco de Porras arrived at Antelope Mesa and undertook to establish a permanent Catholic presence among those "great sorcerers and idolaters." A contemporary account captures not just this Franciscan disdain for Hopi religion, but a sense of what composed Hopi life: "They harvest much cotton; the houses are of three stories, well planned; the inhabitants are great land tillers and diligent workers. Among them it is considered a great vice to be intoxicated, [although] for amusement they have certain games and a race they run with great speed." The people of Awat'ovi had been alerted to the arrival of the missionaries by an "apostate from the Christian [presumably Rio Grande] pueblos" and met the missionaries with suspicion. Under the cover of their military guard mounted on "armored horses," the friars entered Awat'ovi and "set forth through the streets, preaching, the sonorous echoes of their voices at once bringing men and women to listen to them . . . as the Indian now approached without fear, they gave them . . . trinkets such as rattles, beads, hatchets, and knives in order to make them feel that the friars came to give rather than ask."

Eager to receive what in Tusayán were indeed precious and welcome tools and symbols of wealth, the people of Awat'ovi were less than receptive to the friars' message of doom or salvation. Despite the presence in Porras's arms of the original cross of Mother Luisa de Carrión, the indigenous kiva and Katsina priests at the pueblo kept the people alarmed and resistant. Only a "great miracle"— reported by some chroniclers and doubted by others—in which Porras was able to restore sight to a boy blind since birth, shifted the sentiments of the citizenry of Awat'ovi. It followed that "the conversion rose like foam."

Such were the words of Catholic hagiographers throughout New Spain. These chronicles were devoted to weaving stories of mysticism, martyrdom, and imperial expansion into evidence for missionization and saved Indian souls that would continue both royal and papal commitment to a cause that lacked any economic reward. Yet to dismiss these accounts as entirely instrumental would be to overlook the insights they offer on the Franciscan thought world. However vastly different Catholicism may have seemed to the "idolatrous" practices of the Hopis and other Puebloan peoples, Franciscans walked a world in which numinous forces visible and invisible were everywhere, and the natural and magical closely intertwined. Miracles like that of the suddenly sighted boy at Awat'ovi were not inexplicable, or even requiring explanation, for they simply made manifest the power of God. The Franciscan world was alive with miracles, sure evidence that God's kingdom drew near. For example, Friar Alonso de Benavides, whose 1630 chronicle recounts early Franciscan activities in the province of New Mexico, bore witness to them. He had personally visited Mother María de Jesús (1602–1665) in her convent in Ágreda, Spain, and heard from her own lips of her numerous magical "flights" to New Mexico, as many as four in a single day, in which she preached salvation among the Apaches and Jumanos. He even obtained "the very habit that she wore when she went there. . . . the veil radiates such a fragrance that it is a comfort to the spirit." Mother Luisa de Carrión (1565–1636)—whose original cross Porras carried—also claimed to have undertaken many visits to the Indians of New Mexico. Within a few years of Porras's successes with her relic, she would become a victim of the Spanish Inquisition, forced to have her tongue measured "to determine whether it was short, like a witch's." The Hopis and Zunis were not alone in the seventeenth century in punishing signs of sorcery.

However much conversions at Awat'ovi rose like foam, Porras had just a few energetic years of planting the faith among those people until his work came to a quick and painful end. But the friar started with a big vision. Looking to the east from the massive three-story town of ancient Awat'ovi, he could see extensive residential roomblocks, still occupied, a spacious plaza, and mounds of masonry rubble, crumbling adobe mud, and crushed pottery covering more than an acre of the mesa top, the remnants of an adjacent Pueblo dating from the fourteenth century. Doubtless concerned about resistance should he immediately attempt to dislodge the occupants, Porras looked to the plaza to locate mission "San Bernardo de Aguatubi" in honor of the saint's day on which he had first arrived at Antelope Mesa, August 20—Saint Bernard of Clairvaux. Porras set out to construct a church and convento complex so imposing that the residents of the town would be awed by the architectural expression of the power of the Christian god. He laid out a cruciform church that measured more than 8,000 square feet, with foundation walls more than 6 feet thick, and a transept 28 feet wide—one of the largest churches in the province. It would be a monument to Franciscan diligence in announcing the work of Christ.

Alas, Porras's church would not rise much beyond the foundations. By 1633 he received the last rites. Yet, clearly the friar could not have accomplished the construction preliminaries that he did without substantial labor from at least some of the residents of Awat'ovi. His ability to recruit their assistance probably combined intrigue with the new spiritual presence in the community, deft manipulation of symbols potent in the Hopi world (wooden crosses seem to have occupied a mimetic spiritual role as *pahos*, or wooden prayer sticks), psychological persuasion, and physical coercion. Benavides claimed that Porras had mastered the Hopi language in nine months and "converted and baptized more than four thousand souls and instructed the Indians with great perfection." Certainly, an exaggeration both in numbers and perfection—a census report a decade later counted but 900 souls at Awat'ovi and Walpi, combined. Porras's subsequent fate suggests imperfections in his instruction, but the fact that he moved forward in establishing the mission implies some level of success.

Friars were enjoined to communicate an explanation of the significance of the baptismal sacrament, always the first step in conversion. A priest took the measure of a convert's devotion by observing his or her participation in confessions and willingness to receive the sacrament of the Eucharist. Porras distributed gifts of cloth and iron tools as a demonstration of the Church's benevolence, which doubtless attracted interest. Feast days in honor of the mission's patron saint, in this case San Bernardo, were occasions for distribution of new foods like beef, mutton, poultry, and wheat bread, although more often than not it fell upon the Hopis to provide the substantial majority of the meal, which bred resentment rather than gratitude. The Franciscans also attempted to weave instructional pageants of the life and passion of Christ into Hopi customs of public ritual and dance, and even suffered the continuation of dances associated with the Hopi ceremonial calendar if they deemed them free of heretical content—although those celebrating the arrival of the *katsinam* too often fell in that category.

Coercion and studied violence were among the padres' tools, as well. Since the Katsina priests presented perhaps the greatest obstacle to conversion, their kivas and icons were prime targets. Kivas drew the attention of Franciscan architects, who strove to position the altars of their church naves atop those traditional ritual spaces, at once an effort to erase spiritual competition, and to co-opt the spiritual forces that resided therein. This would present a particular challenge for the archaeologists who would later excavate Awat'ovi. Dances featuring the presence of *katsinam* were another target, expressly forbidden by Porras and doubtless cause for offense among the priests who summoned those deities for rainmaking. So, too, was the making and employment of *pahos* prohibited, as Hopi prayers were henceforth to be directed at only one God. Deviation from approved devotional practices could bring public humiliation, flogging, and expulsion from the mission.

Hopi oral histories of the mission era, although recorded nearly three centuries after the fact, suggest initial curiosity with the Franciscan project and customary hospitality on the part of the Hopis. In 1902, Wíkvaya of Oraibi village told Mennonite missionary Henry Voth that the Hopis consented to peace with the Spaniards "and assisted them in building their house." They "gathered stone for them" and lent their labor to the construction of an "assembly house" that had a "tower in which bells were suspended." When this (the church) was complete, the "Tutáachi (priest) told them that he was going to wash their heads." The Hopis "asked him what that was, what that meant," and he told them "that it was something very good . . . and he poured a little water on the heads of those present." After this, the "Hopis had to assemble in the assembly house on Sundays, where the Tutáachis spoke to them . . . and soon they asked the Hopi to work for them. Thus the Spaniards kept the Hopis at work in various ways, and they were not bad to them at first." But relations began to sour, according to Wíkvaya:

For four years everything went along well, and it rained often, too, so that there was water in the cisterns; but at the end of four years things began to change. The priests commenced to forbid the Hopi to have Katcina dances and to make báhos . . . and they did not let [the Hopis] concern themselves about the clouds and the rain.

Trouble lay on the horizon, but it stretches credulity to imagine that the extraordinary constructions accomplished in the first decades of Franciscan missionization could have been effected by simple intimidation, given the very small numbers of mission personnel—generally no more than two priests and a handful of lay brothers—available to exert those arts. Somehow, Porras obtained great effort from Hopi men and women, with men clearing and digging construction spaces, hauling tons of raw stone to the mesa tops, and shaping those into masonry foundations more massive than anything seen since the era of Chaco Canyon's Great Houses. According to friars, churches "were built by women and by boys and girls taking Christian doctrine," for it was "the custom among these nations for women to build the houses." Women probably worked together in gathering the clay, sand, straw, and water—especially the thousands of gallons of water necessary to make adobe bricks—and laying the stones and bricks, with fine finishing the work of women, who undertook that task in pre-Spanish times. Certainly, therefore, Porras drew upon knowledge of political tensions within the pueblos that the Franciscans had cultivated over several decades, since the general pattern defining Catholic sympathizers versus opponents in New Mexico shows that young men, who could not attain power until well along in years, and women, whose influence was circumscribed by their gender, most often proved receptive to the missionaries' messages. Social fissions were nothing new in the Pueblo world, and posed a clear threat to established authority. Early in the summer of 1633, the chronicler Benavides reported that "the old men, evidently angered at the loss of power through the adherence of so many of their tribe to the missionaries, poisoned some food, which the father ate." Porras's agonizing death may have "brought great sorrow to all of the Christians," but Benavides was confident that it was to Porras's "great joy, because he had attained the goal which he had sought, namely, to give his life in the preaching of the Holy Catholic Faith."

Porras died, but the Franciscan project at Awat'ovi moved forward. The archival records fell dim for two decades after Porras's death, and yet the church and convento certainly grew during that period. The most likely successor to the martyr was Padre Andrés Gutiérrez, who was assigned to the *visita* of Walpi, but probably resident at Awat'ovi, and therefore able to administer the last sacraments to the dying priest. Gutiérrez amended Porras's plans to accord with a more modest reality, relocating and down-sizing the church considerably. Recognizing the impossibility of spanning the transept Porras had laid out, he narrowed the church to 16 feet, a more manageable span given the challenge of transporting timbers from the Chuska Mountains, some fifty miles distant. He also moved forward with the construction of a convento (friary) of more than twenty-five rooms that would serve to house the mission personnel and supplies, a sprawling one-story complex that seems to have been completed over the next decade.

Redesigning and repositioning the church proved important for another reason—it allowed Gutiérrez to follow a Franciscan strategy of co-opting the spiritual forces embedded in Hopi spiritual life to their own proselytizing ends. Since the earliest years of Spanish evangelism in the Americas, missionaries had sought to display in architecture the triumph of the Christian god over those of the pagans. At Cholula and Tenochtitlán, Mexico, in the 1520s, the Soldiers of God had torn down temples that stood atop the massive earth-and-masonry pyramids and replaced them with churches, "symbolizing the supplanting of pagan rites by the domination of the cross." More than simply a show of force, Franciscans also knew that the lingering memory of traditional practices and power would doubtless infuse the new churches. Fourteenth-century Aztecs had used similar tactics to invent a fictional lineal descent from the more ancient Toltecs, as had the priesthood at Chaco Canyon designed their Great Kivas to evoke memories of the original pit-houses of their progenitors.

Padre Gutiérrez imposed the same strategy in locating his church, with the difference that in New Mexico, indigenous sacred spaces more often lay underground, rather than atop pyramids. Writing in 1638, Padre Juan de Prada would wax eloquent that "where there were nothing other than the ceremonial chambers (kivas) of barbarous idolatries, today temples may be seen that are frequented by Christians, who acquaint themselves with the Christian faith and good customs."

Indeed, nearly two meters beneath the church altar Harvard Peabody archaeologists excavating in the 1930s would find a perfectly preserved kiva, its roof beams still in place and even the entrance hatch undisturbed. Excavators were immediately struck by the difference between this kiva and what would normally be found in an abandoned Hopi pueblo—roofing *vigas* (timbers) were simply much too valuable to leave in place when a room or kiva fell into disuse, and Hopis salvaged them for new construction. Of the twenty-four kivas investigated at Awat'ovi in the 1930s, only the one beneath the church altar had timbers still in place. Strikingly unusual, too, was the manner in which the kiva had been filled. In all other cases at Awat'ovi, mixtures of household rubbish, broken ceramics, animal bones, and charcoal comprised the fill of abandoned kivas. Beneath the church, however, the kiva had been carefully filled with clean, sifted sand—a deliberate act that not only provided solid support for the foundations as the massive church was constructed atop the kiva, but also preservation of the fourteen layers of earlier kiva murals that had been painted by Hopi priests in their ceremonies. Whether Hopis had earlier used sand to fill the kiva as an act of abandonment ritual—seen occasionally elsewhere in the Southwest—or the mission laborers had filled the kiva with sand in order to establish a stable foundation for the church nave is impossible to know. But what lay between the altar and the kiva roof beams would ultimately prove more puzzling to the story.

Before the discovery of the kiva, and much to their surprise, excavators encountered the bones of a Spaniard. Catholic canon law explicitly forbade burial within a colonial church, but here they found a "secondary" or reburial, in express contravention of that injunction. The man's bones, once defleshed and disarticulated, had been bundled in remnants of European clothing and placed upon a Hopi basket for interment—deliberately and caringly deposited beneath the packed earth of the altar floor. The bundling of the bones vaguely recalls medieval cathedral ossuaries, but more likely reflected Hopi burial practices of swaddling bodies with cotton textiles and personal items like baskets, bowls, awls, knives, bows, and arrows. In this case the arm bones were bound with a cord of yucca fibers and dogbane, which "on discovery, immediately suggested the type of rope associ-

ated with priestly robes." Deposited almost certainly after the ruination of the church in the uprisings of 1680, someone had, after first
allowing his flesh to decompose, lain a European male in his early
20s, dressed as if in Franciscan habits in the liminal space between
Catholic and Hopi ceremonial chambers. Might this body be that
of Francisco de Porras? It seems unlikely, since that martyr died at
nearly fifty years of age. Might he be a victim of the revolt of 1680?
Perhaps. But only if someone had buried him within the altar and
taken pains to replace and resurface it such that it would be invisible to the eye (and later archaeologists). No Spaniards survived those
violent few days, at least so far as the documents tell us. And why
violate Christian rules against burial within the nave?

Just who played some role in this odd transgression of canon law
may never be resolved. We do know that major construction continued under Gutiérrez, and that during those years some fraction
of Awat'ovi's people were drawn physically, as well as spiritually,
closer to the Franciscan presence. As time passed, a "friendly" pueblo
of Christian adherents developed on the far (east) side of the plaza
to house these converts, whether nominal or devoted. This pattern
appeared often throughout Franciscan New Mexico, and expressed
visually the divisions that were developing as Christianity vied with
traditional Pueblo spiritual practices for the hearts, minds, and bodies of Indian people. These new villages are generally of much more
hurried, and fragile, construction than the premission pueblos, and
exhibit a material culture that hints at "lower order" economic status for their residents—very few items of luxury (beads, turquoise,
elegantly decorated ceramics) and bare minimum dwelling size. Yet
their social status may have been something of a rather higher order,

as those drawn to Mission San Bernardo saw themselves as active agents in the transformation of the High Place of the Bow Clan.

At the best-studied of similar sites, the Mission Nuestra Señora de los Ángeles de Porciúncula at Pecos Pueblo east of Santa Fe, the "friendly" pueblo grew to embrace some 300 rooms, with perhaps 100 resident families. With stone and timber resources scarce—yet not nearly so rare as on the Hopi mesas—families obtained their building materials by literally dismantling their homes in the premission pueblo. With the departure of each adherent, fortress Awat'ovi would be losing both citizens and mass. At Pecos, National Park Service architectural historian James E. "Jake" Ivey estimates that by the middle years of the seventeenth century the original North Pueblo "probably looked half-empty and partly in ruins." This new pueblo at Awat'ovi might well have mirrored what researchers claim for Pecos: a "place of greatest power and influence on the *mesilla* during the seventeenth century, with the [premission] North Pueblo a half-empty slum-like backwater occupied by 'unconverted Pecoseños'—Pecos kin-groups that refused to ally themselves with the Franciscans." The insult of Franciscan intrusion would be manifest each day as Katsina priests rose to offer their prayers and corn pollen to the rising sun, for directly in the foreground would be the steadily increasing edifice of the "Christian Indians."

Given the amount of architectural work accomplished during his tenure, we can presume that Gutiérrez's tenure at the mission featured tangible success in recruiting the sympathies of a substantial portion of Awat'ovi's people. That would change, however, with the arrival of Padre Alonso de Posada in 1653. Posada was unequivocally the "dark side" of the Franciscan Order, and a man who doubtless dismantled much of the goodwill that Gutiérrez may have cultivated. Abrasive in style and impudent in act, Posada almost immediately became the subject of Hopi shaming ritual, since "formalized public mimicry and burlesque" was (and is) often part-and-parcel of Hopi ceremonialism, expressed in "clowning" that draws attention to well-known but privately discussed misbehavior. Not a few modern tourists attending Hopi ceremonial dances today have felt the sting of Hopi mockery of white ways, from consumerism to obesity to puritanical attitudes toward sexuality.

Midway into the padre's brief tenure a Hopi convert named Juan stood accused of impersonating Friar Alonso in a ribald and embarrassing performance, while Posada was absent visiting a distant pueblo. Juan "summoned the Indians to the church, where he put on the friar's vestments, took the incense burner and censed the altar, then sprinkled the holy water" in the manner of the priest. Coupled with what the documents coyly describe as a performance of "grave sexual immorality"—of which we will understand more shortly—Juan's parody of the padre drew him a journey to Santa Fe and "a period of service in the convent where he could be instructed in the faith."

Juan's satire likely referenced a rather more "grave" incident at the heart of which lay Posada himself. The Franciscan had taken to keeping a converted woman named Isabel in his chambers for other than Christian pleasures, a fact widely known and resented among the Hopis. When a Hopi man, Sixto, a "leading Indian of the pueblo," began "making trouble" with Isabel, Posada ordered two of the Christian pueblo's *capitanes á guerro* (war chiefs) to murder him, which command they obeyed. Fearing that his guilt might be revealed, Posada then summoned the *mestizo alcalde mayor* of the mission community to "bring the two capitanes to swift and summary trial…upon some pretext of disobedience, and hang them—which he did." The padre's attempts to manage his crisis failed, and in 1656 he found himself a prisoner in the mission convento at Santo Domingo Pueblo south of Santa Fe. Unfortunately for Indian justice, civil governor Juan Manso compelled the friar's release and by 1660 he had been assigned the custodianship of the entire province.

❧·❦

The whipsawing of Franciscan leadership and Hopi sentiment at Awat'ovi continued as conflagration drew near. The decade following the departure of Posada featured a far different Franciscan style, and one that shaped the pueblo's history profoundly. Padre José de Espeleta arrived on the Hopi mesas in 1661, assigned first as guardian to the small church at Shungopovi, and to Mission San Bernardo in 1663. Espeleta, a "highly spiritual man who sensed the value of the mission as Spain's most effective colonizing force," set out to repair the damaged relations with the Hopis. He beseeched Governor Diego Dionisio de Peñalosa to send an organ and trained singers from Santa Fe to help him communicate the soothing words of Christ in music. Soon he earned the governor's approval to excuse any Hopi singers from labor or tribute requirement, and devoted intense effort to inculcating in the already ritualistically inclined Hopis a love for choral singing and associated liturgical dramas. Navajo oral histories recorded in the early twentieth century seem to recall Espeleta's tenure, for as Navajos herded their sheep and goats beneath the escarpments of Antelope Mesa, they marveled at the music drifting down into the canyons and washes. They gave Awat'ovi the Navajo name

Tallahogan—the Singing House, or Place of the Singers—evoking a history strikingly incongruous with the ways its meaning has descended to us today.

Espeleta also began a program of taking Hopi boys into the mission for intensive Christian education. Residing in the convento rather than the Christian pueblo, the boys learned Spanish and Latin, to write, to recite the rosary and the catechism as the essential and fundamental contents of the Catholic doctrine, and to spread their knowledge among their kinspeople. Only one of these boys survives in the historical record, but "Francisco de Espeleta," as he was known among the Franciscans (and "don Francisco" by Spanish governors), plays a powerful, if ambiguous role in the story ahead. Writing several decades later, Friar José Narváez Valverde would claim that the Hopis "remain in their heights in primitive freedom" under the command of one Francisco de Espeleta "because of his having been brought up and taught to read and write by one religious whose name was Espeleta. . . . since this uprising (1680) it has not been possible to reduce them."

If Narváez were correct, it would not be the first time that a devotee turned on his teachers and became leader of native resistance. Perhaps the most famous of such figures is that of Opchanacanough—He Whose Soul Is White—a Powhatan leader who first received tutelage in European ways as a boy christened "don Luís." Taken from his natal village of Kiskiak to Spain at the age of seventeen and educated there, he returned to help spread the faith in the short-lived Jesuit mission at Ajacán on the Virginia Chesapeake. But within a year don Luís led the revolt that extinguished the mission and fulfilled the Jesuit missionaries' desire for martyrdom. Closer to home, the Naranjo family of the Tewa pueblo at Santa Clara fielded mission-educated

participants in the Pueblo Revolt, as well as to the Spanish reconquest thirteen years later. Francisco de Espeleta, however, is one of
the most opaque characters in the story of Awat'ovi's demise and
the Hopis' rejection of Catholicism. He seems to have been torn in
his sympathies and himself driven from pillar to post in negotiating
the intense clan and village politics of Tusayán during the period of
the Pueblo Revolt.

The end of the Franciscan Espeleta would come shortly after his
successes at Awat'ovi. Even during the years when Espeleta brought
music, choral voices, and a semblance of social harmony to Antelope Mesa, other forces were combining to sabotage his work. Other
Franciscans who joined the missions in the Hopi country proved
more in the cut of Padre Posada than of Espeleta. One such was
Fray Salvador de Guerra, first stationed at Shungopovi in 1652 and
transferred shortly to the eastern Towa pueblo of Jemez, where his
superiors could better monitor his abusive behavior to his charges. At
Shungopovi, de Guerra had invaded Hopi homes in search of cotton
cloth to demand as tribute, and when he discovered "some feathers"
and "idols," he seized the people and doused them with turpentine
"so as to set fire to them." One of his victims ran for a distant water
spring where he could douse the flames, but de Guerra—fearing he
meant to report the grotesque punishment to other Franciscans—
mounted a horse and ran the man down, killing him. Authorities
in Santa Fe heard of the crime and brought him east. When called
before the ecclesiastical court to account for his actions, he defended
himself by claiming that he only "occasionally used beating and lard-
ing to punish idolators and boys and girls for 'culpas particulares.'" By
1664, just one year into Espeleta's term, de Guerra turned up at Hopi
again, appointed to Awat'ovi.

Espeleta could not control the rogue friar. Although he may have lessened his physical cruelties, he intensified his demands that the Hopis weave cotton mantas for him, doubtless for resale in the markets of Santa Fe. The courts again found against him, declaring "the said father is incorrigible, overbearing, and arrogant," and removed him from Hopi to the eastern mission at Quarai for penance. And then inexplicably assigned him to the mission at the southern Tiwa pueblo of Isleta on the Rio Grande.

Complaints against de Guerra from Isleta provide a window into the tensions that would reach a flash point in the summer of 1680. The absence of rain had become so severe, and the temperatures so brutal, that it distressed even the Spaniards. No doubt more concerned about his own survival than that of the Pueblo Indians—who "perished of hunger, lying dead along the roads, in the ravines, and in their huts"—Governor Bernardo López de Mendizábal finally "consented and gave permission to Christian Indians . . . to perform this dance (of the Kachinas) in public." At Isleta this permission shattered what little decorum Padre de Guerra still maintained: "Not being able to restrain them in any other way, [he] went throughout the pueblo with the cross on his shoulders, a crown of thorns, and a rope about his neck, beating his naked body, in order that they might stop the dance." The Isletans found his performance so disturbing that one group, probably the Christian faction, "came after him weeping, saying that they were not to blame, because the governor himself had commanded they dance."

Elsewhere, Franciscans harshly suppressed the ceremonies and prosecuted the Katsina dancers for idolatry. In 1675, the local Inquisition hanged three Katsina priests in Santa Fe, and forty-three others suffered floggings for crimes of sorcery and sedition. Among the flogged were prominent spiritual leaders like Po'pay, from Okhay Owinge (San Juan Pueblo), Antonio Malacate of Tesuque Pueblo, the Keresan Alonso Catiti, and Luis Tupatú of Picurís Pueblo, who over the next several years quietly set about organizing an effort to expunge the Spanish curse from the region. The rebels sent runners to distant pueblos like Acoma, Zuni, and those of the Hopi mesas, using a knotted cord to indicate the days yet to pass before the rising would commence. Their careful timing went awry when Spaniards intercepted messengers from Tesuque Pueblo and tortured them to reveal the rebels' plans. Lest the Spanish have time to raise a defense, on August 10, 1680, the Eastern Pueblos erupted in rebellion, followed a few days later by the Hopis. Widespread warfare, raiding, and sacking of outlying settlements delivered 422 Spanish subjects to death or captivity. The surviving 1,946 colonists, missionaries, servants, and allied "Christian Indians" were expelled from the northern colony for more than a decade.

Padre José de Espeleta died not at Awat'ovi, where he had been

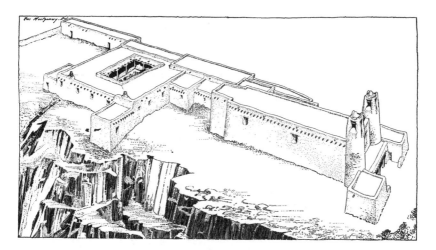

Mission San Bernardo de Awat'ovi in 1680, on the eve of the rebellion.

recently replaced by Fray José de Figueroa, but at Oraibi. His end is recalled in the histories passed down to Wikvaya. At "the moment of the yellow dawn" Hopi assailants woke him by pounding on his cell door, and rushed in once he had slid open the bolt. Espeleta resisted the assault and found himself dragged outdoors, where the attackers slit his throat and threw his body off the edge of the mesa for the ravens and coyotes to devour. Similar fates befell the other three documented priests at Hopi on that fateful day—Fray Figueroa at Awat'ovi, where the residents quickly began to loot the church of its paraphernalia and timbers; Fray José de Trujillo at Shungopovi, who was bound and burned over a fire fueled by timbers from the mission; and along with Espeleta at Oraibi the recently arrived Fray Augustín de Santa María, his throat slashed as well. No records exist of the fate of the lay brothers, carpenters, and any family members who lived at the missions, but no memories of their survival exist, either. Nor do Hopi traditional narratives recall the destiny of the "Christian Indians" who had participated in the Franciscan decades at Awat'ovi. The Hopis' Navajo neighbors, however, recall that "some of the Catholics escaped to shelter among the Navajos, and some were driven over the cliffs." By the end of August no living representatives of the Spanish Empire and its Catholic faith walked Antelope Mesa. And yet something powerful remained.

❧·❦

The stunning success of the rebellion's early days disintegrated over the course of one year, although it would take more than a decade for the Spaniards to reexert their authority. Po'pay and his corevolution-

Nuestra Señora de la Macana (Our Lady of the War Club), a rare depiction of the Siege of Santa Fe in 1680, and the iconic Virgin that survived.

aries understood that the Pueblo world had been utterly transformed during the eighty-some years of Spanish colonization. Pushing a program of nativistic purification and return to the "old ways," the rebels urged the complete destruction of the mission churches and their liturgical paraphernalia, as well as rejection of the Spanish-influenced lifeways of livestock herding, wheat farming, tools, and architecture. Freed from the yoke of the missionaries, many Pueblo Indians set out to desecrate, dismantle, and reuse the adobe bricks, heavy timbers, and extensive construction of the mission complexes—yet often converted the churches and conventos into corrals for the sheep, cattle, and horses that they were wont to preserve, rather than reject. The deep divisions between traditionalists and those who had been drawn to Catholicism reemerged quickly, since they drew not only upon religious sympathies, but the inequities in power that had crosscut Pueblo society for generations. Pecos Pueblo experienced an internal civil war, and the southernmost Pueblo peoples—the Piros and Tompiros—refused to follow Po'pay's leadership, distant as he was among the northern Pueblos. Enraged, Po'pay "began to act like the Spanish tyrants he had expelled," executing dissidents and accumulating women for his pleasure. Deposed from leadership by dissatisfied Tewas and replaced by the northern Tiwa Picurís captain Luis Tupatú, Po'pay was dead by 1688. The Keres captain Alonso Catiti also died, and in the resulting leadership vacuum the Keresan pueblos fractured into competing raiders.

In contrast to the mythology of a "bloodless reconquest," soldiers like don Diego de Vargas and the Franciscans who followed his mounted columns were forced to mix fierce fighting with complex recruitment of Pueblo allies, and a negotiated reimposition of the Catholic faith that included some sufferance of traditional

Pueblo religious practices. In the same year as Po'pay's death, Spaniards began forays into their former colony with reconquest in mind. Brief yet bloody engagements at Zia Pueblo suggested a waning rebel defensive capacity, and intelligence gathered in those entradas suggested that to the west, the Zunis and Hopis had begun raiding each other for their stores of corn. Finally, over the winter of 1691–92, embassies from the pueblos of Jemez, Zia, Santa Ana, San Felipe, and Pecos—combining Towa- and Keres-speaking peoples—reached the Spanish encampment at El Paso del Norte to parlay with the Spaniards, and invited their return to the devastated north. Pacification of the Rio Grande Valley pueblos occupied Spanish attention for several months. No words had reached them about the fate of the missions in the western provinces of Zuni and Moqui.

What the Spanish *reconquistadores* found when they finally reached Tusayán would only deepen the mystery of the Singing House. History did not stand still in the absence of Europeans.

4

Wolves from the East

And when all of these people act like bandits, I do not know what
protection there is for a poor religious alone at his mission.
What can one ant do against a thousand bloodthirsty wolves?
—FRAY ANTONIO CARBONEL, JUNE 1696

The Spanish reconquest of New Mexico took place across four long years and in several halting stages, far messier and traumatic than the "Bloodless" reconquest celebrated today in the annual Fiestas de Santa Fe each September. Indeed, the reconquistador don Diego de Vargas entered the province in that month of 1692 to little opposition and achieved a symbolic reoccupation of the villa of Santa Fe without bloodshed—yet the fortified Casas Reales (now Governor's Palace) remained in the hands of Pueblo Indians who had reclaimed the settlement they once called Ogap'oge (White Shell Water Place). As winter enveloped the province, Vargas led an expedition to the west, receiving the (equally) symbolic subjugation of the Acoma, Zuni, and, after tense confrontation at the foot of Antelope Mesa "in the midst of 800 Moqui Indians, all armed," a pledge of loyalty from "the chief, Miguel by name" of Awat'ovi, outside the gated walls of which he established an encampment and parade ground. This phase of his resettlement campaign fulfilled, he departed south for his base in El Paso. He would learn the conquest was incomplete.

Vargas returned as winter drew near in 1693, this time with recolonization his aim. He brought a substantial expedition—100 men-at-arms, 70 families, 18 Franciscan friars, and dozens of Indian allies herding some 2,000 horses, 1,000 mules, and 900 head of cattle, sheep, and hogs. The force arrived outside of Santa Fe in December to find the villa's residents "shameless and sneering," deeply suspicious of the colonists' intent. Making an encampment "two harquebus shots" distant from the former provincial palace's adobe walls, he negotiated for two weeks, until December 28, when the Indian occupants suddenly turned militant. Huge bonfires burned within the plazas of the palace, and war songs reverberated throughout the night.

As it turned out, the fighting would prove particularly fierce due to the defense offered by some seasoned warriors resident in the former Casas Reales. These Indian fighters, from the Galisteo Basin pueblos south of Santa Fe, had been the majority force in sacking the villa in 1680, and had rebuilt the ruined complex as an Indian pueblo during the decades thereafter. Their martial skills had been honed in defending their own villages (and associated missions) against Apache raiders during the seventeenth century, and through service as auxiliaries to Spanish campaigns against the Navajos during the same decades. Settling in the former village of Ogap'oge was a decision that removed them from daily anxiety about Apache raids in the Basin and confirmed their centrality to the revolt.

Known in Spanish accounts as "Tanos," these peoples comprised one branch of the Kiowa-Tanoan language family that occupied much of the Rio Grande Valley north of the Sandia Mountains, and extending to encompass the Jemez and Sangre de Cristo mountain ranges. Just when the subgroup of Tanos hived off from their Tewa kinspeople is unclear, but by the fourteenth century they were coalescing into major agricultural towns in the fertile former ocean bed of the Galisteo Basin. The first European mention of Tano settlements dates from the 1540s, when Coronado's expedition passed through the Basin on their ill-fated quest to find Gran Quivira.

At least eight major towns, numbering more than a thousand residents in each, flourished when Spanish colonists arrived in 1598, profiting by exchanging their corn and beans with Plains Apaches in return for bison meat, hides, and slaves. Franciscan fathers established missions at the Pueblos of Galisteo and San Lazaro by 1616, and three more at San Marcos, San Cristóbal, and La Cieneguilla by 1626. Ostensibly devoted to the salvation of Indian souls, the Franciscans also saw the missions as economic engines for the colonial enterprise, especially in animal husbandry through the raising of horses, mules, and cattle for the new colony. Tanos resented the labor demands placed upon them, but also garnered important new skills in the livestock trades—iron forging, leatherworking, and gunsmithing. Providing military protection for the missions against seasonal raids by Apaches—newly mounted on escaped horses, the Vaqueros and Faraones were precursors to later Lipans and Mescaleros—Tanos were the most familiar with Spanish arms and tactics among all the 1680 rebels. Thirteen years later, with Vargas outside their walls, they would fight again, suffer defeat, and begin another migration.

Once the rebellion erupted, Tanos proved avid in the cause. Burning mission churches, killing friars, and marching north to turn the tide during the siege of Santa Fe, Tano fighters gained reputations as not easily intimidated. After expelling the surviving Franciscans and colonists, they rewarded themselves with the spoils and claimed Ogap'oge. They transformed it into a fortress, adding second and third stories of solid adobe ramparts from which they could command all the approaches.

Now, with Vargas's forces surrounding their citadel, they employed defensive tactics that recalled medieval warfare during the reconquest of Spain. The Indians drew up their ladders from the exterior walls, "barred the main gate, and manned the ramparts, shouting their defiance" while letting loose a volley of arrows and sling stones at Vargas's emissaries. An initial Spanish charge to the battle cry "Santiago!" was repulsed, and required more deliberate tactics. Spanish sappers set out to undermine the fortress walls, but the defenders "melted snow in iron kettles, and poured boiling water down upon them." In response, de Vargas's men built "shielded ladders" that helped them reach the battlements. Even then the fighting lasted throughout the freezing night. Only after the attackers breached the walls of a makeshift kiva that had been constructed adjacent to the fortress did the Spanish gain entrance to the two interior plazas. So intricate were the stronghold's internal defenses that it took more than fifty of Vargas's men to subdue the defenders, and even then it took "the whole blessed day until nightfall" to be sure that the surrender was complete. Seventy Indian fighters would eventually be captured and hanged. Two Indians, "without hope at the thought of defeat," hanged themselves before the Spaniards could seize them. Tanos would remain staunchly opposed to the Spanish in

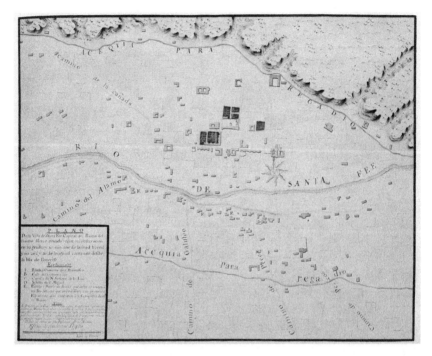

The earliest known map of Santa Fe, as drawn by Joseph de Urrutia in 1767. The Governor's Palace (the Pueblo citadel in 1693) is marked with the letter *B*, and the open square south of it is the present town plaza.

the years to come, and that enmity would shape events far distant on the Hopi mesas.

The villa regained, Vargas sought to stabilize the colony and to reestablish missions among the Pueblos as efficiently as possible. But resettling the Galisteo Basin pueblos seemed doomed to failure, since without either a presidial guard or the fortified mission complexes for security, and the livestock economy in shambles, the residents would be entirely vulnerable to Apache violence. Or, perhaps depart the colony all together and align themselves with those former enemies and trading partners. Vargas and his Franciscan advisors decided that requiring the defeated Tanos to settle north of Santa Fe, in the better watered and more secure valley of the Rio Santa Cruz would be the wiser course. The Spaniards called the reestablished pueblo San Cristóbal de los Tanos, known as *Tsaewari* ("wide white band," or "dance sash") by its inhabitants. A second expatriate community from the Basin was established as New San Lazaro, or Tewige, by which time some 500 Tanos had joined their Tewa cousins in the basin lying between the Jemez and Sangre de Cristo ranges. In the autumn of 1695, Vargas expelled the Tanos from New San Lazaro, in order to clear the site for anticipated new colonists, and all the Tanos were united at Tsaewari. Tewige would soon become the Spanish village of Santa Cruz de la Cañada.

The Franciscans were charged with renewing the Catholic faith among the resettled and deeply resentful Tanos. Vargas demanded that the Tanos build their padre a "house and chapel" in which he could sing the Te Deum Laudamus. These isolated priests, scattered throughout the colony in ramshackle missions, would spend their nights in fear of their lives (or anticipate martyrdom at the stroke of a stone axe). It was from new San Cristóbal/Tsaewari that Friar Carbonel wrote an anxious message to his custodian, Fray Francisco de Vargas, in which he characterized living among and attempting to proselytize the Tanos as being an "ant" (*hormiga*) surrounded by salivating wolves. The following spring would prove him right.

❧⨾⨾❧

Far to the west, the "Moquis"—as the Spanish called the Hopi peoples of the province of Tusayán—also knew of the Tano's ferocity. Although they had succeeded in expelling the Franciscans from their mesas in the rebellion of 1680, the region had not enjoyed peace in the decade that followed. As one major source of corn, beans, and squash in the west, the Hopi villages suffered seasonal raids each autumn by Utes, Paiutes, Comanches from the north and Apaches from the south, who waited until after harvest time to sweep through the cornfields that flourished in the sandy washes beneath the four mesas. Raiders also fought "their way into the villages and took food, women, and children," who might find themselves forcibly adopted kinspeople among their captors, or sold to Spanish slave traders for transshipment as far south as the silver mines of Durango and Zacatecas.

External enemies were not the sole threat, however. According to Hopi oral accounts, intervillage conflict proved even more frequent and devastating. Albert Yava of First Mesa would later recall "sometimes other Hopi villages attacked them too. The people of the Hopi villages did not consider themselves as belonging to the same tribe. They considered themselves Walpis, Mishongnovis, Shongopovis, Oraibis, and so on. Their village was their nationality, you might say." Neighbors attacking neighbors would foster grievances that festered well before (and after) the conflagration at Awat'ovi. The internal violence concurrently weakened the defensive capability of the whole Hopi coalition.

Especially vulnerable was the community of Walpi at First Mesa. Today the most iconic of Hopi towns, in the seventeenth century Walpi actually lay on the western flank of the mesa below where it now stands (in order to be close to the spring that served its people) and was known by the name Keuchaptevela. Harassed by foreign raiders and antagonistic neighbors alike, after the revolt of 1680 the beleaguered Walpis sought a better defensive site by relocating atop the *peñole* (rock outcropping) of First Mesa where the village stands today. Even then, as threats intensified, they knew their situation was perilous. Walpi needed to increase its strength. One strategy toward that end could draw upon a centuries-deep custom on the Hopi mesas: the addition of "outsiders" to their community. This process of recruitment involved practices long in use before the Spanish conquest, given the "braided" nature of Hopi historical identities and the array of oral traditions about Hopi clan migrations and the formation of new communities on their mesas.

Popular notions of timeless Indian "tribes" and a body of federal Indian law that recognizes only "tribal" entities have created a fog of misunderstanding around the complexity of the deep past. Albert Yava's comment about Hopi village "nationalities" points to this at the local level. Indeed, there may be no Indian people in the Southwest with more variegated origins than those known today as the Hopis. Each of dozens of ancient "Hopi" villages, including Awat'ovi, was populated over the centuries by small groups of migrants from across the Southwest, often carrying language and traditions discrete unto themselves, if similar to some of the broader cultural patterns across the region. As migrants sought entrance and acceptance to established villages, they would be challenged to show how their presence might help to sustain the community.

At Oraibi Village an elder recalled the process thus: "When a clan arrived usually one of the new arrivals would go to the village and ask the village chief for permission to settle in the village. He usually asked whether they understood anything to produce rain and good crops, and if they had any cult; they would refer to it and say, 'Yes, this or this we have, and when we assemble for this ceremony, or when we have this dance it will rain. With this we have traveled, and with this we have taken care of our children.' The chief would say, 'Very well, you come and live in this village.'" Once accepted as new members, however, the village chief tested their loyalty, requiring that newcomers "participate in our cult and help us with our ceremonies." Only then would he distribute cornfields according to the rank of their arrival, a procedure that tended to reinforce the subordinate status of each new immigrant group.

As archaeologist Wesley Bernardini explains, "although the Hopi *region* may have received a large number of immigrants . . . in fact each Hopi *village* received a different set of socially distinct immigrants groups who shared in common only a brief period of co-residence at their most recent place of occupation." As these small social groups coalesced in villages on the Hopi mesas, numerous points of potential friction arose. Different languages made communication difficult, especially around esoteric ceremonial traditions. A strong tendency to "rank" each newly arriving group as socially and ceremonially beneath the status of "founding" clans fostered enduring resentment, and the limited resources in Tusayán intensified an impulse toward intervillage tensions. In order to avoid chaos, communities of disparate peoples "would have required new efforts to integrate populations and consolidate social identity." Any deviation from those social identities could produce chaos (*koyaanisqatsi*) and require reintegration, most often through roles associated with clan or Katsina obligations, which created relationships that reached across village and valley divides to align people of diverse origins. If those avenues failed, reintegration might require violence.

Thus had communities formed in Tusayán over the centuries, as diverse and volatile as they were ancient and enduring. After the revolt of 1680, however, the pace of foreign arrivals intensified. Some time after the revolt, probably in response to an autumn 1681 foray by Governor Antonio de Otermín with 146 Spanish men-at-arms and 112 pueblo auxiliaries, the Keres of Sandia Pueblo left their village and set out for the west. Before their departure, the Sandias had transformed the Franciscan convento into a "seminary of idolatry," adorning the standing walls with Katsina masks "arranged very carefully, after their barbarous custom." Otermín ordered the remains of the convento put to the torch, destroying the images of the sacred beings. According to several stories, the fugitive Sandias reached Second Mesa in Tusayán and, after convincing the resident Hopis of the value of their ceremonies, were allowed to settle and establish the fortified village of Payupki (the Hopi name for the Keres of Sandia). Around the same time, some refugees from Jemez Pueblo also sought shelter among the Hopis, establishing a village on Antelope Mesa remembered as Akokavi, or "Place of the Sunflowers." These refugee communities, with firsthand knowledge of the tensions that led to the revolt and the persistence of Spanish efforts to regain their colony, would lend their own bitter experience to Hopi attitudes about the Franciscans.

The people of Walpi sought a more assertive solution. After a discussion among clan leaders, survival of the village seemed impossible without the aid of new allies. Since their own Hopi kinsmen acted more antagonistic than sympathetic, recruitment of battle-hardened Pueblo cousins from the Rio Grande presented an alternative. And events unfolding in the Rio Grande region lent themselves well to the Walpis' scheme.

There, the winter of 1695–96 visited hardship on Indians and Spaniards alike. The turmoils of the preceding year had prevented successful planting and tending of agricultural fields. The harvest of 1695 had proved lean. A viciously cold season depleted what few stores remained in the pueblos, and the Spanish colonists had even less food on hand. Vargas sent soldiers to the pueblos to levy corn but found the granaries bare. One padre assigned to the Tanos complained of thin attendance at mass, "because they are traveling about soliciting food, since they are suffering seriously from hunger, for during the course of the war they had no harvests whatsoever." In March of 1696, Fray José Arbízu wrote from San Cristóbal/ Tsaewari that "the natives of said pueblo . . . are leaving me, and in the sierra they have placed their corn supplies and clothing . . . [they are] openly in rebellion," having "prepared covered pits and traps at the ascents to the mountains so that the horses of the Spaniards will fall into them," and erected stockades at the entrance to their camps. Vargas estimated the fugitive Tanos in their mountain strongholds (apparently reoccupied fourteenth-century villages in the valleys of the Rio Chiquito and Rito Sarco, above Chimayó) to number some 600, a formidable challenge to his authority in that they seemed "more intent to make war than peace."

Lending additional concern to Vargas were the reports he received throughout early 1696 from padres among the Tanos of the presence of "Moquis" (Hopis) at San Cristóbal/Tsaewari. Some of these seem to have been guided into the mountain refuges by locals "where they had, and still have, all of their food supplies and weapons of war and have set up stockades to make themselves invincible." Vargas feared that the Tanos might be recruiting allies from the Western Pueblos, as well as from neighboring Apache and Navajo bands. He misunderstood the direction of the alliances, however. Hopis sojourning with the Tanos signaled that the process of recruitment designed by the Walpis was underway in 1696, beginning a process of stitching the two peoples into a shared history that continues to the present day.

As cold weather persisted into the spring, delegates from the highest-ranked clans at Walpi—the Bear and the Snake—set out to the east. Traveling some three hundred miles afoot, they sought out the villagers of Tsaewari and extended an invitation "to make a home in our country" far distant from the travails of the Spanish colony. The Tanos considered the request, but more urgent matters prevented a decision.

Late in the evening of June 4, violence erupted at San Cristóbal/ Tsaewari. The residents who had not yet fled for the mountains killed Fray Arbízu and his guest, Fray Carbonel, stripped them to their underclothes, and lay their bodies in the dirt plaza, placing one atop the other "in the form of a cross, face up." Also killed were settlers Simon de Molina and Diego Betanzos, a young Mexican Indian servant, and a fourteen-year-old Indian boy from El Paso who spoke Spanish, probably a *doñado* (a child given to the Church for upbringing and instruction) attached to the mission as personal servant to Arbízu. Some soldiers, who had been "drinking chocolate with the reverend fathers," had departed just before the killings began.

Rebellion flamed elsewhere in the colony as well. At San Ildefonso Pueblo, Fray Francisco Corbera was slain. Fray Antonio Moreno, normally resident at Nambe Pueblo, who was visiting Corbera for "spiritual consolation," and a Spanish family took shelter in the convento, only to have it put to the torch, where they "were suffocated by the smoke." In the province of the Jemez 2 padres died, as well as 10 colonists, their children, and a soldier. In all, 5 priests and some 25 colonists and their dependents died in the uprising.

Vargas recovered quickly from the shock, ordered that far-flung missions and Spanish settlers convene in Santa Fe to prepare a defense, and gathered his forces for retaliation. The 100 *presidiales* who arrived in New Mexico in 1693 had been reduced through warfare and disease to a mere 48, and thus his capacity was severely limited. The Spanish found support, however, among the Keres-speaking Pueblos of San Felipe, Santa Ana, Santo Domingo, and Zia, who had long-running conflicts with the Tewas and Tanos (probably predating the Spanish settlement of New Mexico), and thus were willing to contribute auxiliary warriors to the Spanish cause. The leadership at Tesuque Pueblo (Tewa) north of Santa Fe also favored the Spanish, although others in the village remained hostile. Pecos, too, was deeply divided, as it had been in 1680. Rebel leaders were captured and executed at Nambe Pueblo and Santo Domingo, but it was "the accursed Tano nation" that Vargas held responsible for the uprising.

On June 28, he mustered sufficient force to "set forth to make war against the Tewas and Tanos," and ventured into the mountains above Chimayó. Alerted to his approach, the Tanos fled higher into the mountains but left behind their meager stores of corn. Vargas found but one *coscomate* (bin) of maize in the refugee site, seven *coas* (planting sticks), and evidence of preparations for a long siege—"a tall square shed with adobe walls and a door to store supplies. . . . [as well as] ditches and acequias to bring irrigation water to their *milpas* (fields). They had built a dam across a very large arroyo that comes down to the milpas through the cañada." Captain Don Antonio de Valverde led a column into this "Cañada de los Tanos," high up on the Rio Chiquito, and "occupied all their milpas, establishing himself in the middle of them." The Tanos retired and established another fortified encampment in the high valley above Nambe Pueblo, but it, too, was overrun as the inhabitants fled.

In one month of campaigning, Vargas chipped away at rebels throughout the colony, his forces killing at least 90 and taking several hundred prisoner, most of whom were distributed as household slaves among the colonists. One key rebel, Lucas Naranjo, a Tewa-African "lobo," was killed by a fortuitous harquebus shot on July 24 during an engagement near the Mesa Prieta (Black Mesa of the north). Throughout the month, too, Vargas received regular reports of western Pueblos, Zunis, and Moquis, circulating among the rebel Pueblos, who were also said to be crafting alliances with Navajos and Apaches. The Moquis were almost certainly not potential allies for the Rio Grande uprising, but most likely representatives from Walpi who were carrying forward their own plan of recruitment.

Three more visits followed the Snake and Bear clan chiefs' first efforts in the winter of 1695–96, perhaps on an annual basis after harvests were gathered in Hopi country, and therefore spanning the years 1697–1699. On the fourth, the Tanos finally agreed to make the migration. This time, the Walpi clan leaders had brought "a bundle of prayer feathers, *pahos*," representing three promises—"male and female pahos together meant people" and signaled their willingness to allow the Tanos "to take Walpi's sons and daughters as husbands and wives" toward the growth and unity of a village community. The third was a plain, unpainted prayer stick, representing the lands that the Tanos would receive at First Mesa for a new village and cornfields below the mesa. "Land and people, that was the pledge," a promise still memorialized today in the masked dancer who carries "a tall stick with cotton strings and feathers attached, representing land and people." The symbolic generosity extended in these *pahos*, unfortunately, would not be realized in practice, which would shape the Tanos actions in the years immediately ahead.

After departing Tsaewari, the Tanos stopped briefly at the Tewa village of Kha'po Owingeh (whose Franciscan mission was dedicated to Santa Clara) on the western side of the Rio Grande, where they recruited additional migrants. Based on the presence of lead-based glaze-ware ceramics, a Tano clan seems to have left the Galisteo Basin in the early 1500s and journeyed north to the Pajarito Plateau, taking up residence with Tewa clan relatives at the village of Puye for at least a generation, before following their kinspeople in moving off the plateau to the village of Kha'po Owingeh, closer to the river. Two centuries later their Tano relatives would ask them to join the journey to Hopi, and thus crafted today's enduring relationship between the linguistic cousins on First Mesa and those of Santa Clara Pueblo.

Stories curated and retold over the centuries at Santa Clara Pueblo count several pauses in their Tano relatives' migration under the leadership of a man named Agaitsay (Yellow Star). Some 400 people made the journey, perhaps 100 families, according to these histories. At each of four locations, the Tanos planted "sacred things" in order to assure a safe journey and perhaps to create a living trail of ties back to their homeland. Some see these pauses to plant as indicating one migratory leg each year, as cornfields were planted in each location, harvested, and the journey recommenced each autumn. Others see the planting pauses as symbolic, a matter of a few days or weeks to mark the journey with ceremonial plantings (corn, tobacco). Tewas today mark these *"parajes"* (resting places) as "chains of belonging" that link their homeland with the migrant village at First Mesa—Cañoncito north of Laguna Pueblo (Tohajiilee Navajo country); Awpimpa, or Duck Spring, near Grants, New Mexico; Bopaw, or Reed Spring, near Gallup, New Mexico; and Kwalalata, Place of Bubbling Water, at Keams Canyon just a few miles distant from First Mesa.

When at last the migrants reached First Mesa, they discovered they were not, as they had expected, welcome. Rather than receiving a defensible site atop the rocky peñole, their Walpi hosts insisted they make their home below, on the eastern slopes of the mesa, where Polacca Village now sits. "How pitifully ignorant must have been our ancestors to believe the Hopi," recalls one narrative. "Little did they know they would be so pitifully deceived . . . not permitted to ascend the mesa when they arrived at Hopi, but forced to make camp below." Hungry after their long migration, they "petitioned Walpi women for food . . . they were told to cup their hands to receive a corn-meal gruel," which was poured into their hands "boiling hot. The Hopi women laughed and berated them for being weak and soft."

Even while suffering these affronts, the Tanos proved their military skill by repelling a Ute raid on the cornfields below the mesa. In contrast, Tanos claimed that when the enemy was around, "the Hopi hid trembling in their houses, like mice in a granary." And yet, "when our ancestors had defeated the Utes and made life safe for the Hopi, they asked for the land, women, and food which had been promised them. But the Hopi refused to give them these things. Then it was that our poor ancestors had to live like beasts, foraging on the wild plants and barely subsisting on the meager supply of food. Our ancestors lived miserably, beset by disease and starvation. The Hopi, well-fed and healthy, laughed and made fun of our ancestors."

The Tanos lost hope for residence on First Mesa and began to explore alternative village locations with Hopi villages to the west. News of the rejection had also reached those relatives in Tsaewari, and a delegation arrived among the Tanos "to take their friends back." Only then did the Walpis "make reparation," and "restored the confidence of the Hano." The Hopi chief offered a location north of Walpi on First Mesa for a new village, and allocated planting lands to the Tanos toward the east, on the slopes of Antelope Mesa. And yet deep suspicions remained. When the Hopi chief reminded Agaitsay that the agreement included the Tanos' rights to "take some of our women for wives," the Tano leader demurred. "Wait, let us not go too fast. . . . first we have to see how well our villages live together." He feared that should Hopi women marry into the Tanos, and tensions arose again, they "might have to break apart. It would be too hard for us to have to go away from here and leave our children and grand-children behind. . . . later we can talk about taking Hopi wives."

Frustrated, Agaitsay laid down a curse that would shape future relationships between the Tanos and Hopis that endures today. Handing a small ear of corn to the Hopi chief, he asked that the Hopi "chew it up but do not swallow it." Once the Hopi had done so, Agaitsay demanded he spit the chewed corn back into his hand, and once done, he took the chewed corn into his own mouth, and swal-lowed. "What is the meaning of this?" asked the Hopi.

"It means that we will take from your mouth the language you speak. We will speak Hopi."

The Hopi replied, "It is good you will speak Hopi. Now you chew some corn and give it to me." Agaitsay chewed some corn, but at the last moment spit the corn into a deep hole that the Tanos had dug at the very edge of the lands allotted for their new village. His people then hastily filled the hole with earth and "covered it with heavy rocks." Shocked, the Hopi asked again the meaning of Agaitsay's actions.

"It means that you will never have our language in your mouths. We will speak Hopi and Tewa, but your people will never speak the

Tewa Village in 1893, looking north from the edge of the community as defined by the "language curse."

Tewa language. If you were to speak Tewa you would be able to infiltrate into our rituals and ceremonies. . . . We want you to know we will remain Tewas forever." The hole into which Agaitsay spit the chewed corn remains the most important shrine at the village today, marked by a large boulder of petrified wood.

The Hopis of Walpi had gained battle-tested fighters to protect their eastern flanks from enemies, whether Utes or Navajos or Apaches or Spaniards. The residents of Tewa Village guard their identities fiercely, however, and even today distinguish themselves as holding specialized ritual knowledge associated with warfare. Although intermarriage between Tanos and Hopis became common in the centuries that followed the migration, and clan linkages bind the Tewas to ceremonial kinspeople across all three Hopi mesas, "few Hopis have even a passive knowledge of Arizona Tewa." The strength of the curse laid down by Agaitsay and embraced by all the descendants of the migration endures. But in those first years after founding of Tewa Village, the question of just where the Tanos would find wives to sustain and increase their numbers remained an open one. Tensions around this issue remained central to Hopi-Tano intercultural relationships. Inter-marriage between original and arriving clans had always been resolved on the Hopi mesas, at least in part, by the familial and emotional ties that marriage created. Events soon to unfold to their east, on Antelope Mesa, would provide an alternative to the rigid boundaries that Agait-say had spit into the sandy soil that memorable day.

The wolves from the east were biding their time.

Map showing route of Tano migration to Hopi mesas.

At Play in the Fields of the Lord

*We are facing a highly involved political situation, and if we
don't get the permit renewed, the general statement is going to be
that the Hopis don't want us to work. This, of course, is not so.*

—J. O. BREW, CAMP JOURNAL, MAY 26, 1939

In 1935, archaeologists in the Peabody Museum at Harvard University also cast hungry eyes westward to the Hopi Mesas. Bill Claflin, curator of southeastern archaeology at the museum, and Peabody director Donald Scott saw a major excavation at Awat'ovi as an important bridge between the earlier focus of archaeologists in the region on the pre-Columbian era and an emerging interest in the Spanish colony and Franciscan missionization. Awat'ovi promised "an unprecedented opportunity . . . for linking precontact Hopi settlement to what was known about historic Hopi life and thus to modern Hopi culture." They recruited a twenty-nine-year-old doctoral student, John Otis Brew, to craft a research proposal that could be used to solicit funding for such a project.

Little about "Jo" Brew's background and training suggested he was the ideal man for the task. A 1928 graduate of Dartmouth College with a degree in fine arts and an interest in the archaeology of the classic world, his first archaeological fieldwork took place in Illinois. In 1931 he joined a Peabody expedition in the Alkali Ridge region of southeastern Utah, his first exposure to ancestral Puebloan prehistory. Despite Brew's inexperience, his work there proved so well designed and meticulous that the Peabody appointed him director of the Alkali Ridge project, which would occupy him until 1934, when he took a year to excavate hill forts and lake island dwellings in western Ireland.

When Brew returned to Harvard the following year to write up his Alkali Ridge dissertation (which proved much delayed; he would not defend and earn his doctorate until 1945), he set to work on the research design for Awat'ovi Pueblo. His vision was robust. "Taken in conjunction with ethnological work and present and projected developments in physical anthropology [the study of human remains] . . . a carefully considered archaeological project lasting with sufficient funds over a period of years should produce in Northeastern Arizona the most complete Southwestern study yet attempted." His plan, he promised, "would go back much further in time and come down to the present in the time-scale." Ambitious, and yet, as Brew would come to realize, fraught with political challenges in the "present" that no archaeologists had yet faced.

Brew consulted the earlier reports authored by Victor Mindeleff, Jesse Fewkes, and A. V. Kidder, who had briefly explored Antelope Mesa in the 1920s. He quickly grasped that a project devoted to "deep chronology" ought to encompass more than the single site of Awat'ovi, since investigations to date had not reached the lower

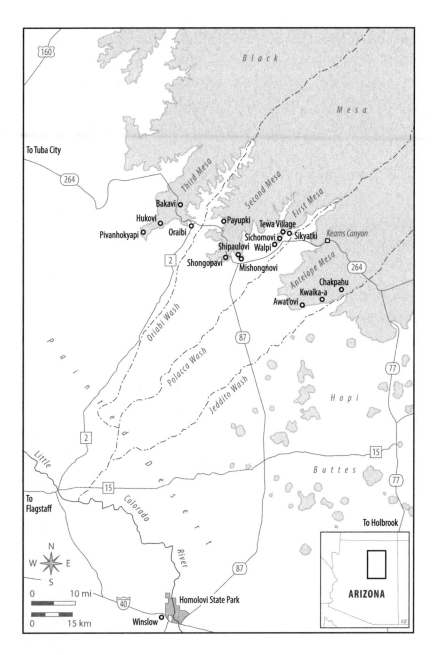

Map of the Hopi mesas and associated settlements.

levels of that site, and thus it might not represent the baseline of cultural development in Tusayán. The full expanse of Antelope Mesa, therefore, became the field the expedition would explore. Kawaika'a, Chakpahu, Lululongturqui, Ne Suftanga, and Kokopynyama would also be surveyed and in some cases, excavated, in an "attempt to trace the cultural development in the area back to Basket-maker [the earliest Puebloan culture, dating to c. A.D. 600]. . . . [the project] would be of inestimable value to Southwestern Prehistory." The breadth of the venture would be the most ambitious to date, and raise questions about the evolution of Pueblo culture and identity that remain unresolved today.

In March 1935, Claflin, Scott, and Brew met to discuss his report over lunch at the Union Club in Boston. Brew proposed a budget for the first year's fieldwork of $2,500 (the first in a series of budgets that would underestimate costs and require deficit spending by the museum). They also discussed the politics at Hopi and potential resistance to the research design. Brew cautioned that he would seek permission for the project from the Bureau of Indian Affairs "without applying to the Hopis themselves." He explained that disgruntled Hopis had expelled Jesse Fewkes from Antelope Mesa forty years before, and only should the Hopis identify the "expedition with the Government" would they realize "the *work could not be stopped* [emphasis in original]." He proposed that it would "be wise for the leader of the expedition to adopt and maintain scrupulously a double attitude toward the Hopi." Friendly relationships might be key to "management of the labour," but neither should the Indians "lose sight of the official nature of the expedition." Whatever they might think of the project, they must understand that it "is useless to act." In a hint of prescience, he noted that John Collier, President Roosevelt's new commissioner of the BIA, might reform practices such that it "necessitates getting permission from the Hopis." If this proved to be the case, he proposed negotiating with the "Council of the First Mesa Chiefs at Walpi, [for] the small units which compose the Hopi 'nation' do not agree particularly among themselves." It would be best to have the "nearest neighbors 'for' rather than 'against' the project." At the lunch's end, Scott appointed Brew, who had never visited the Antelope Mesa or the Hopi mesas to the west, director of the project.

Anticipating a 1935 summer-fall field season, the Peabody sought an excavation permit from the Department of the Interior under the Antiquities Act of 1906. The act was the first United States law to provide general protection for any general kind of cultural or natural resource. As drafted by Edgar Lee Hewitt, who would go on to found the School of American Archaeology in 1907, Section 3 of the Act required that "the examination of ruins, the excavation of archaeological sites, or the gathering of objects of antiquity" on lands administered by the Departments of Interior, Agriculture, or War be carried out only after a permit to do so had been issued by the secretary of the department responsible for the land in question. The permits were to be issued only to institutions "properly qualified to conduct such examinations, excavations, or gatherings. . . ." Furthermore, the objective of these permitted activities was to be "for the benefit of reputable museums, universities, colleges, or other recognized scientific or educational institutions, with a view to increasing the knowledge of such objects." Finally, the act required that the collections of materials from these investigations be placed in public museums for preservation and public benefit.

Peabody's plan of work encompassed only the 1935 field season, and Brew presumed that renewals would be pro forma in the

years ahead. Although they would take several years to erupt, con-
tradictory forms of federal paternalism would converge to create yet
another crisis at Awat'ovi Pueblo. Reformers in the Roosevelt admin-
istration laid the terrain in 1934, with the passage of the Indian
Reorganization Act championed by Commissioner of the Bureau
of Indian Affairs John Collier, Sr. Alarmed by the disintegration of
tribal lands in the wake of the Dawes Severalty Act of 1887, which
surveyed tribal lands and allotted parcels to individual Indian own-
ers in the hopes of producing "yeoman" farmers and ranchers in
the idealized Jeffersonian model, and ashamed by the collapse of
Indian economic and cultural self-sufficiency that followed, Collier's
"Indian New Deal" sought to reorganize collectively held tribal lands
and provide self-government to tribes through constitutional forms
of government.

Collier appointed Oliver La Farge, anthropologist, director
of the National Association on Indian Affairs and 1930 Pulitzer
Prize–winning author of *Laughing Boy*—a romance set among the
Navajos, and soon to be a major motion picture—to negotiate the
crafting of the Hopi constitution. This would prove a daunting task
that confirmed Albert Yava's description of the Hopis as peoples
who "did not consider themselves as belonging to the same tribe."
One student of the question cautioned that "to write a workable constitution for the politically diverse Hopi villages was hopeless from
the start . . . the extreme parochialism and distrust among them pre-
cluded the successful creation of a single governing instrument for
them all." These culturally internal challenges were perhaps intensified by the fact that La Farge's primary fieldwork and research had
been among the Navajos, with whom the Hopis were waging a struggle over the allocation of Reservation lands. La Farge assured Collier

that he could be "pro-Hopi" in working toward a tribal constitution, yet betrayed prejudices in the correspondence between the two men. "A cantankerous and tight-minded group of Indians . . . [who] quarrel constantly and the talking never ceases," he said of them, and worried that formalizing a democratic and secular system of governance would encounter "melancholy results . . . [since] the chiefs and the religion still govern 80% of the people."

Traditional forms of Hopi governance, especially the behind-the-scenes customary power of each village *kikmongwi* (chief), presented particular challenges to La Farge's efforts to convince the Hopis of the utility found in adopting a western-styled democratic system of popular sovereignty. The *kikmongwi* opposed any unifying government that would eliminate the sovereignty of their individual communities, whereas the "boilerplate" constitutions utilized by the Indian Reorganization Act aimed to centralize governance that could further the causes of the federally recognized tribes. La Farge shuttled from mesa to mesa and village to village, needing to be "everywhere at once, to spend hours with numerous individuals as well as groups, at widely separated points."

He gained Collier's approval to customize the IRA constitution in order that the new tribal council could exercise no authority in strictly village matters, and that in the traditionalist villages the *kikmongwi* would appoint council members who answered directly to him, whereas in the "progressive," often-Christian villages council representatives would enjoy popular election. Thus composed, the council would represent the whole Hopi tribe in dealing with the outside world.

On October 26, 1936, about half of the Hopis eligible to vote cast ballots decisively in favor of the new constitution, 651 supporting and

104 opposed. Whether or not these 755 voters truly represented a majority of voters remains hotly contested, yet even if they surpassed the 50 percent margin, those who "voted with their feet" by ignoring the referendum clearly represented a negative majority. The lack of confidence among Hopis doomed the council's ability from the very beginning, therefore, and by 1940 participation in and the legitimacy of the council fell so low that it was disbanded; external-relations decisions reverted back to the Bureau of Indian Affairs. La Farge, who had initially congratulated himself and Collier on their "outstanding success," would later lay the blame on Hopis themselves, rather than on what critics like Frank Waters called "a white man's concept utterly foreign to the nature and background" of the Hopis. La Farge may have agreed, although in tone rather differently than Waters. "The council stopped meeting, no new representatives were elected, the constitution went into abeyance. Above all, no village, I think, was prepared to surrender any part of its sovereignty or to lay aside any of its quarrels with other villages."

Yet, at least in the case of the Peabody Expedition to Antelope Mesa, and the memory of Awat'ovi to the Hopi people, the short-lived constitution would prove a powerful new historical force. And La Farge's comments may have echoed issues at work within Tusayán many centuries earlier.

❧·❦

Peabody's Awat'ovi expedition commenced its first field season on September 24, 1935, and ran for ten weeks. Brew served as leader, with the assistance of Alden Stevens, J. A. Lancaster as crew foreman, and Lyndon Thompson as cook. Brew hired eight Hopi crew-

Peabody Expedition Camp, with the Western Mound in the middle distance. The Hopi crew's tents are in the far distance, right.

members, three from First Mesa and five from Second Mesa. Each man was paid $2.00 per working day, compared to $3.00 per day for Thompson. Six from this inaugural crew—Gibson Namoki and Sylvan Nash of First Mesa and Everett Harris, Alec Dennis, Leland Dennis, and Jacob Poleviyum from Second Mesa—would serve in subsequent years and emerge well schooled in archaeological fieldwork methods. Brew would write that the Hopi excavators were so "familiar with the materials of ancient construction that they recognized plaster walls, adobe floors, etc., immediately. . . . They have sharp eyes, too, attested to by the number of tiny square and other shaped pieces of turquoise we are getting which seemed to have dropped out of the turquoise mosaics."

The expedition formed a tight-knit and largely self-sufficient community, dubbed "New Awat'ovi," even as the days grew short and nights cold in the high desert autumn. "We are quite comfortable in camp, with stoves in the tents," Brew wrote. The camp was "a scene of great activity: men in the trench, engineering department with

plane table, range pole, pegs, and flags all over the site; a crew digging fence post holes; a team of horses and scraper; one Hopi making
boxes, and the cook making cinnamon rolls, angel cake, and pun'kin
pie (out of sweet potatoes)." The Hopis proved diligent workers, but
kept largely to themselves, sharing a smaller tent-camp complex
somewhat apart from the main camp. At the main camp, the archaeologists converted the pottery tent to an evening "concert hall," from
which they offered "an answer to the Hopi songs that drifted over to
us after dinner from the camp of the Hopi workmen."

Brew's plan of work involved three elements: reconnaissance
mapping of Antelope Mesa in its entirety; survey and test excavations
on the large sites of Awat'ovi, Kawaika'a, Chakpahu, Lululongturqui,
Ne Suftanga, and Kokopynyama; and investigation of several "small,
early sites" in order to assess the temporal depth of settlement on the
mesa. In all, surveyors identified sixty-one archaeological sites, ranging in age from Basketmaker III (A.D. 600–800, with the innovations
of bean cultivation to augment corn agriculture, pottery-making, and
the adoption of bow-and-arrow weaponry) to the end of ancient settlement on the mesa with the destruction of Awat'ovi in 1700. Thus,
more than 1,000 years of human occupation lay before their eyes,
from the humblest of pit-houses to the great pueblos numbering several stories and hundreds of masonry rooms encompassed in massive
villages. At its peak during the classic period (A.D. 1150–1300), the
mesa, fine springs, and farming lands below the caprock may have
supported a population of more than 4,000. At last, southwestern
archaeology had a single location in which the sweep of Ancestral
Puebloan prehistory and history lay open to the eyes, hands, and
minds of scientific exploration and analysis. Although the earliest
periods, ranging from Basketmaker III through the Pueblo I (A.D.

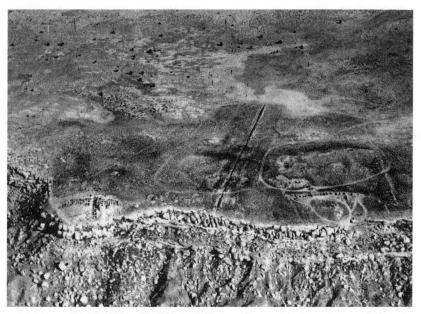

Aerial view of Awat'ovi from the south. Surface of Antelope Mesa, with Awat'ovi in the foreground. The honeycomb area in the left foreground is the excavated portion of the Western Mound; to the right, the Eastern Pueblo and Mission San Bernardo de Aguatubi.

800–1000) and Pueblo II (A.D. 1000–1150), were the least well understood elements of this prehistory, the impressive and enigmatic ruins of Awat'ovi Pueblo would act as a magnet for investigation in the seasons ahead.

The Peabody's permit was renewed for the following year, and on August 3, 1936, in the swale of the Great Depression, the first major season of excavation began across a full four months. During the course of the season Brew would employ twenty-seven Hopi crewmen, providing a welcome source of cash to their families. This season would focus almost exclusively on Awat'ovi Pueblo itself, especially what Brew called the "Western Mound," a mass of architectural rubble towering some twenty-five feet above the bedrock of the mesa top. Brew surmised that "in this mound was to be found the oldest large structure on the site."

The Western Mound proved to be a monumental excavation task. The initial tactic was to scrape the surface of windblown sand to expose the outlines of room walls "in a strip two to four rooms wide" to expose the general structure of the complex. "Attacking the core of the mound" to expose whole rooms in the sequence of their construction would follow. Working level-by-level, ninety cleared rooms revealed a stratigraphy several centuries old. When the Hopi laborers finally reached the ground surface bedrock of the mesa, it became clear that the room walls extended continuously to this preconstruction level, with the recovered ceramics indicating continuous occupation of the settlement from the late thirteenth century to the historic era. The mix of ceramic styles in these lowest levels attracted Brew's attention. Two distinct types composed this lowest level, a geometric black-on-white tradition associated with Puebloan peoples of the Kayenta district to the north of the Hopi Mesas (in today's Navajo National Monument), and a black-on-orange tradition associated with Puebloan peoples who lived along the Little Colorado River some sixty miles due south of the Hopi Mesas (in today's Homolovi State Park).

Brew surmised that the founders of early Awat'ovi hailed from two regions some two hundred miles distant from one another, those from the Kayenta region probably arriving sometime between A.D. 1275 and 1300, since their homeland villages were depopulated by the latter date. They were probably refugees from the last years of the Great Drought that crippled the Four Corners region between 1276 and 1299. The peoples from the Little Colorado apparently arrived at the same time, or slightly later. Yet the mixed nature of the ceramic assemblage suggested that the peoples themselves mixed in the early years. The migrants from the Homolovi core communities, however, were probably drawn to Antelope Mesa, rather than pushed from their homelands, since those towns remained occupied well into the fourteenth century. Whether or not these very different ceramic traditions signaled peoples of different language or cultural identities was (and is) impossible to discern, yet the Peabody excavations seemed to highlight the heterogeneity of the peoples who established the great towns of Antelope Mesa.

By mid-season, more than 80,000 potsherds had been tabulated, and more than 5,000 each day went to the classifying tables. A long-term occupation of Western Mound was obvious, with clear changes in ceramic styles that seemed to indicate evolution, rather

Western Mound excavations, 1936.

than replacements, in the peoples of the town. By the fourteenth century, a distinctive form appeared and was classified as Jeddito Black-on-Yellow, evolving gradually over the next century to a local form termed Awat'ovi Black-on-Yellow. In each case the styles were defined by the rich creamy yellow background color, a result of the makers employing coal as their fuel for firing the pottery. Only in the Antelope Mesa region did bituminous coal seams extrude beneath the hard sandstones of the mesa tops, allowing their mining and use in firing kilns that archaeologists found on the lower benches of the mesas. Brew later estimated that several thousand tons of coal had been mined from these seams over the centuries, a form of resourcing and manufacture unique to the Hopi country. Given the scarcity of firewood in the region, coal (for both cooking and ceramic firing) gave the settlers of Antelope Mesa an edge in the regional ceramic economy, and provided a valuable trade commodity. As the Homolovi villages to the south were the primary agricultural region for cotton growing and yarn production, it became clear, given the prevalence of yellow wares in the Homolovi cluster, that a lively trade existed in which pots and bowls produced on Antelope Mesa were exchanged for cotton yarns, blankets, and shawls from the south. By the sixteenth century, the local art of pottery production reached its apex in the style known as Sikyatki Polychrome, a splendid expression of artistry that would decline with the arrival of the Franciscan missions. Yet the style would reappear in the late nineteenth century in a revival inaugurated by the legendary potter Nampeyo, and come to be seen as the archetypical Hopi ceramic tradition today.

Whether or not these systems of exchange involved peoples related by blood and culture, or whether they bound together "multi-ethnic" networks through the transfer of unique resources remained (and remains) an unsettled issue in southwestern archaeology.

As the 1936 season drew to a close, attention of the excavators turned to the kivas located within the room blocks of the Western Mound. In 1901, archaeologist Walter Hough had tested the site of Kawaika'a about one mile north of Awat'ovi, and discovered in one kiva "a painted wall showing part of a human figure and a bird in tallow, green and white." Nothing like these images had been discovered previously in the Southwest, and a portion of Brew's research plan included investigation of similar phenomena at Awat'ovi. Fragments of painted plaster in room fill led the workers toward their first kiva, in which layers of wall plaster revealed, upon close examination of a cross-section, twenty-three such paintings layered upon one another. With this discovery hopes rose and found remarkable affirmation. Over the course of the last month's work, painstaking work unveiled forty-one fragmentary murals, all but one located in kivas.

These images ranged "from pure geometric design, through formalized bird and animal representations often resembling elements on Sikyatki pottery, to apparent crude attempts at realism." Brew recognized their significance immediately. These paintings, he thought, made for the possibility "that some of the figures represented can be identified with modern [Hopi] ceremony and story." Furthermore, since they were almost exclusively associated with kivas, it seemed also possible that he "could obtain from them information as to the societies by whom the kivas were used." They held the potential "signatures" by which Hopi sacred societies indicated their ownership of, and the practices within, spaces generally prohibited to non-Hopi eyes.

Watson Smith and team scraping Kiva murals at Awat'ovi Pueblo, with *katsinam*.

After photographing and creating scale color drawings of the mural art, the field session wrapped up with high hopes for the coming year. Primary among those goals would be a shift forward in time, toward "extensive excavation of the mission quadrangle and the town during the historic period." Things were about to get even more interesting.

The 1937 excavation season began on July 12 and remained in the field until November 5, as winter bore down on Tusayán. Brew's primary goals were "the complete clearing of the rooms of the Franciscan Friary and church and excavation of two sections of the contemporary town," as well as test excavations in search of additional kiva murals in the sites of Kawaika'a and Chakpahu, the next major villages north on the rim of the mesa. The latter were designed to determine the extent of the kiva mural tradition on Antelope Mesa, and would find that to be extensive across both time and space. In these efforts a member of the team, Watson Smith, would pioneer new techniques for recording the artwork, then peeling each painted layer of plaster away from the underlying art, thereby permitting preservation of each image and the creation of an artistic record for the region.

It had become clear to Brew in 1936 that the Western Mound town was but lightly occupied by the time of the sixteenth-century Spanish entradas and the establishment of the mission in 1629. A substantial village had arisen just to the east of the Western Mound, which Brew referenced as a community "contemporary" with the Franciscan constructions. Yet it was also evident from the surface ceramic collections that the eastern community also predated the Spanish presence, especially when excavations began in the mission and friary complex. As density of occupation in the Western Mound increased over the centuries and construction there reached three to four stories of roomblocks perched atop one another, the architecture had become unstable, and so the community had gradually expanded eastward on the mesa top. When the Franciscans began laying out their church and residential areas, therefore, they did so by occupying a living village. The fact that the church altar had been placed directly above the thoughtfully and ritually "closed," or decommissioned, kiva, empty of artifacts and filled with clean sand, suggested some Hopi acquiescence in its location.

Ironically, after the revolt of 1680, once the priests were slain and the church itself burned and tumbled down, the people of Awat'ovi returned many of the rooms in the convento to an earlier purpose—modest residences. As Brew's team probed into the rubble of the sprawling convento, they realized that the ruin represented two occupations—first, the friar's presence between 1629 and 1680, and second, the remodeling and inhabitation of the convento by Hopis in the twenty years that preceded the annihilation of November 1700. This second occupation was unusual, since in most other post-Revolt missions the convento was destroyed at the same time as the church, neither restored nor reoccupied until after the Spanish reconquest, with buildings left to decay and collapse on their own. Yet in the convento of Mission San Bernardo, "the friary rooms . . . upon excavation were found to have been subdivided by narrow masonry walls of the kind found in the native Hopi houses of the 17th-century town." The Hopis, it seemed, had "very sensibly moved into the friary after they had martyred its occupants." In fact, the new occupants had much increased the residential potential of the convento, nearly quadrupling the number of rooms in the Franciscan building and adding more than a dozen masonry rooms to the exterior of the building. What had for fifty years served as a symbol of European notions of elite accommodation—a combination residence, office, school, and place of worship for perhaps a half dozen priests, neophytes, and native servants—became a bustling community building of more than one hundred rooms, housing perhaps forty or fifty residents. Ignoring the rebellion's call for a rejection of all things Spanish and a return to the ways of the ancestors prior to 1540, the fill in these new rooms evidenced a fertile mix of material culture. Just three rooms held "fragments of [a] large bell . . . four metates, twenty-five manos, fragments of painted wooden prayer sticks, and . . . five hundred sixty-eight potsherds, including six . . . restorable jars." The convento yard itself "was covered with sheep manure," laid down after the rebellion. The violence of the revolt at Awat'ovi, at least, targeted Spanish priests and their attendants, and the church itself, but not the living and working quarters that the Hopis themselves had labored so hard to build. One faction, perhaps, had decided they felt so at ease in those surroundings that the setting became a new home.

Other discoveries marked Awat'ovi as unusual. The presence of the young European male interred in the makeshift "third" altar had been discovered during the search for the "superpositioned" altar-kiva relationship, yet evinced little discussion in the fieldnotes or publications on the 1937 season. In 1949, however, Ross Gordon Montgomery would address the interment in his architectural history of the mission, and concluded that the data "points with calculable sureness to the bundle of inarticulated skeletal material as an intrusive element." The archaeology suggested that the "wrapped remains were apparently deposited under the altar mayor at a time when the mission premises were involuntarily surrendered. . . . This could have been accomplished only between 1680 and the early summer of 1700." Montgomery, ever convinced that Hopis could not have harbored a reverence for the altar, conjectured wistfully that perhaps "several pious soldiers re-buried a comrade under the high altar on one of the several occasions when they were in the vicinity of Aguatubi during the *Reconquista*." The very Hopi style of the interment—bundled, wrapped in native cotton, and bound by yucca cords, and laid upon a Hopi basket—failed to garner his interpretive attention. The mysterious body would, however, soon attract the notice of others.

Testing of the church nave multiplied many times over the number of burials, and the complexity of their removal, given the need to maintain stratigraphic control on their temporal deposition, pushed the excavations of the church and friary into the following field seasons. But the world outside "New Awatovi" and its ancient namesake was beginning to intrude.

In late August of 1937, prior to the discovery and exhumation of the young European from the church altar, a visitor arrived on Antelope Mesa. The Reverend Victor Rose Stoner was conducting rounds of Civilian Conservation Corps camps in Arizona. Having recently completed an M.A. degree in archaeology at the University of Arizona in Tucson with a thesis on the Jesuit missions of the Tucson Basin, Stoner, a secular priest of the Tucson Diocese, was an avid protoprofessional who mixed ardent Catholicism with an enthusiasm for the human sciences. Brew and his team were less than thrilled by his interest, however, since he proved a nuisance, interrupting work and eating more than an appropriate share of the camp's "excellent cuisine." Stoner insisted, as he received a tour of the mid-excavation mission, that—since he carried an altar stone and vestments with him on his rounds—he be permitted to conduct "the first and only Mass at that spot since mid-August, 1680." Brew agreed grudgingly, if only to move their visitor along, and on September 5, 1937, Stoner did so, addressing a congregation of six members of the expedition "with the same Mass last said by a Spanish padre" at the mission, according to the *Tucson Daily Citizen*.

It would not be the last Brew would hear from Reverend Stoner, however. The following June he received a letter forwarded by the Peabody Museum from Stoner, who pointed out in a penned comment on the letterhead that he had "recently been elected president" of the Arizona Archaeological and Historical Society "for the third term." After complaining that his work toward his doctorate had been slowed by the requirement that he have "reading knowledge" of

German, he mentioned that in April he had heard news of "the discovery of the Padre's body beneath the altar at Awatovi last fall. . . . A movement is afoot to have the martyrs of the Pueblo Revolt of 1680 declared saints—canonized, as the term is." He wondered, "What steps would be necessary to take in order to get the body back here in Tucson?" A complete account of the discovery of the body was of essence, as the Catholic Church was "very, very careful in permitting the veneration of a relic when there is any doubt to its authenticity." If the body were placed in the care of the Bishop of Tucson, it would "make the case stronger" when "canonization eventually takes place." Surely, Stoner argued, "Harvard would be willing to let us have the body when Harvard's interests are purely anthropological, while that of the Church reaches far deeper."

Stoner's tone was solicitous, but he had been working less sanguine angles since April. In July, Brew received a copy of a letter from Commissioner of Indian Affairs John Collier, addressed to the Bureau of Indian Affairs Superintendent to the Hopi, Seth Wilson, in which the commissioner raised an alarm. Collier reported that Arno Cammerer, director of the National Park Service, had recently been contacted by Arizona senator Carl Hayden who desired a reply to charges leveled by a certain Reverend Victor Stoner that "the first European settlement in Arizona" was being "destroyed by Harvard." Most specifically, Stoner claimed that an act of desecration had been committed by Peabody's archaeologists' who "tore down the altar" and "removed the body of a Franciscan priest . . . undoubtedly either Padre Porras who was poisoned by the Hopis in 1633, or Padre Figueroa who was killed in the Pueblo Revolt of 1680." Collier further alerted Superintendent Wilson that "a suggestion has been made to the Senator that the site should be established as a national monument," and that his office had not found "a record of a permit under the provisions of the act for the preservation of American antiquities having been granted to Harvard University to make archaeological examinations of this place."

Brew launched damage control. He wrote to Stoner that he would be "very glad to talk over . . . the whole question of the disposal of skeletal remains which may prove to be the remains of early Spanish friars or soldiers," while cautioning that "Professor Hooten and Dr. Woodbury" were still undertaking examinations to "determine its racial affiliations." He assured Stoner that "Harvard will be willing to cooperate with the Church in making the best disposal of any European skeletons we find," but did not mention that as early as January 1938 he had received a preliminary report from the Peabody analysts that the individual from the altar burial "should be assigned to an individual of the European race." To Superintendent Wilson he replied that all the skeletal remains uncovered at Awat'ovi would reside with the Peabody Museum "according to the terms of our permit" (he dodged the question of whether the permit had been renewed for 1938). He attempted to reassure the regional Park Service official, Dr. Jesse Numsbuam, superintendent of Mesa Verde National Park, that "Harvard is not interested in skeletons beyond the historical information that we may obtain from a study of them," and pointed out that no desecration of the burial was intended, but the altar had to be excavated and removed in the quest for the superimposed kiva that they surmised lay beneath the church.

By January of 1939, Brew had decided that cooperation with the Archdiocese of Tucson might be the wisest political course, and began a correspondence with the Franciscan Fathers stationed at the Saint Joseph Indian Mission in Keams Canyon, Arizona, toward a "repatriation" of the body buried in the Awat'ovi altar. He cautioned, however, that "its youth (twenty-one years or younger) precludes the possibility of its being either Father Porras or Father Figueroa." Yet, he went on, "since there were very few Spaniards at Awatovi who were not connected with your Order, and since a man buried beneath an altar would, I should think, almost certainly be closely associated with the Order, I am sending the skeleton to you."

On February 15, Father Arnold Heinzmann wrote from Keams Canyon to announce that "the box containing the precious parcel arrived by mail this morning and I thank God fervently for this great favor. It was very amusing to hear the mail man exclaim as he drew up to the house; 'What on earth are you expected [*sic*] that is very light and might be valued at $500.00?' For the moment I could not guess. Then I saw the name of the sender and all was clear." Father Stauble weighed in as well, penning a note of gratitude for the "great privilege to possess and honor the remains of one of our predecessors in bringing the light of the Gospel to the Hopis." In the fog of relief felt by all the parties, no one seemed to question why the remains of a young European male might have been curated and reburied, presumably by Hopis, after the violence of the great revolt. And the story persists in its confusion, for although the body remained at the mission for "a good many years," it subsequently went missing at St. Michael's. Watson Smith would later write, "it thus appears a mystery has been compounded upon a mystery, and one may only hope that the uneasy bones have somewhere found a resting place." Time would reveal that his were not the only "uneasy bones."

Yet events were closing in on Brew and the Peabody Expedition. Jesse Nusbaum and Superintendent Wilson had communicated the news of the proposed National Monument at Awat'ovi to the Hopi

Tribal Council during the autumn of 1938. It was not well received. The council had already decided that no further permits for excavation should be issued without approval of the clan most directly descended from Awat'ovi. At least three, Badger from Second Mesa and Reed and Snake from First Mesa, contended for that right of priority. Both the BIA and the Department of the Interior, in the reformist atmosphere of Collier's Indian New Deal, felt Hopi approval preceded the government's right to let the permit. Brew worked behind the scenes to secure the permission of Luke Kawanusea, of Mishongnovi, who Brew claimed as "chief of the badger clan having control of the abandoned city of Awatovi, agrees to the renewal of permit." Brew placed little credence in the sense of offense that the Hopis felt, arguing instead "that the really important point lies in the various claims for control of the surrounding farmlands. The most important dispute seems to be between the Second Mesa Badger Clan and Sequi's Clan at First Mesa. There are secondary disputes, however, within each Mesa. These disputes probably go back hundreds of years, and I imagine played an important role in the sacking of Awat'ovi." By June 22, however, Wilson reported that all three clans were willing to allow the permit, but now felt that the *kikmongwi* at Walpi and those at Second Mesa must agree as well. In this, at least, Brew's strategy to play the federal government against the "contentious men," decision-makers among the Hopi, did indeed display remarkable historical insight, if questionable professional ethics.

Whatever their internal clan and leadership entanglements, the Hopi Council used their new, if ephemeral, tribal constitution and attendant political muscle to oppose the excavations and, implicitly, the establishment of the National Monument. In April of 1939 a formal delegation traveled to Washington, D.C., and requested that neither the BIA nor the Department of the Interior approve the excavation permit beyond August 26 of that year. Among those delegates was Byron Adams of First Mesa, who although he had opposed the constitution and Tribal Council as "merely an institution organized by the white man, and has no jurisdiction in the minds of the Hopis over clan lands," saw the visit as a chance to make a powerful public statement. In a newspaper article that appeared in April entitled "Indians Ask Science to Leave 'Sodom and Gomorrah' Buried," he laid out the Hopi perspective. "There were certain conditions when Awat'ovi was destroyed. The other villages got together and decided to destroy it because evil things were done there. There was no decency. It was agreed that it should never be touched again afterward, if any of the villagers were left, and they went back there, they would go insane. 'What good does it do to dig there?' the villagers want to know. If it were on some other mesa, where no one was living, we might feel differently. But we are still alive. Our civilization is not dead. They are digging up our ancestors and they are touching things we have said shall not be touched."

The message reached the right eyes. On May 30 the Department of the Interior notified the Peabody that, after consultation with the Indians of the Hopi jurisdiction, "these Indians would not renew this permit to conduct any archaeological work on their lands." Brew scrambled to move his field season start date up to July 7 from August 7 in hopes of getting his work completed by the August 26 deadline. His report on this final season, published in 1941, concluded with a curt statement "with the fieldwork finished the expedition staff is now engaged upon the final reports . . . in order to make the findings of the Awatovi expedition available to students as soon as possible."

He wasn't counting on World War II. Many of the expedition's key scientists volunteered or were drafted into military service. Eleven reports were, in fact, published. The last made it to print in 1978. In the meantime, members of the expedition and their Hopi workmen had decided to hold a reunion at Antelope Mesa. It took place in the summer of 1975. Times had changed.

6

You Will Find Me Poor, While You
Return in the Grandeur of Plenty

———————•◆•———————

*It is not hard to see why Hopis experienced the factional
dissention of Orayvi . . . as the repetition of a cycle of
events, the outcome of which could be prophesied on
the basis of knowledge of the past.*

— JERROLD E. LEVY, 1992

When Harvard lost its excavation permit in August 1939, Jo
Brew's investigation of the ancient Hopi past ran up against
the "ethnographic present," the complex realities of Hopi internal
and external politics. Thirty-six years later, a reunion of the Awat'ovi
Expedition on Antelope Mesa would illuminate changes in the
willingness of Hopis to express an even stronger sense of cultural
sovereignty vis-à-vis outsiders who wished to study their history
and culture. Proposed by Stanley Olsen of the Harvard Peabody
Museum, who had conducted the analysis of "piles and piles" of ani-

mal bones recovered during the excavations and with the "enthusiastic collaboration of the tribal officers," the daylong reunion took place in the spring of 1975. Six Peabody Expedition veterans took part, as did seven Hopi workmen from the 1930s—Gibson Namoki, Max Namoki, Sylvan Nash, Emory Coochwikvia, Eric Lalo, Kenneth Polacca, and Patrick Williams.

After "exploring the site thoroughly" throughout the daylight hours, the reunion party convened for dinner at the new Hopi Cultural Center at Kykotsomovi village on Second Mesa. Ill health prevented Jo Brew's attendance, so Watson Smith presented his overview of the project and its significance to southwestern archaeology. During the question period that followed his lecture, however, the Hopis expressed "clearly a feeling of dissatisfaction with what had been accomplished, not because we had dug, but because we had not dug enough, or had dug the wrong things . . . forty years ago, they didn't give a damn." Furthermore, "they say we shouldn't have taken all that stuff away [to the Peabody Museum]." Smith seemed startled by a new assertiveness among his formerly congenial excavating crew. "The Hopis, it was plain, felt that our efforts directed to the Spanish mission had been misapplied. . . . it did turn out in the end that perhaps from the Hopi point of view a disproportionate amount of effort was put into that church. The Hopi village was kind of pushed off to one side. They desired a more thorough focus on the native village."

The intervening thirty-six years had delivered a heightened sense of confidence and cultural protectiveness among Hopis. Like the men from the Peabody, many had seen military service during World War II (including rolls as code talkers, less celebrated than their Navajo neighbors), as had their children in Korea and Vietnam. Further empowered by the rise of Native American activism in the 1960s and

1970s, many Hopis felt able to express their long-held distaste for the manner in which the site excavations were handled.

Clearly, the expedition's shift in emphasis from exploring the pre-Columbian Hopi village to the seventeenth-century Franciscan mission complex, and fascination about the annihilation of the residents of Awat'ovi, suggested to the Hopis that the centuries predating the Spanish intrusion on Antelope Mesa were somehow less meaningful than the short century of the mission period. An untoward fascination with the Christian era and the fate of "the Christian Indians of Aguatubi" came at the expense of more ancient and richer Hopi history. Why dig in ruins that held less than a century of history, when the older village embraced a story many centuries deep? The kiva murals that Watson Smith himself had uncovered and curated told of the arrival of the sacred *katsinam* in the thirteenth or fourteenth centuries—surely more spiritually meaningful than the brief, and failed, experiment with Christianity.

Yet Hopi ambivalence toward the anthropological enterprise had much deeper roots. Franciscans, Spanish soldiers, and archaeologists were not the only "Pahaana" (white men, from the East) who intruded on the Hopi mesas over the centuries. Foreigners—whether mythic or real—played prominent roles in Hopi narratives about the past and the future. Thus white men's "science" found itself confronting an entirely different mode of perceiving history in Tusayán, the first glimpses of which were witnessed nearly a century before.

❧·❧

In the Euro-American mind, history marches from past to present. Each event—birth, death, marriage, divorce, war and peace—accrues in a sequence that shapes the next in knowable ways, although their precise relation may prove elusive. We attend to the past to better comprehend our present. Yet, invert this. What if our present were already active in our past? What if our present is nothing more than a past foretold? This swirl of cause and effect, effect as cause, not linear but cyclical and untethered from western time, more closely captures the way many Hopis understood (and understand) the ruination of Awat'ovi Pueblo.

Euro-Americans encountered this swirl well before Jo Brew sensed a "deep time" to the politics involved in the denial of his permit. Perhaps not surprisingly, it came through the notebooks of "Many Buttons." Although best known for his research among the Zuni, Frank Hamilton Cushing found himself cast as a character in Hopi history at the mesas in 1882, in a complex dance of intrusion and evasion between anthropologists and Hopis that, in some ways, continues today.

In December, Cushing had journeyed north from Zuni to attend winter ceremonies in the Hopi village of Oraibi, and to acquire pottery, weaving, and paraphernalia for the collections of the Smithsonian Institution in Washington, D.C. To do so, he established a "little shop" in the plaza at Oraibi, from which he intended to exchange manufactured goods from the East for Hopi goods, preferably of a ceremonial nature. Oraibi's *kikmongwi*, Loololma, a "progressive" who favored the Americans and their education for his people, had approved Cushing's endeavor.

On the evening of December 20, Cushing received visitors in the quarters assigned him by Loololma, however. One "small elderly man threw his robes from his naked shoulders" and demanded that he cease trading. "Stranger *Tehano* (American, literally, 'Tejano'). . . .

You are a heap of dung in our plazas, you stink of your race. Leave or we will throw you off the mesas, as we throw dung out of the plazas." Cushing protested. He demanded to understand "why you hate the Americans," so that he would know "what to tell my fathers, [in] Washington. . . ."

After a discussion among themselves, the Hopis ordered Cushing to "get paper and a writing stick quickly." He settled himself by the fire, and scribbled deep into the night. At last they "gave him in substance" what Cushing termed "a myth," although much of it proved an "infuriated argument interspersed with the most insulting messages to Washington." In his notes, the first detailed record of a "prophetic myth . . . of a complex of prophetic myths," Cushing found himself, by allusion, cast in the role of "older brother ('the Americans')," who "came out of the cave-worlds first" and "journeyed to the land of the sun" while the Hopis undertook their migrations and finally "settled where we now get being." Older brother "left us and journeyed toward the land of the sun," so said the ancients, but with a prophecy to carry in memory:

> Many men's ages shall pass while we are apart. Your children shall fill the world whither you go. Then you will turn back towards the place of your birth, seeking a country more spacious wherein to dwell. It is then that you will meet me again. You will find me poor while you will return in the grandeur of plenty, and the welfare of good food. You will find me hungry and offer me nourishment, but I shall cast your morsels aside from my mouth. You will find me naked and offer me garments of soft fabrics, but I shall rend your garments and trample them under my feet. You will find me sad, and perplexed, and offer

me speeches of consolation and advice; but I shall spurn your words, reproach, revile and despise you. You will smile upon me and act gently; but I shall scowl upon you. Aside as I would cast filth from my presence will I cast you. Then will you rise and strike my head from my neck. As it rolls in the dust you will arrest it and sit upon it as upon a stool-rock, a glad day for me, for on that day you will but divide the trail of your own life with the knife which severs my head from my body, give immortal life, liberty, surcease from anxiety to me. . . . Thus have spoken the ancients through many ages of men.

A grim, and yet ambivalent, prophecy, in which Cushing seems assigned the symbolic role of Pahaana, or representative of the intruding non-Hopi world from the east. Reviled as "filth" (or turd, synonymous with "witch" in some Hopi narratives) and rejected by the villagers, Cushing-as-Pahaana would behead his erstwhile kinsmen, while simultaneously liberating them to enjoy a pure, harmonious, and immortal new life. One student of the prophecy explains it as an ancient and malleable story aligned with Hopi origin narratives, one that "assigns order to a chaotic, stressful and constantly besieged world," yet also raises questions about that order. "The most fundamental purpose of all of the versions of the Pahaana prophecy is to maintain ambivalence, paradox, and anxiety, not to relieve it." Elder Brother, as Hopis term the key figure, embodies a paradox— Elder Brother as Punisher *and* Elder Brother as deliverer from anxiety—a paradox that signals "a state of complex and alternating state of conflict and cooperation [between outsiders] and Hopis and with each other."

The Pahaana prophecy represents a Hopi variant of apocalypse-

and-rebirth themes widespread across the ancient (and New Age) Americas, resonating with similar themes found among the Mayas (Kukulkan), Aztecs (Quetzalcoatl), Venezuela's Makiritares (Watunna Wanadi), and closer to home in the Zunis' Beginning narrative and the Navajos' Blessingway. In each of these, a revered ancestor departs to the east and only returns at a moment of crisis among his kinsfolk, bringing transformation and rebirth in often violent fashion. The most familiar version, given much elevation, perhaps, by Franciscan chroniclers, was that the Aztecs conjoined the story of Quetzalcoatl with the arrival of conquistador Hernán Cortés on the coast of Mesoamerica in 1520, thereby easing the Spanish conquest.

Among the variations offered by individual Hopi clans, certain elements of the Pahaana prophecy, as lodged within the larger emergence narrative, remain consistent. An "Edenic" world becomes corrupt, either through overcrowding or immorality, or both, and as life descends into chaos (*koyaanisqatsi*), a righteous few find escape to a new world as destruction is visited upon their recalcitrant kin. Pahaana/Elder Brother, who appears shortly before the apocalypse with revitalized teachings from Masaw, a deity associated simultaneously with death and life, usually effects both annihilation of the corrupt and ascent of the chosen few. Once in the new (fourth, or our current) world, the narratives shift to tracing the migrations of the unique clans who would ultimately find a home in the center-place, or the Hopi homelands. Bear and Badger Clans are most commonly cited as the first arriving and hence highest-ranked of these migrating peoples.

Frank Hamilton Cushing may have been the first to have the prophecy directed at him, but he was certainly not the last. No precise term exists in the Hopi language that translates as "prophecy;"

rather, the compound word *wuk-navoti* ("revealed knowledge") is generally rendered as such. The Pahaana prophecy is "grafted on to the emergence myth," with its cycles of crisis and renewal, and thus Pahaana is a central agent in the perpetual tension of the Hopi historical imagination. The fact that recorded versions of the prophecy only begin with Cushing in 1882 is evident in many of the "signs" that the dialectic of destruction and resurrection is imminent—World War I, World War II, the dropping of the atomic bomb, the Korean War, the Vietnam War, Apollo 11's moon landing in 1969, the intrusion of New Age "false prophets" into Hopi ceremonial life, and, more recently, the attacks on New York and Washington in 2001, or the rising crisis of global warming. Yet the prophecy's prominence in Hopi engagements with outsiders surely occurred much earlier, perhaps even before Europeans entered Tusayán. Rebirth following world destruction is sometimes contingent upon the survivors' promise to follow the "simple life that [Masaw] had prescribed," perhaps as a method of assuring that migrants to the Hopi mesas would adhere to the prevailing ceremonial orthodoxy. That one version specifies only "those who had strayed—*popwaqt* (witches)—would have their heads cut off" strengthens this defense-of-orthodoxy theme.

The people of Tusayán had certainly experienced the arrival of strange beings with numinous powers before the Franciscans, in the form of the *katsinam* (Rainmaking Spirits from the Gods) who overwhelmed earlier religious traditions beginning in the late thirteenth century, and whose arrival affected both cultural trauma and social rebirth. In the later decades of that century, these new ideas and their supernatural expressions began to stride across the peaks, plateaus, and canyons of the Southwest. Uncertain in origin and much debated in genesis, the *katsinam* arrived at a moment of crisis among Puebloan peoples and provided rejuvenating beliefs, ceremonies, iconography, and ways of social belonging to peoples frayed, frightened, and fighting in the cataclysmic world of the centuries before the arrival of the Christian god and saints. Numbering some 250 individual beings, if current patterns may be read into those of the past, the panoply of Katsina spirits appeared in Puebloan communities each year after the Winter Solstice and before the spring rains, when "men ask the sun to return so that the crops will grow." The arrival of these new evangelicals is often recalled today as benign. The predominant interpretation of the social significance of the Katsina religion, or "cult," focuses on its extraordinary ability to bridge divisions of ethnolinguistic identity and create new forms of transcommunity identification. Katsina societies existed in more than one community, building semiotic and symbiotic communities that functioned in the interests of social solidarity. But that success seems to have been hard won. Real struggles unfolded between older Pueblo Medicine societies, Sacred Clown, Hunting, and War sodalities and the agents of the Katsina religion, often expressed in narratives of gods in conflict with the mortals. Among the eastern Rio Grande Pueblos, the *katsinam* gradually experienced "domestication" and were subsumed within the earlier sodalities, but in the west, at Zuni and Hopi, the *katsinam* prevailed.

Few narratives of the *katsinam* survive among the Eastern Pueblos of the Rio Grande region, but the spirits' arrival in the area is manifest in the rich rock art iconography that suddenly appears on the valley's black basalt outcroppings. Where abstracts, zoomorphs, and stick-figure humans once prevailed, in the fourteenth century clearly identifiable "masks" of classic *katsinam* figures appear by the hundreds, usually in close association to images directly related to conflict and warfare—shield-bearers, bows, axe-bearers, and Venus "stars"—all masculine symbols. Similar concentrations of Katsina

Katsina imagery at San Cristobal Pueblo, New Mexico.

and war imagery may be seen along the mesa escarpments to the west at the proto-Hopi settlements of the Homol'ovi cluster.

These images and iconography resonate vividly in Hopi oral history, where, in several accounts of "tales of destruction" visited upon early Hopi villages, *katsinam* figure as allies of village chiefs who immolate their own communities when they discern wickedness or sorcery, *koyaanisqatsi*, spreading among their people—just like Ta'polo at Awat'ovi. Efforts to return the people to a condition of *suyanisqatsi* (a life of harmony and balance) are effected not through gentle reform but through overwhelming supernatural force, as when the *kikmongwi* (crier chief) of the Third Mesa village of Pivanhokyapi summons the Yaayapontsa (wind and fire *katsinam*) from the San Francisco Peaks to march as a firestorm and immolate his own followers. In this case, the corruption that inspired the violent cleansing lay in "women who began to leave their homes and abandon their husbands and children" in a desire to "go into the kivas" and join men there for the gambling game of *totolospi*, as well as to engage in sex with the men and boys.

Women figure centrally in all extant Hopi narratives of destruction, either as objects of desire who lead men to corruption, as *powaka* (sorceresses) who use love medicine to attract powerful men, or as the focus of violence between men from opposing villages. The fact that *katsinam* appear prominently as allies of senior men in their efforts to maintain political control of their own people suggests deep underlying tensions within Hopi villages, a theme consistent with much more recent Hopi history. That women in the Eastern Pueblos were quite explicitly cordoned off from most aspects of the Katsina Religion is also significant; young males, even noninitiates, were informal members of the ritual organization, with formalization coming at puberty; whereas women, associated with moieties, served as "pathmakers" when *katsinam* visited the villages. This period seems also to show archaeological evidence for women's disfranchisement from the most powerful aspects of ceremonial life. Small kin-or-clan kivas in scattered hamlets had long served both as domestic dwellings and ritual chambers, thereby displaying women's material culture (especially grinding stones) along with that of men. Yet from A.D. 1300 forward, women among the Eastern Pueblos seem increasingly excluded from kivas as they grew larger and oriented toward community-level ritual—similar to the process by which women were excluded from the Great Kivas at Chaco.

With the arrival of the Katsinam, kivas again became the domain of men, thereby signaling "a decline in the power and prestige of women."

Franciscans appeared at the Hopi mesas as yet a new variant in "cycles of evangelism" that Indians had been experiencing for centuries, as "outsiders" who brought the power to disrupt and the power to reshape. Between 1629 and 1680, Franciscans at Mission San Bernardo doubtless heard the Pahaana prophecy as well. It seems probable that Hopis made sense of the arrival of padres Porras, Gutiérrez, and Concepción in 1629 in terms of the Pahaana prophecy. The missionaries were initially "received with some coolness, because the devil was trying in all possible ways to obstruct and impede the promulgation of divine law." Among the threats that the people of Awat'ovi had been alerted to by an "Indian apostate from the Christian [Rio Grande] pueblos" was that the "Spaniards with tonsures and vestments were nothing but impostors" and that they intended to "behead their children," certainly an allusion to Pahaana. The "miraculous" healing of the blind boy affected by the laying of a Cross upon his eyes may have further convinced Hopis that the Castillam were associated with Pahaana, as evidence of their capacity to "make anew." Franciscan conversion pedagogy also mirrored themes in the prophecy. The friars, "soldiers of the gospel, girded themselves with the armor of prayer in order to subdue and conquer the wiles of Lucifer . . . set forth through the streets, preaching, the sonorous echoes of their voices bringing men and women to listen to them, compelled by a mysterious impulse." While announcing their message of salvation, they likewise dispensed "rattles, beads, hatchets, and knives"—the "grandeur of plenty"—yet found the Hopis cautious, for they had been warned that if they "accepted anything from the friars they would die." Despite the caution, Porras pursued a deeper communion with the people of Awat'ovi and neighboring towns, mastering their language, which was "very barbarous and difficult," and in a period of nine months claimed to have converted and baptized more than "four thousand souls."

Like Pahaana, the friars' methods displayed compulsion as well as attraction. Wíkvaya, keeper of oral histories at Oraibi Village, recalled in 1902 that Hopis called the priests *tuutachi*, a term approximating "dictator" for their habit of giving orders, such as traveling long distances for water to make adobe bricks or timbers for mission construction, as far away as Black Mesa, some fifty miles from Hopi lands. He also accused the priests of preying on Hopi women while the men were away, of destroying *pahos* and ordering the backfilling of kivas with rubble and sand. If these orders were not followed, the priests threatened that the Hopis "would be slashed to death or punished in some way." Punishments other than slashing included flogging, or, in extreme cases, enslavement through the sale of one's labor for a period of time, as much as ten years. At once reviled as "filthy" outsiders and revered as representatives of Elder Brother, the Franciscans lived in a liminal state in many Hopi's minds. Ambivalence, paradox, and anxiety, all of which lay at the core of the Pahaana narratives, were part of daily life at Mission San Bernardo. When the revolt came in 1680, it may be that some "converted Indians of Aguatubi" died at the hands of the rebels, who were, in their own way, fulfilling the purification aspects of the Pahaana prophecy.

Likewise, the Pahaana prophecy probably resonated with the Franciscans' vision of apocalyptic conversion, in which they "believed themselves a divinely inspired elect whose role was the *renovatio* of the evangelical life in the last age of the world." Influenced by Joachim of Fiore's vision of history, in which mankind evolved through three successive stages "culminating in an age . . . of bliss and understanding," Franciscan apocalypticism "emphasized events near the end of time which included the salvation of all the world." Salvation, in the Franciscan worldview, required the birth of the Antichrist and the martyrdom of the prophets Elijah and Enoch, as well as the conversion of the Jews. Only then would "nations of the world enter into the church" to herald "a time of peace before the final judgment." The Franciscans, therefore, shared many of the fundamental performative and philosophical elements, at least, of the Pahaana prophecy. When martyrdom did visit Mission San Bernardo, Hopis and Franciscans alike may have sensed an "end of days" narrative unfolding. Only early in the twentieth century, however, would the force of prophetic history be manifest for all to see.

❧·❦

If the central theme of the Pahaana prophecy lies in destruction and rebirth as the essence of Hopi history, no event illuminates this more clearly than the "split," or fissioning in the Third Mesa community of Oraibi. The crisis came to a head in 1906 and reverberated over the years to finally produce five new villages (Kykotsmovi, Bacavi, Hotevilla, Upper Moencopi, and Lower Moenkopi). The Oraibi fission, at least for many Hopis, is seen as "the culmination of a series of events presaged by past cycles, indeed, foretold by them."

Perhaps the most ancient of the settlements in Tusayán, with archaeological evidence dating back into the twelfth century, Oraibi was among three populous towns chosen by Franciscans as the location for Mission San Francisco (later changed to San Miguel) in 1629. By 1664, the mission census reported 1,236 "souls" (converted), "very good church . . . good provisions for public worship, a choir with many instruments, and a good convento." In the revolt of 1680, two priests resident at Oraibi, Augustín de Santa María and the former priest (and choral master) at Awat'ovi, José de Espeleta, suffered death at the hands of Warrior Katsinas from the Badger Clan, after which their bodies were tossed from the cliffs. In June and July 1701, Spanish governor don Pedro Rodríguez Cubero, after learning of the attack on Awat'ovi the previous autumn, led a military expedition to punish the "apostate Indians of the province of Moqui." The thin documentary record indicates the campaign proved a failure, beaten back by the "multitudes of the enemy . . . especially as the Moqui had with them the Tanos Indians, who, after committing outrages, had taken refuge among them and had risen at their command." And yet Hopi memory of this event leans toward a different angle. In 1936, Edmund Nequatewa, casting back to these troublous times, recalled that although the Spanish were indeed repulsed, it was not before a member of the Strap Clan of Oraibi identified the ceremonial leaders behind the assault on Awat'ovi. Seized by the Spanish captain, Juan Domínguez y Mendoza, the men were executed by musket fire. Thus the Spaniards, as Pahaanam, appear as judge, punisher, and redeemer in marked similarity to the story that Cushing heard some fifty years before.

Even after the expulsion of the Franciscans and the destruction of Awat'ovi, Oraibi would retain its prominence in Tusayán in the centuries ahead, among the Hopi villages and in encounters with Mexicans and Americans. Following the American conquest of New Mexico in 1847, Hopis welcomed James S. Calhoun, the first American superintendent of Indian affairs for the New Mexico Territory by sending a delegation to Santa Fe, composed from the leaders of each of the pueblos, including the largest, Oraibi. Each of the pueblos "was an independent republic, having confederated for mutual protection," but Oraibi was clearly the most prominent, and populous. In 1851, Antoine Leroux, guide to the Sitgreaves Expedition, counted 2,400 residents at Oraibi and a total Hopi population of 6,720.

Before the end of that decade, white Americans became an everyday presence in Hopi life with the arrival of Mormon colonists who cast their own missionary efforts at conversion, based on their belief that Hopis descended from the Welsh adventurer Prince Madoc and his A.D. 1164 expedition to colonize new lands beyond the western sea. Between 1858 and 1873, Mormons dispatched fifteen official missions to the Hopis, who were, at least initially, well received, since Hopis could obtain farming and blacksmithing implements from the missionaries. Mormons, too, held apocalyptic beliefs, based on their reading of the Book of Revelation in the Bible, and founder Joseph Smith's own revelation of the White Horse Prophecy. Whether or not Hopis absorbed these into their cosmology isn't clear, but a certain resonance may have existed with that of the Franciscans. Still, Hopis maintained discrete categories for these new arrivals, terming them Monomam to distinguish them from Pahaanam (other Anglos). A few Hopis did convert—Tuuvi and his wife, Katsinmana, from Oraibi, visited Utah and upon their return welcomed the establishment in 1873 of the Mormon town of Moencopi, where Oraibis cultivated summer gardens, in part to gain their military protection from Navajos, who often raided Hopi cornfields. In 1876, Mormons founded Tuba City (named for Tuuvi). Although pressure from the U.S. government forced Mormons out of Hopi country by the late nineteenth century, their insinuation of modern farming technologies and crops—peas, potatoes, beets, radishes, lettuce, alfalfa, onions, turnips, wheat, and barley—would later be viewed by some Hopis as harbingers of a negative transformation in Hopi lifeways, according to ethnographer Peter Whitely.

The U.S. government also established a presence among the Hopis at Keams Canyon in 1873. The people of Oraibi seemed unique in their hostility to the government presence, refusing annuity goods and refusing to take part in the annual census. Keams Canyon also hosted a small school for Hopi children, but Oraibi seems not to have allowed any from their village to attend. An invitation for Oraibi chiefs to attend a Washington, D.C., council in 1878 was also rebuffed—the chief at Oraibi said that if the government so wished to consult, the president ought to visit Oraibi.

The intrusion of outsiders like Frank Cushing accelerated rapidly in the 1880s. The Union Pacific Railroad extended down the Little Colorado Valley, establishing the town of Winslow, from which vastly more American goods and visitors traveled northward on horseback and in wagons to visit the mesas. This was especially so after the publication of John Gregory Bourke's *The Snake-Dance of the Moquis of Arizona* in 1884. So avid was fascination with a priesthood whose "magic" included the ability to lull rattlesnakes into a slumber

Street in the Pueblo of Oraibi, c. 1888, Tusayan, Arizona, De Lancey W. Gill.

that would allow the dancers to perform with them clenched in their mouths that special tours were arranged by the Fred Harvey Company, which had built a hotel in Winslow.

Cultural pressures also intensified with changes in U.S. Indian policy in the 1880s. With the Indian Wars largely in the past (although the Wounded Knee Massacre would take place in 1890), government reformers sought a quick path to acculturation and assimilation for all Indian "wards" of the nation. Even as ethnographers like Cushing sought to preserve ancient "myths and traditions," reformers sought ways to "kill the Indian, and save the Man." Foremost among their programs was a belief that the collective ownership of tribal lands, especially suited for market-oriented ranching and farming, stood as a barrier to Indians' ability to become full-fledged citizens of the United States. Thus a two-pronged program of education for Indian youth toward wage labor and the cash economy, as well as allotment of land to individuals and families and out of clan control, took root in the U.S. Indian affairs policy discussions. Hopi youth who learned English, and the American "system of values," would help to shape citizen-farmers who could leave traditional ways behind and effect a gradual transition to full citizenship.

In the fall of 1887 the Bureau of Indian Affairs opened a boarding school at the Keams Canyon Agency, thirty-five miles from Oraibi. Schooling would lie at the heart of factionalism that grew increasingly volatile over the next two decades. Hopi Agency superintendent David L. Shipley made clear that the aims of his model of education would be to erode the pagan influences that had stunted Hopi development and instill the light of Christian values among his charges. Little wonder, then, that the oldest and most conservative Hopi village would prove reluctant to send their children away for months at a time, and see them transformed in the manner Shipley proposed.

Oraibi resisted the call for students far more than other villages. Since they had declined annuity goods over the years, the agency had little leverage with which to persuade them. In June 1890, the BIA invited five Hopi village chiefs—Loololma from Oraibi, Simo and Ahnawita from Walpi, Honani from Shungopovi, and Polacca from Walpi—to Washington. In addition to enjoying the National Theater and a session with President Harrison that included ritual tobacco smoking, they traveled to the Carlisle Indian School in Pennsylvania, and viewed industrial workshops in Terre Haute, Indiana. These leaders came to an agreement with Harrison to accept the government's education program, Christian missionaries, and the allotment of land in severalty to individual titleholders.

Whether they requested so or not, the government built each leader a model home of stone masonry and pitched, gable roofs, which the Hopis termed *palakiki* (red houses), as their tin roofs rusted following summer rains. These were to serve as model homes for the "yeoman" farmsteads that the Bureau hoped to see scattered across the Hopi reservation once acculturation was complete. Yet that autumn saw little enthusiasm for the boarding school, with student enrollment ranging from two to eighteen on any given day. Loololma, who seemed deeply impressed with the power of Anglo culture and society after his trip east, was unwilling or unable to convince others, opposing the boarding school idea, to send their children away. Accordingly, Commissioner of Indian Affairs T. J. Morgan imposed a quota system that would ultimately require each village to furnish seventy-five children to the school, or leaders would suffer arrest and imprisonment. Only after an Army patrol entered Oraibi did the parents form their children in a line. From this group Superintendent Ralph P. Collins seized all he wished, thereby forcing Oraibi to surrender its children to the U.S. government.

Even as the education program devolved from attraction to coercion in its methods, the land allotment program exacerbated a division between *pavansinom* (Hopis like Loololma convinced of the benefits of acculturation) and *sukavungsinom* (those hostile to such measures), and intensified even stronger resistance from hostile Hopis. Especially offensive was a provision that required Hopis to abandon their homes in the mesa-top villages and settle in *palakiki*-style houses on their individual allotments down in the valley bottoms. The BIA saw the old villages as entrenched resisters to the acculturation program, and allotment would, it was thought, serve to undermine resistance to assimilation. But Hopis pushed back, pulling up survey stakes overnight, destroying survey monuments, and warning that they might descend on the school to free their children.

In June 1891, hostile disruptions reached the point that Lieutenant L. M. Brett was dispatched to Oraibi to arrest their leadership. Met by some fifty armed and well-positioned hostile men, Brett withdrew and recommended a larger detachment return, backed by Hotchkiss guns, which had six months earlier wreaked death upon the Lakota and Hunkpapa Sioux Ghost Dancers at Wounded Knee. Nine men suffered arrest and confinement at Fort Wingate, including key ritual leaders from among the hostiles. While imprisoned, the BIA built the Oraibi Day School down below Third Mesa, in hopes of addressing the resistance to children's distance at Keams Canyon. Attendance hovered around thirty youngsters, yet no children from the hostile faction attended.

To the surprise of reformers in Washington, Hopis and many local, knowledgeable whites joined to oppose the allotment program. Traders like Thomas Keam, early anthropologists like Alexander Stephen, Frank Cushing, and James Mooney, missionaries like Mennonite minister Henry R. Voth, and military men like General A. D. Cook lent their names to a Hopi petition numbering some 125 totemic signatures, at least 50 of which represented *pavansinom* (those presumed friendly to the government). Motivations may have varied, since Indian traders and anthropologists alike saw Hopi traditionalism as a resource valuable both to Hopi peoples and to the burgeoning art market, and thus worthy of preservation. By 1894 the BIA discontinued allotment at Hopi, one of the few Indian reservations to successfully resist that devastating policy.

Yet tensions between *pavansinom* and *sukavungsinom* remained unresolved, and would prove the vortex around which the centrifuge at Oraibi would rotate. One ironic outcome of the BIA's survey and land allotment study, only grasped much later by ethnographers (perhaps also by Hopis at the time, but who resisted its enunciation), was the realization that "a restricted and tenuous resource base required that Hopi society structure itself on an inequitable distribution of land," according to ethnographer Jerrold Levy. Since planting fields and orchards were distributed in accordance with the "ranking of clans" in a priority of their ceremonial responsibilities, and as determined by their arrival on the mesas in ancient migrations, the only way that the scarce agricultural resources could be preserved over the long term meant that during periods of drought, surplus population had to be "sloughed off" in an orderly manner. Conversely, Hopi collective agricultural labor required a high degree of "cooperation and social integration." Thus, an "internal contradiction" existed that kept Hopi society in a "state of dynamic tension, a tension that intensified or eased as droughts alternated with wet periods."

The internal contradictions at the heart of Hopi society mirrored in key aspects the "ambivalence, paradox, and anxiety" embodied in the Pahaana prophecy. While the intrusion of Anglo ways in the form of schooling and efforts to instill a consumption ethic among the Hopis fostered strains in society, a series of drought years beginning in the 1890s likewise signaled a growing cultural crisis. The missionary Henry Voth reported that no rains fell in 1902 and that the ground had grown so hard that it was nearly impossible to plant corn. In 1903 two train carloads of corn from Kansas were imported to relieve the hunger at Oraibi. Reliable springs, the very reason that the mesas had hosted settlements for centuries, began to dry up. Women waited for hours to fill *ollas* from seeps of water in the sandy-bottomed springs. A ceremonial ritual order designed to ensure rainfall and plentiful harvests seemed to be failing.

Drought struck Hopis unequally, however. Powerful ceremonial clans—Bear, Parrot, Patki, Bow, and Snake—for instance, held rights to fields high in the Oraibi Wash that could be flood-irrigated when scattered-but-often-fierce rains did fall. Others, like Water Coyote, Lizard, and Sand, although large in membership, held farming lands less well situated to catch runoff on the alluvial fans of tributary watercourses, or none at all. In fact, careful analysis of land allocation shows "an almost perfect correlation between the ceremonial scores [status rank of clans] and the quality of land controlled. The system of clan ranking by ceremonies is nothing more than a translation of economic reality into the realm of the sacred," according to Levy.

Ironically, the land distribution system envisioned by reformers took need, as determined by individual family size, as a crucial variable, but failed to understand that Euro-American–style "nuclear" families were not the fundamental component of Hopi kinship. Clan and matrilineage crosscut the western model of family in ways that fee simple allotments could never equitably address. Circumstances grew dire. "Drought, depression, deprivation, arroyo cutting [which prevented irrigation ditches from drawing floodwaters to fields] and land gridlock" combined to create a widely perceived sense of imminent crisis. Rapid growth and competition for grazing land from neighboring Navajo outfits compounded the atmosphere of threat from without.

When it came in 1906, the "Oraibi split" is commonly explained as the culmination of tensions between the *pavansinom* (conciliatory, if not entirely friendly to white society and reforms) and *sukavungsinom* (hostile to the threats to Hopi lifeways embodied by white society and reform efforts). It began with struggles over the two factions' ceremonial responsibilities. The hostiles, who held responsibility for the Niman (Home) Dance—performed each July as the "going home" ceremony for the rainmaking *katsinam*, who attend to the precipitation essential for Hopi farming between the Winter and Summer solstices—were prevented by the friendlies from performing the ritual. *Pavansinom* blocked access to the Niman shrine and thus the ability of the dancers to send the Katsinam to their spiritual home. With the Niman postponed, the Snake Dance, also the ceremonial duty of the *sukavungsinom*, was likewise delayed. The standoff seemed to threaten the very essence of Oraibi's religious obligations.

Adding to the tension was the arrival in Oraibi of some fifty ada-
mant "hostiles" from the Spider Clan at Second Mesa's Shungopovi,
who had recently clashed with Superintendent Theodore G. Lemmon
while resisting his attempt to seize their children for the Oraibi Day
School. They reinforced their clansmen there, and began a campaign
to undercut the ceremonial authority of Tawaquaptewa, the friendly
kikmongwi of Oraibi (who had followed his uncle, Loololma, into the
chieftainship).

Finally, on September 6, Tawaquaptewa heard that the hostiles
intended to assassinate him. Through a long night, each faction held
councils in village houses, and the *pavansinom* decided they would
drive the sukavungsinom from the town the following day. With
several whites they had summoned as witnesses (including Elizabeth
Stanley, acting principal of the Oraibi Day School and her colleague,
field matron Miltona Keith), the friendly faction rushed into the hostiles' council and began to force the hostiles out of their gathering,
even to the point of literally lifting them from their feet. These captives were carried beyond the village bounds and set down. The hostiles, oddly, outnumbered their attackers by as much as four to one,
yet seemed to lodge little objection beyond their passive refusal to
walk out of the village.

The women and children of the hostile faction joined their men-
folk on the outskirts of Oraibi, while groups of *pavansinom* peri-
odically threatened them to maintain their exclusion. Throughout
the afternoon there were exchanges of words between the factions.
The unfriendlies seemed to understand that a prophecy required
one group of disputants to leave the village, yet wished it not to be
them. Finally, a line was drawn in the dirt and they found themselves on the outside. Still, the friendlies remained nervous, for they

understood the prophecy to augur that those who left might return and claim vengeance on the village.

An anxious stalemate held until October, when the BIA stepped in with a "Program for Dealing with the Existing Hopi Troubles." This included the abolition of the Oraibi tribal government, the expulsion of the leaders of both factions and the stipulation that they remain banished for life, as well as that allotment be restarted despite the decision twelve years earlier to halt the project. When Superintendent of the Navajo Agency at Fort Defiance Reuben Perry, who had been placed in charge, interviewed the hostile leader Yukeoma, he learned that the hostiles wanted nothing of the boarding school uplift program, wished simply to live as they had for centuries, and that if the government desired to resolve the dispute, ought to abandon any hope for assimilation and behead the leadership of the friendly faction—clearly a reference to the role of white elder brother in the prophecy.

Perry declined Yukeoma's request, but did, on two occasions, attempt to stage a pistol duel between Tawaquaptewa and Yukeoma, in each case giving only one a firearm, however. Neither shot the other. Perry seems to have stage-managed the scenes in an effort to undermine each chief's authority, to demonstrate that neither was really willing to carry the dispute, and perhaps the prophecy, to its logical or prophetic conclusion. He warned both leaders that if they persisted in their conflict, the government would remove each from authority. Now Perry brought troops to the hostile encampment at Hotevilla, where they were settling in for the winter, and seized eighty-two children who were taken to the Keams Canyon Boarding School. The hostile men were given the option of returning to Oraibi or being placed under arrest.

More than half refused, and were put to hard labor at the Keams Canyon Agency. The majority of women and children remained at Hotevilla and fended for themselves through a harsh winter, hunting rabbits for subsistence. The friendlies at Oraibi agreed to make peace with their expelled kinsmen. The hostile men, once released from their prison labor, looked for a new village site and settled on one at Bacavi Springs, about one mile from Hotevilla. The leader of the Bacavi hostiles, Kewaninptewa, gave Hopi Agency Superintendent Horton H. Miller a symbolic handful of thirty-two beans that stood for the number of children from his faction who were now enrolled at Keams Canyon, and even floated the idea that a school be established at the new village of Bacavi. Thus ended, at least for the moment, the crisis at Oraibi. Two new villages had been established, removing the hostile element from Oraibi, and effectively splitting the sukavungsinom into two, weaker, threats to government order.

Yet this version leaves several vexing questions unresolved. First, all accounts make clear that the *sukavungsinom* significantly outnumbered the *pavansinom*, both in overall village membership and during the expulsion of the hostiles, by at least two-thirds. A census of the hostile encampment at Hotevilla in October 1906 counted 539, which Superintendent Lemmon estimated as a substantial majority of Oraibi's total population. That they were expelled from the village by the smaller faction and that the *sukavungsinom* did not resist with their weapons (guns, and bows and arrows) surprised him as well, for he knew from experience they could be fierce fighters. He noted also that Elizabeth Stanley and Miltona Keith, who observed the struggle, expressed surprise at the calm demeanor of those who were carried from the village bounds. Commissioner of Indian Affairs Francis E. Leupp, after reviewing these and other eyewitness accounts, wondered just how much the opposition to civilization really lay beneath the dispute, and he mused that internal political issues may have lain much closer to the core disputes.

Of course, internal politics among the Hopi involved more than the Americans were likely to grasp. Agency Superintendent Lemmon, only two days after the struggle, interviewed Tawaquaptewa and other members of the *pavansinom,* who explained the whole affair was simply the fulfillment of a Hopi prophecy and that the expelled faction would journey, as had so many in the past, to new homes elsewhere (perhaps the Keet Seel ruin in Navajo National Monument, some one hundred miles to the north). Later, Lemmon heard virtually the same narrative from members of the *sukavungsinom,* which suggested a level of concordance, at least around the prophetic structure of the crisis.

That white outsiders were recruited, if only by the *pavansinom,* to witness the climax of the fission hints that at least some elements of the Pahaana prophecy were at work. Their presence, as symbolic representatives of Pahaana, and the explicit references to whites as potential agents for "beheading" leaders of the opposition—invoked not by Tawaquaptewa, leader of the friendlies, but by hostile leader Yukeoma, suggests that each faction had a certain common understanding of the meaning of the split in the village. In narratives shared long since the crisis, in the 1980s, a deeper significance began to emerge. All parties, while not excusing the other of wrong thinking or wrongdoing, held mutually a belief that the culture-changing intrusions of white society (for better or worse) *as well as* internal struggles over ceremonial and village leadership constituted an atmosphere of *koyaanisqatsi*, or chaos. "A corollary of *Pahaana's* return," writes Peter Whiteley, "is that it will coincide with a stage when Hopi life becomes corrupt and decadent." Each faction doubtless thought the other *popwaqt*, or sorcerers whose power had grown beyond acceptable levels. The Hopi philosophy of history, as expressed in the emergence myth's cycles of destruction and rebirth, *required* that the crisis be brought to a head. Once the chaos fomented in the collapse of the current ritual order was abolished, cultural renewal, either as envisioned by *pavansinom* or by *sukavungsinom*, would come to fruition. "By splitting the village," Whiteley explains, "the leaders could simultaneously solve the symptoms of ritual corruption—that is, the land, water, and population problems. . . . The education program and the general acceptance of the white man's ways were chosen as the necessary catalyst."

Ironically, Yukeoma, leader of the hostiles who founded Hotevilla, cast back to ancient tradition and established his clan, Kookop, or Fire Clan, as the first arriving clan of that new community and therefore the highest-ranking clan, with priority rights to farming lands. The Fire Clan, however, held no important ceremonies and would in time find its primacy challenged by others. The revival of the Pahaana prophecy in the decades leading up to 1906 served as a tool of religious leaders to foster a regeneration of the ritual ceremonial order as foretold through the concept of revealed knowledge. Yet in many respects the fissioning left Oraibi, Hotevilla, and Bacavi with such fractured leadership and ceremonial knowledge that "the collapse of the ceremonial calendar" did not allow for the reconstitution of a revived piety. Hotevilla did become, and remains, a conservative stronghold of

Hopi ceremonialism, if only a shadow of what it once was, and more oriented toward farming and sheep grazing than many of its neighbors on the mesas. Bacavi has grown more progressive than its neighbor. Oraibi dwindled in population to fewer than 100 residents (from more than 800 in 1900). Tawaquaptewa held the leadership position of *kikmongwi* until 1948, then briefly reclaimed it in 1956. Shortly before he died in 1960, he ordered that "he be buried with all his ceremonial equipment," apparently in an effort to force "an end of ceremonies" and the prophetic rebirth of Hopi religion. His son, Stanley Bahnimtewa, however, continued the Soyal ceremony when he stepped into the *kikmongwi*'s role in 1978.

Clear, however, is the truth buried within Jo Brew's later observation, in 1939. The Peabody's Awat'ovi Expedition was "facing a highly involved political situation" that mobilized "claims for control of the surrounding farm lands," long-running disputes between clans around ceremonial and political rank, all of which went back "hundreds of years, and . . . played an important role in the sacking of Awat'ovi." What he may not have realized were the number of centuries that underlay these disputes.

7

Across This Deep and Troubled Land

Aliksa'i. They say they were living at Awat'ovi.
Great numbers of people were at home there, so many, in fact,
that some people did not know each other. . . .
There were settlements all across the land.
The residents of Awat'ovi were wont to do all sorts of things.

—THIRD MESA VERSION, 1993

Jo Brew sensed that storm clouds born of internal strife, many centuries deep, underlay some aspects of the tensions that forced the Peabody Museum's exit from Antelope Mesa. As Hopis began to recount stories of their ancient past to ethnographers interested in preserving these histories and the original language in which they were maintained, a sense of the extraordinary depth they curated began to emerge. These were rendered in "mytho-historic" form, wherein accounts are "laden with actors and agents . . . with greater-than-human faculties: gods and goddesses, culture heroes and evil sorcerers, terrifying spirits, animals capable of speech." Little in the Hopi versions of history do not find comparable form in the epic histories of the Western world—from the fall of Troy to the founding of Rome. In a sense similar to the cultural lessons contained in *The Iliad*, Hopi accounts of violence in their deep history "anchor the present generations in a meaningful, significant past, functioning as eternal and ideal models for human behavior and goals, " in Christopher Vecsey's words. Or, as in the case of Paris's insult to Menelaus's hospitality, cautioning against individual hubris that will lead to ruination.

Periodic eruptions of violence were common among peoples of the ancient Southwest. But these seldom merit rehearsal in the epic narratives of Hopi history. Rather, tales of wholesale destruction of communities warrant memory and retelling. Ranging from locations long lost to mapmakers to those as recent as Oraibi, these histories attend to key tenets of life in the Puebloan Southwest.

Palatkwapi (Red-Walled City of the Southern Lands) is among those places that defies a precise location, yet establishes one strain of history that runs throughout Hopi accounts of migration, settlement, and dislocation. Some believe the town to lie as near to the Hopi Mesas as Montezuma Castle in the Verde Valley of Arizona, as far distant as Paquimé in Chihuahua, Teotihuacán in the Valley of Mexico, or even Palenque, Chiapas. "Some Hopi scholars and cultural advisors," caution T. J. Ferguson and Micah Loma'omvaya, "suggest that Palatkwapi may have been an *era or epoch* rather than a place per se. According to these advisors, Palatkwapi is a sequence of events that happened when Hopi ancestors resided in a region south of the Hopi mesas . . . associated with a number of locations where ancestors of the various Hopi clans lived." Thus *time*, rather than *place*, is the primary referent of the Palatkwapi narrative.

Founded by a coalition of migratory bands who would coalesce into the Water Clan, Palatkwapi was, according to Edmund Nequatewa, "small at first, then it grew large, and by the time it was large there were numerous persons in the village who rejected virtue." The people, once attentive to the lessons learned in the collapse of the Third World and their rescue by Masauwu, who led them through the *sipapuni* into the Fourth World, could not answer the crucial question: why are we here? "Evil and corruption had entered the village. Instead of gathering in the kivas to examine the meaning of life, men and women used the kivas for playing *totolospi*, *kokotukwi* and other gambling games." Fields lay neglected, and no longer were *pahos* created as gifts for the spirits. A Butterfly Dance became popular, performed first by young maidens as was appropriate, but soon "young married women were taking part, and instead of putting it on during the day time in the plaza, they were dancing in the kivas at night." Things went from bad to worse. Married women abandoned their husbands for the company of other men. A shadow descended on Palatkwapi.

The *kikmongwi* of Palatkwapi, Tawayistiwa, met with clan leaders to share his dismay at the growing corruption of life in the village. In an effort to halt the slide into *koyaanisqatsi*, they selected the chief's nephew, Siwiyistiwa, to impersonate the Tsaveyo ogre, a disciplinarian represented by a black mask with horns and protruding eyes. Called to the plaza, the people of Palatkwapi heard Tsaveyo admonish them to return to their former piety. "Unless Palatkwapi returns to a good way of life it will cease to be a living village."

For a short time, people heeded the warning, but soon returned to their heretical ways. Tawayistiwa then sent Siwiyistiwa on a mission to a high mountain ridge in the south, there to find a deer and, in exchange for *pahos* made by his uncle, to obtain the one prong of the stag's antlers. Once returned, Tawayistiwa crafted four Katsina masks for his nephew, the most significant of which was that of Masauwu, "the Owner of Fire and the Spirit of Death." Dressed in this "dreadful and fearful costume" Siwiyistiwa ran back to the high ridge and struck a fire, from which he gathered coals into his Masauwu mask. When he breathed upon them, fire would erupt from the mask's mouth. The youth began haunting Palatkwapi each night, sneaking into the town and, as bidden by his uncle, perching on rooftops and emitting fire from the Masauwu mask as he ground corn in a metate, singing to announce his presence. The people of Palatkwapi heard his voice and witnessed the fire in the darkness, and began to grow fearful. After several nights of growing anxiety, a group of men trapped Siwiyistiwa as he tried to leave the town at dawn, and dragged him down into a kiva. After stripping his masks, and finding the "ghost" one of their own townsmen, they killed him and buried him in the plaza, leaving, at his pleading, however, one hand exposed.

Each of four dawns thereafter, the people of Palatkwapi visited his grave and saw that for each morning one of his four fingers had folded down into his palm. Not knowing what this portended, they continued to "value pleasure above a good life," carrying on in their kivas. On the fourth morning, when each of Siwiyistiwa's fingers were clenched in a fist, they heard a "rumbling in the distance . . . the earth began to shake . . . large stones slid from their foundations and the walls of the houses cracked. . . . Out of the gray cloudless sky rain poured down, and a cold wind swept through the plaza." As the plaza filled with water and became a lake, "the head of the great water serpent Balolokong appeared . . . out of Siwiyistiwa's grave and its head reared higher and higher as his body emerged from the earth." On the top of the serpent's head rose the one-pronged antler from the stag, and his "eyes turned this way and that, surveying the crumbling walls of Palatkwapi." People fled in terror as the floodwaters from above and cracking earth from below destroyed the village. Children were lost and the old and crippled left behind.

Finding refuge on high ground beyond Palatkwapi, the survivors hastened to make *pahos* and find a way to quiet Balolokong. They chose a young boy—Choong'o—and a girl—Kachinmama, both "of clean hearts and innocent" to act as couriers to the serpent. Balolokong received the children gently and taught them songs that would accompany, in the future, a Winter Solstice ceremony (the nine-day Soyal, marking the return of the *katsinam* to Hopi from their long sleep in the San Francisco Peaks) to commemorate what had happened at Palatkwapi. If done properly, the serpent promised to "send rain when the people are in need. When a stranger comes to the village, feed him. Do not injure one another, because all beings deserve to live together without injury... when people are old and cannot work anymore, do not turn them out to shift for themselves ... defend yourselves when an enemy comes to your village, but do not go out seeking war. The Hopis shall take this counseling and make it the Hopi Way."

Meanwhile, the former residents of Palatkwapi regrouped themselves into their clans and shouldered their few remaining possessions. They set out on yet another hegira, "walking to the north, toward Situqui (Flower Butte [the Hopi Mesas today])." Balolokong gave the children new seeds, and instructed them to look to the north for campfires at night, "for that is where your people are now." Before they departed, however, he gave one more instruction: "The single horn you saw on my head is my symbol. Therefore let the priests of the Kwan society wear a horn in this fashion to symbolize the knowledge of things I gave the Hopi."

The destruction of Palatkwapi, if representative of a time rather than a place, shows several elements of "Hopis in the making." Having escaped the end of their Third World, they had established new communities in the Fourth, organized around the forms of piety instructed by Masauwu. As the village grew in population, the social order began to erode, especially as women began to violate ceremonial and sexual norms. Generational tensions emerged, too, as did challenges to the *kikmongwi*'s authority. Calling upon others of the priesthood, Tawayistiwa delegated his own authority to his nephew Siwiyistiwa and marked the young man for sacrifice. Siwiyistiwa's execution and burial calls forth the punishing and purifying powers of Balolokong. This being seems a variation on the feather-and-horned serpent ubiquitous across the Puebloan Southwest, and almost certainly a merging of a migratory idea that combines the water powers of Tlaloc, the Aztec rain spirit, and the Feathered Serpent, Quetzalcoatl, whose origins lie in Mesoamerica and whose iconography coincides with the arrival of the Katsina religion in the Southwest Borderlands. Palatkwapi is destroyed by earthquake and flood, perhaps a reference to the eruption of Sunset Crater near Flagstaff, Arizona, in A.D. 1085. Expelled from their crumbling and flooded city, the survivors divide into clan groups who traditionally comprised migratory units, and move generally northward, chastened and renewed in their adherence to orthodox forms of piety. Among the migrants travels the members of a new sacred society, that of the Kwan or One-Horn, one of the four societies that convened the Wuwutcim initiations at Awat'ovi in the autumn of 1700, and

which remains important to Hopi life today. In their journey northward toward the Flower Butte, these "becoming-Hopi" peoples created new towns, often described as "winter villages," at places again
without precise locations—Kunchalpi, Hohokyam, and finally to a
place with specific reference, Neuvakwiotaka, a cluster of archaeological sites on Anderson Mesa, Arizona, at a relatively high altitude
of 6,200 to 7,200 feet. "After many harvests, where they lived very
prosperously," at Neuvakwiotaka, probably at least a century, they
continued to the Hopi towns of Homol'ovi.

Ceramic analysis of the six settlements on Anderson Mesa and
Chavez Pass indicate they were founded in the middle decades of
the thirteenth century A.D., beginning around 1225, and peaking in
population between 1275 and 1300, with depopulation by 1325. One
of those villages, today called Grapevine Pueblo, is a likely candidate
to figure centrally in another history of conflict in ancient towns, the
demise of Hovi'itstuyqa, as does its distant neighbor, Tupats'ovi.

In Tupats'ovi lived a homely boy, Pitsinsivostiyo (Cotton Seed
Boy), and his grandmother. They were of the "lower-class people" and
lived on the southwest edge of the village plaza, an area of midden
dumps and where others went to "relieve themselves." The two often
ate only the thrown-away food of their neighbors, while suffering
their disdain. On the northwest corner of the plaza, where dwelled
the "upper-class people," lived an "exceedingly beautiful, industrious,"
maiden named Nagai-si, whose desirability as a wife attracted suitors
from within the town and beyond. She found none, however, who
stirred her heart, and was annoyed to be drawn away from grinding
corn or preparing meals for her family. She finally announced a challenge, that the first young man to bring her a red fox—she wished "to
own one as a pet"—would gain her love.

None, however, proved able to capture the red fox she so wished to own. Six years passed, without a single suitor delivering the prize, nor gaining her hand in marriage. Pitsinsivostiyo knew of the challenge, yet saw no way that he might prevail, when other, more athletic and higher-ranking boys had failed. His grandmother, however, saw how crestfallen he had become, and discovered the source of his discouragement. She began to instruct Pitsinsivostiyo in the rudiments of hunting—how to identity the best shoots of the Apache plume from which he might fashion arrows, the oak from which he could shape and smooth and bend a bow by binding it wet across a ladder and allowing it to dry. She taught him to twist sinew cords to make a bowstring, and soon he had all that was necessary to hunt the fox.

Yet, to the boy's surprise, when his grandmother sent him to the "rocky hill" where he might find the red fox, she laid out an unusual strategy. She told him to gather the seeds of the "giant dropseed grass" en route, and, once atop the ridge, to find a "large empty place" where he might churn the ground with his feet until it was "really messed up." He was to shoot his arrows into the ground "all over the empty space," and then to lie among those shafts so that it seemed as if "you were attacked by enemies and killed." One arrow he was to tuck in his armpit; another, the obsidian point anointed with pitch, he should stick directly above his heart. "Be lying there when the sun goes down," and sprinkle the "giant dropseed all over yourself," as well as some in "your mouth. These seeds look just like maggots." She had supplied him with several dead mice, several days old and beginning to decay, which he was to chop up and smear on his body "to give off the odor of a rotten corpse."

Pitsinsivostiyo's stinking body drew a coyote, which howled to his pack that a body lay waiting to be devoured. As they gather around, the boy peered through his eyelashes and saw, just to his right hand, that among them stood a red fox. Seizing the fox in his hand, he rose and yelled to frighten the coyotes away, then secured the fox. He spoke to the fox, assuring it he meant no harm, but that he wished only to make a gift to Nagai-si; "I am sure that girl will be gentle with you."

Even while Pitsinsivostiyo was training as a hunter and executing his grandmother's plan, potential husbands continued to call on the maiden. Among them was a "very handsome" young man from the distant village of Hovi'itstuyqa, a town larger and more prosperous than Tupats'ovi. Carrying the name Sikyaatayo (Red Fox Boy), he, too, had failed to bring her the animal itself, but proved an avid suitor nonetheless, and one whom Nagai-si secretly hoped might succeed. When Pitsinsivostiyo presented the tamed red fox to Nagai-si, and she accepted his proposal of marriage, all were astonished that a poor and homely youth had succeeded where so many better young men had failed. Their marriage raised the boy and his grandmother in the esteem of their neighbors, for they realized that only people "endowed with greater-than-human powers" could have captured the fox and brought him so willingly to the maiden. The people of Tupats'ovi began to talk among themselves, wondering if the boy's grandmother might be the Old Spider Woman, gifted with numinous powers.

In time, Sikyaatayo heard that Nagai-si had married Pitsinsivostiyo, and yet he still desired her, more even than before. He began haunting the neighborhood of Tupats'ovi, watching Nagai-si in secret as she went around her daily chores. Discovering that she went at dawn each day to "speak her morning prayers to the sun," he lay in wait overnight, anticipating the yellow dawn.

As Nagai-si returned from the shrine, Sikyaatayo seized her and threw her to the ground. Her fox "cried and howled," attempting to alert Pitsinsivostiyo of the assault, but to no effect. When Nagai-si finally returned to their house, Pitsinsivostiyo saw "that she was not herself," she had "let it happen without resistance." The fox, however, spoke to Pitsinsivostiyo "in plain Hopi. 'I am sorry for you. This morning when I ran along with your wife for the prayer to the sun, I saw something unpleasant,'" and described what he had seen that morning.

Sikyaatayo abducted Nagai-si and took her to Hovi'itstuyqa, a long day's travel to the northwest. Disconsolate and "bent on revenge," Pitsinsivostiyo again turned to his grandmother for advice. But poor and friendless as they were, they had no allies or even kinsmen upon whom to call to avenge the dishonor. Old Spider Woman advised he seek help from among the distant Kisispaya (Yavapai?) people, who lived well beyond the Hopi country to the southwest. They did not dwell in pueblos, but in "roundish huts," and spoke a different language, but one that sounded familiar enough through their trading visits that he could have a conversation. The chief of the Kisispaya called his warriors together, and then Pitsinsivostiyo spoke, describing the offense to his honor and his request: "I would like you to raid the village of Hovi'itstuyqa in my behalf and destroy it. You can do whatever you want. If you're interested in the women and girls, you can round them up. If you want to kill them along with the rest, that's all right, too. The loot such as food and other items of value that you find, you can distribute however you see fit. My only wish is to see that place destroyed."

The Kisispaya warriors gathered weapons and packed dried venison for the four-day journey to Hovi'itstuyqa. Pitsinsivostiyo went ahead to scout. Slipping into the village after nightfall, he snooped into houses through the ladder openings in their roofs. At last he found where Sikyaatayo and Nagai-si lived, and, peering down, he saw them making love. Nursing his rage, he returned to find the Kisispaya camp "in a spot out of site of Hovi'itstuyqa" where they were straightening their arrow shafts over a fire's embers, and testing their bows. Pitsinsivostiyo described what he had witnessed, and claimed the right to kill Sikyaatayo himself, after which he would yell to call the warriors into the pueblo. "Deal severely with them. I do not want you to spare any man or boy."

The next night Pitsinsivostiyo again entered the sleeping village, while the Kisispaya encircled the walls and quietly drifted through the plaza and alleyways. Pitsinsivostiyo found the couple in their home, illuminated by firelight on "unfolded bedding ... clinging to each other." Peering down through the ladder-entry, he pulled an arrow from his quiver and fixed it in the sinew bowstring, drew the bow tight, and "aimed right at the heart of Sikyaatayo." The arrow flew true, penetrating the young man's heart and exiting his back. Pitsinsivostiyo released a cry of revenge and the Kisispaya attackers "scattered through the village ... rushing from house to house where they killed the men and boys. The women and girls were all herded together." Plunder followed—"necklaces, earrings, provisions, and everything of value."

The village in flames, the Kisispayas herded the women and girls back to their encampment. Dividing the captives among themselves, the Kisispaya chief selected Nagai-si as his own reward, to which Pitsinsivostiyo agreed. "Very well, I promised the women to you. This one here did not want me and followed that boy here. I can't treasure her anymore." He "laid out a road marker in the direction of the Kisispaya homes and they departed." Pitsinsivostiyo returned to Tupats'ovi and reported the annihilation of Hovi'itstuyqa to his grandmother. She "felt sorry for the people of Hovi'itstuyqa," and when she saw that the red fox had followed Pitsinsivostiyo home, she made a *paho* for the animal, now grieving the loss of his mistress, and ordered that her grandson return him "to his people." The fox, relieved and honored, told Pitsinsivostiyo that "his people had always desired a prayer feather," and now, with this gift, he directed that in Katsina dances henceforth, the feather should be worn, along with the pelt of red foxes.

Yet, soon Pitsinsivostiyo "was troubled by what he had done to the people of Hovi'itstuyqa. . . . He should not have murdered all the people there. After all, not all of them had wronged him. Sikyaatayo alone had hurt him by stealing the love of his wife." Anguishing over his role in the massacre, he "blurted it all out to his grandmother." She knew, she replied, that "when you plotted this wicked scheme that it would be troubling you one day." She had sided with him out of loyalty, but was herself tormented by the events. The only solution, she felt, was to flee. "If we stay here, we'll never be able to forget. . . . we should just get up and go to the southeast . . . where we came from in the first place." The two left under cover of night, leaving all their meager belongings behind, and living off wild plants as they traveled. When the people of Tupats'ovi found that the two were gone, they discovered that "their cotton was beginning to give out." It was at this point it became clear that Cotton Seed Boy was more than just a name for the homely young man, that in fact he had "owned the cotton. When he left, he took it with him. . . . too late, they treasured what they had had in him. . . . From that day on they could no longer grow any cotton." A young man's rage at the loss of his wife brought ruin not only to a distant town, but to his own people as well.

Neither of these towns are identifiable today, although the general location along the Anderson Mesa/Chavez Pass regional community seems likely, with references to the rocky heights where the fox was captured suggesting the Mogollon Rim, and the importance of cotton-growing consistent with that cultigen's presence in fourteenth-century Hopi life. Perhaps the tale of Hovi'itstuyqa's destruction lies in an intermediate zone, between a "time" and a "place" that moves closer to full focus as the narratives develop. Tension between Puebloan towns was ubiquitous throughout the Southwest, since arable lands were always at a premium, and microenvironmental fluctuations could leave one community destitute while a distant neighbor enjoyed plentitude. The biological necessity of seeking marriage partners from outside one's community is amply demonstrated in Puebloan courtship and marriage practices, given the relatively small population of these villages. Pitsinsivostiyo's quest for vengeance for the loss of Nagai-si is an assault to which the maiden accedes. Her virtue surrendered is vehicle for her ruin. Sikyaatayo's higher status is attractive when compared to the poverty and low status of Pitsinsivostiyo and his grandmother. Preparations for courtship and the red fox motif, Pitsinsivostiyo's grandmother's knowledge of bow-and-arrow making and hunting powers texture the story, even as it speaks of allies and enemies in the ancient Southwest. The Kisispayas (Yavapai hunters and farmers of the Verde Valley) are agents of revenge. Summoned from within the doomed town, the attackers kill the male inhabitants, and make captive the women and girls to distribute them among themselves—the fate of Awat'ovi's survivors. Crops fail and the regional Neuvakwiotaka community disintegrates, setting the stage for the founding of the Homol'ovi cluster that will specialize in cotton growing and weaving in the century ahead.

The people of Tupats'ovi, like so many before, moved on in their migrations toward the Flower Butte, doubtless via Homol'ovi, and finally, with many other migrating clans, to those beckoning mesas with their ever-reliable springs. There they would establish new towns, amid the swirl of history and prophecy and danger that composed Hopi life. Just three miles northwest of Old Oraibi on Third Mesa lie the ruins of Huk'ovi, "Windy Place on High." Analysis of the ceramic scatter at the ruins of Huk'ovi, Jeddito black-on-orange and Jeddito black-on-white, indicates that the village was established in the middle years of the twelfth century and no longer occupied after the last decade of the thirteenth century, perhaps a consequence of the prolonged drought of 1276 to 1299.

During its heyday, Huk'ovi was equal in population and power to its nearby neighboring village of Pivanhokyapi on Third Mesa. Although occasionally at odds with each other over ownership of planting fields in the valleys below the mesa, it was also common for courtships and marriage to link the towns through kinship. Ceremonial calendars in each village featured dances and feasts staggered in such a way to encourage visitation from neighbors, as did clan linkages allow a wider sense of lineage and kinship than those within each village. Clan exogamy, however, which required youth seeking marriage partners to wed outside their clans, thereby recruiting new resources to each clan, afforded opportunities for social mixing. And the peril of conflict, when greater-than-human powers were at work.

In Pivanhokyapi lived a "very handsome" young man, who caught the eye of a maiden at Huk'ovi during one of their joint ceremonials. She would often encounter him when he was out gathering firewood for his mother, and yet she could not get him to pay the least attention to her. She even asked his friends to bring him over to her home

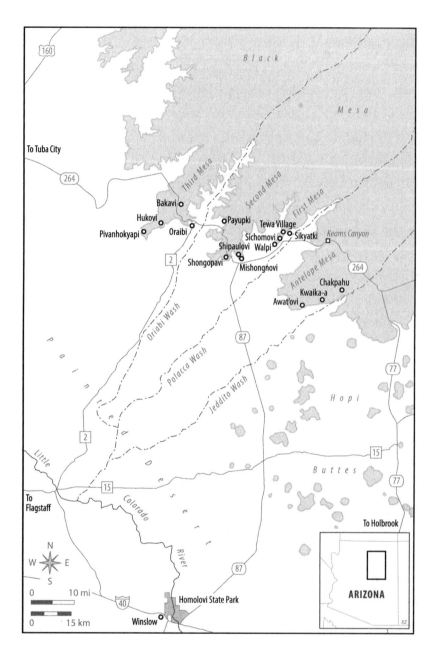

Hopi Mesas and the villages of Huk'ovi, Pivanhonkyapi.

at Huk'ovi at night, but he refused, suspicious of her ardor. "No way will I go over to her place."

It came time that the residents of Pivanhokyapi staged their famous Ladder Dance, an event that drew an audience from many of the distant villages. On the edge of the mesa were four deep holes drilled into the rock, into which tall pine poles carried miles from the heights of the San Francisco Peaks, some fifty miles distant, were inserted. Four dancers, impersonating *katsinam*, would climb the poles and leap acrobatically from one to the other, in teams of two, often crossing in mid-flight, barely missing a collision. The watchers waited for these moments, and often cried out when the dancers were in mid-flight, so close were there bodies. It was a great spectacle and demonstrated the grace and power of the dancers.

The girl from Huk'ovi again approached the young man when he was gathering fuel wood out on the mesa, and again he ignored her. "Am I so ugly you run away from me," she asked. "Do I look so much like an old woman that you're avoiding me?" He admitted that she was, in fact, "a pretty girl," but still resisted her enticements, even when she offered her body, "come over here and enjoy yourself on me, you can have my body."

The boy refused, with the excuse that he would soon be a member of the important ceremony, and the senior men prohibited such sexual liaisons before ritual performances. The girl returned to Huk'ovi, furious at his rejection. "And she would find a way [to punish him], since she was a witch (*powaqmana*) and a master at her craft. By using her magic powers she caused a crack in one of the holes into which the pine poles had been inserted. . . . with that crack . . . the pole would give way and crash down over the rim with the boy still on it." Since the postholes lay just a few feet from the edge of the mesa, a fall to the rocks below would surely be fatal.

As the Ladder Dance ceremony neared, the men of Pivanhokyapi gathered in their kiva for preparations. To their surprise, Old Spider Woman called down to them and asked permission to descend. "A girl from Huk'ovi has caused a crack alongside the hole in which your tree is planted," she warned. "It can't stay the way it is." She offered them a special "mushy paste" with which to repair the crack and make the dance pole stable.

On each of three mornings thereafter, however, new cracks were discovered in the rock of the mesa in which the poles would be inserted, and in each case, Old Spider Woman provided the paste with which the cracks could be repaired. When the day of the dance finally came, "the people of Pivanhokyapi and some from Huk'ovi" turned out to watch. The dancers performed "beautifully and uttered cries that were pleasing to the onlookers." Each team of two would climb the poles, and dance upon their narrow summits, sometimes leaning so far as to make all believe they would fall from the mesa top to the rocks below. As the dancers leaped from top-to-top of the poles, passing each other in the air to the sounds of the drum and grating noise from rattles made of bone scapulae, "the spectators below roared."

The maiden from Huk'ovi stood among the audience, and wondered that none of the poles had broken during their twisting and bending. At noon, when the dancers paused to eat, returning with the priests to the kiva, she examined the holes in the mesa top and discovered that her cracks had all been mended. Enraged, "by means of her witchcraft, she broke one of the roof beams in the kiva" where the men were resting. The roof suddenly collapsed, crashing "down on all inside."

Those within the kiva struggled to escape, and the people of Pivanhokyapi tore back the roofing vigas, latillas, and earth in desperation. But "all the men had perished," suffocated under the heavy beams and dirt roofing. "How the people lamented . . . in hysterics about the terrible event." Each villager had lost "at least one relative or acquaintance in this tragedy." The dance, of course, was at an end, and mourning for the dead and their burial took its place.

As night fell, lamentations echoed across the valleys and mesas. One man, crying in sorrow atop a high roof, was startled to see a "light . . . moving straight toward Pivanhokyapi," a flame that wove and disappeared then reappeared ever closer. Finally, it entered the village plaza, and the people edged closer in the dark to examine its source. It stopped at the shrine in the center of the plaza, and people could see, to their amazement, that it was a woman, "terrifying to look upon." She showed herself as Tiikuywuuti, "Child Sticking Out Woman," a spirit from a woman who died in the deep past in the midst of childbirth, the mother of all game animals and to whom hunters pray for success when seeking to take prey. Although she wore a hideous mask, she was a beautiful young woman beneath, captured forever at the moment of her death. She was sympathetic to the trials that Pivanhokyapi had experienced, since she abhorred the use of *powa*, "the power to change," toward selfish ends. She revealed her knowledge that the young woman from Huk'ovi was a sorceress, and offered, if the people of Pivanhokyapi wished: "I will take revenge for you. If that is your desire, I want some of you to make prayer sticks for me and deposit them here at this shrine. I will then take on this task."

When the man who spoke with Tiikuywuuti told the survivors in Pivanhokyapi of her offer to avenge their loss, several men "set to making prayer feathers." Deposited at the shrine, the villagers awaited nightfall, crowding the rooftops of the pueblo.

Once again the distant flame appeared, and approached the mesa in a halting, zigzag line, weaving in course between where lay Pivanhokyapi and Huk'ovi. As it drew close to the mesa, however, it homed in on Huk'ovi, circling the village and finally entering the plaza. Once inside, Tiikuywuuti "went through the motions of grinding corn and singing," drawing the residents to gather around. Yet as the audience drew near, she quickly dashed from the village toward the west, leaving the people of Huk'ovi bewildered.

When Tiikuywuuti appeared in the plaza the second night, the men decided to lie in ambush and seize the creature. Yet when they rushed upon her, she turned and gazed upon them with blazing empty eye sockets and bared, jagged teeth, frightening them away. Night after night she entered the Huk'ovi plaza, singing her "eerie song," building a growing fear in the village. "She's coming here for a reason, we must catch her by any means, this ugly demon." Yet each time they tried, fear overcame them. A deep foreboding encompassed the village.

Haunted by Tiikuywuuti each night, the clan leaders of Huk'ovi met and pondered a solution. They knew there lay a purpose behind her visitations and were thankful that she had not "harmed anyone yet." After much debate they decided that to abandon the village might be their only way of escaping the ogre. "Let's move away from here . . . we're bound to find a place to live somewhere else." The villagers packed hurriedly over the course of the night, and set out to the southwest in search of a new, and hopefully safe, home. Yet each night when they made an encampment, Tiikuywuuti would check to make sure Huk'ovi was empty of inhabitants, and then turned to follow the fleeing inhabitants of the deserted village. When they saw her flame approach, they reshouldered their burden baskets and set out again as she prodded them onward. "The people had no choice but to move on."

Eventually, far beyond the mesas to the southwest, the people of Huk'ovi established a new settlement where, it is said, they became the progenitors of the Mission Indians of California. But the lesson remained: "because of a witch girl . . . the village of Huk'ovi was abandoned and fell into ruin." The witch, however, may have traveled with them.

A thin membrane separated the world of gods and spirits from the world of common people in Hopi history and culture, and the story of Huk'ovi's abandonment shows that membrane in all its permeability. Gods existed with their own concerns, especially their role in shaping everyday Hopi lives toward "good living" in the interests of community. Common Hopis were attentive to their responsibilities in demonstrating their fealty to the teachings of Masauwu, even while they remained subject to universal human frailties of self-interest, lust, and rage. Between these resided those spirits with evil intent, and the *popwaqt*, human actors that were defined variously by Spanish padres as *hechiceros* or *hechiceras*, and by Anglo chroniclers as witches, wizards, and sorceresses. Again, perhaps universally across cultures, people who could draw upon numinous powers in ways commoners could not were often the source of admiration *and* subject to vilification. The constant challenge in any society with such thin boundaries between the supernatural and natural worlds lay in discerning the purposes to which "greater-than-human" powers were aimed. The root of the term *powaqa* (or *powaka*)—witch or sorcerer—is at first glance innocuous: *powa-* simply means "change," or "transform," which is then coupled with the element *qa/ka,* "one who/that which." Variations abound that have little or no negative connotation: *powata* (to make right/cure/exorcise); *powalti* (to become purified/healed as from insanity); *powa'iwta* (be purified/be back to normal). A *powaqa,* therefore, is someone with the powers of change or transformation who puts those powers to "personal gain or advantage, usually with negative consequences, including death, for their fellow humans." The dual nature of *powa-* probably emerged from deep in the ancestral Puebloan past, long before agriculture and consolidation of small groups into larger communities, from those women and men who anthropologists term "shamans"—people capable of communicating with the spirit/animal world, and often able to take animal form in Nagualism—"a phenomenon that involves animal metamorphosis paired with the faculty of deriving powers" from the transformation.

The "witch girl" of Huk'ovi sought self-serving ends, although just what she might have gained from marriage with the handsome youth from Pivanhokyapi is obscure. It may be that the youth's spectacular skills in the Ladder Dance suggested equal skills as a husband and provider, and a fine career ahead in the ceremonial sphere. Perhaps she stood in for a sense of inferiority between Huk'ovi and its neighbor, since it was Pivanhokyapi that seems most renowned for its ceremonial traditions. Women's role as agents of *koyaanisqatsi,* however, is ubiquitous in Hopi history, as is the suffering of whole communities for the transgressions of an individual.

Ironically, Pivanhokyapi and its residents would themselves suffer immolation and ruination in time. Although well regarded for their piety and adherence to the ceremonial calendar, as years passed their piety led also to a sense of tedium. The first expressions of this showed when frenzy arose around a game of chance, *totolospi*. First men took to the kivas to gamble away the hours, and soon women joined them. Women offered themselves as prizes, and "no one belonged to anyone anymore. It was total promiscuity." Finally, even Talawasyi, the *kikmongwi*'s wife, joined the craze, ignoring her nursing child through the night and refusing to correct her ways. The *kikmongwi*, seeing that the *koyaanisqatsi* was consuming his community, entreated the Yaayapontsa (Wind Gods) for assistance. At his pleading, they agreed to bring fire from the San Francisco Peaks and purify the community by setting it aflame, even while the gamblers were inside the kivas, thereby killing most of the people. Only the children, who had been spirited away from Pivanhokyapi, lived to renew the pious life. Both Huk'ovi and Pivanhokyapi would suffer similar fates, although many of the former would migrate westward, while only a few of the latter would carry their message into later generations.

Purification through obliteration, called down by one's own leader, brings these stories to the cusp of the historic era with the demise of Sikyatki. This community, located on the northeast slopes of First Mesa, its ruins now largely covered by windblown sands, looms large in contemporary Hopi culture by virtue of the stunningly complex and beautiful pottery crafted during its heyday in the fourteenth and fifteenth centuries, when it grew to some 600 rooms in size with a population of perhaps 800 residents. Between 1325 and 1400 the total occupation of the Hopi Mesas seems to have doubled, "likely corresponding to an influx of immigrants" from the south—Anderson Mesa, Chavez Pass, and Homol'ovi—as well as less well understood arrivals from the north—Kayenta—and the east—

Keres-speaking peoples from the Rio Grande and San José river valleys.

Sikyatki was no longer occupied when the first Spanish entradas began in 1540. Yet its significance endures in the form of Sikyatki Polychrome pottery. Characterized by extraordinary artistry and highly expressive, asymmetrical, often abstract renderings of life forms—plant and animal—and fired in an oxidizing atmosphere that yielded a rich, creamy yellow background, Sikyatki Polychrome (and associated Matsaki and Fourmile styles) suggests a geographically wide-ranging explosion of creativity that probably superceded linguistic boundaries. So distinctively different was this form, which extended eastward to encompass the whole of Antelope Mesa, that archaeologists have long wondered if these communities might have come from a different linguistic stock than those of Second and Third Mesas, echoed in the Hopi notion that not everyone across the three mesas "knew each other."

When Jesse Walter Fewkes excavated portions of Sikyatki on behalf of the Smithsonian Institution, he collected some five hundred of these remarkable vessels. Ironically, among his workmen was a Hopi man named Lesou from Walpi Village, who was married to a Tewa woman of Tewa Village, a descendant of the immigrants who arrived to fortify the northern approaches to First Mesa between 1696 and 1700. Nampeyo, his wife, "was so enchanted with the artistic designs and aesthetically-pleasing colors" that Lesou showed her on sherds collected from the excavations that she began reproducing the images and forms in her own wares. Inspired by Sikyatki, Nampeyo initiated a renaissance in "Hopi" pottery fabrication and decoration that continues today through her descendants and affines. Archetypical Hopi pottery today, therefore, may draw upon a dis-

Whole Sikyatki Polychrome jar.

tinctive tradition and renaissance artist neither of which derived from "original" Hopi stock.

Just a few miles southwest of Sikyatki Pueblo, well out of sight and on the opposite flank of First Mesa, lay the older, emphatically Hopi community of Qöötsaptuvela, or Ash Slope, which the people of Walpi today consider their ancestral home. Viewed from above, from Walpi today, it wears its name well, several mounds of masonry rubble with a distinctive ashy cast, with the name Ash Slope doubtless referring to its aspect after the residents moved up onto the mesa top around 1700, seeking a more defensive location in anticipation of the Spanish effort to punish them for their role in the annihilation of Awat'ovi.

Given the proximity of the two villages, their diverse origins and languages, and the limited arable lands below in Polacca Wash, tensions between their peoples probably ran deep and long. As is so often the case, however, material tensions were second to those inspired by passion and power.

In Sikyatki at this time lived a couple with a beautiful daughter, who drew suitors from within the village, as near as Qöötsaptuvela, and as far as Awat'ovi, miles distant on Antelope Mesa. The girl would receive visitors while grinding corn, allowing them to speak to her through the vent hole of the upper rooms of her family's house. In time she grew tired of the interruptions, however, and narrowed the field to just two youths, both from her own village of Sikyatki.

These two young men came from different clans, Coyote and Swallow, and their rivalry for the girl's attentions began to create daily stresses within the village, as each clan sided with their clansman and spoke poorly of the other. The girl knew she was the source of unpleasantness within her people, and at last decided to bring piki bread to the home of Coyote Boy, thereby signaling her willingness to be his wife. Coyote Boy's "uncles and other male relatives were readying the wedding garments for their new daughter-in-law." They set to weaving her wedding robe and the large sash and fashioning the wedding boots from soft deerskin.

Swallow Boy, however could not accept the girl's decision, an arrogance born of the fact that he and his relatives "were all witches who were powerful and great troublemakers." Among their powers were those of metamorphosis. "If they intended to travel somewhere, they did not do so by the strength of their own legs but in the guise of coyotes, wolves, owls, and crows." Their neighbors called them with contempt "turds," but feared them terribly as well.

So powerful were Swallow Boy's relatives that they stalled the wedding by calling for a contest between the two youths, to make a final determination of who would take the maiden as his wife. The Sikyatki *kikmongwi* accepted this delay, since he feared what would become of his people should the tensions grow more violent. The sorcerers laid out the contest, a footrace that would unfold over vast distances as a footrace between Coyote Boy and Swallow Boy, who would run first to the southeast to the Little Colorado River, and carve their clan symbols in a rock there, each marking his arrival with his sign, the second arrival placing his below the first. From there they would race northeast to the Rio Grande, again leaving their clan marks, and turn to the northwest to run to the Big Colorado, and finally return to First Mesa. The winner would cross a line gouged in the sand, on either end of which was thrust a stone knife. "The one who comes in first will pick up his knife and wait for the loser. As soon as he arrives, the winner is to sever his head."

Coyote Boy was by far the fittest and fleetest of the two, and yet his clansmen knew that Swallow Boy would transform into a swift animal or bird in order to win the contest. His clansmen promised a solution, and once the race was underway, retired to their kiva to consider their strategy.

When the race began, Coyote Boy moved easily into the lead. When he turned to look behind, he seemed so far ahead that he had lost sight of his rival. Yet when he reached the Little Colorado, he found the Swallow Clan mark already incised on the rock. In his running he had noticed a nighthawk swooping overhead, and realized that Swallow Boy had adopted that form for any leg of the race where there were no spectators. At each juncture, he found the Swallow Clan mark in rock before his own, and lost hope that he could ever overcome the other's sorcery. His clansmen in the kiva, however, knew of his trouble and were smoking their pipes, blowing clouds of smoke into the sky. These clouds gathered into "thick thunderheads" over the trails the boys were racing, and suddenly let loose great sheets of rain. Swallow Boy in his nighthawk guise was drenched and forced to change back into his human form. Coyote Boy overtook him and now had hope he might prevail.

As the thunderstorm ebbed, however, the lead changed back and forth as Swallow Boy was able to resume the race as the nighthawk. Coyote Boy received from one of his clansman a magical gourd that could itself be made to fly, and with this he was able to keep pace until they both drew near First Mesa and the crowds that had gathered on the rooftops of Sikyatki Village. They could see Coyote Boy in the lead and raised a cheer. Swallow Boy's kinsmen saw the boy slowing, falling into a trot, then a stumbling walk, but he had no choice but to remain in his human form. Coyote Boy crossed the line first, and awaited the dawdling rival. "The moment he arrived, Coyote Boy ran up to him and grabbed his long hair from behind. Then he thrust the knife into the boy's throat and cut off his head. The witch boy died instantly."

With the victory, the boy's uncle, head of the Coyote Clan, demanded that the Swallow Clan leave the village forever. "You caused your own misery, because you are people without compassion. You are so mighty that you could not show any pity." Yet, "under no circumstances were the witches going to submit to the wish of the Coyote clan people. They had no intention of causing their own ruin by leaving. They were extremely powerful and declined to leave."

In this atmosphere of unresolved conflict, "the people of Sikyatki settled down to their daily routine again, but life was not very peaceful." The sorcerers, or Turds, resented the fact that they were beaten and caused every possible trouble for the rest of the villagers. Finally, the *kikmongwi* of Sikyatki, "who held all of his children dear," decided "to terminate this corrupt way of life. He wanted the witches wiped out and the village destroyed." Lacking the power to do so, however, he finally called upon the *kikmongwi* of Qöötsaptu-vela for aid.

The Sikyatki chief explained that he would soon call for a communal harvesting party that would draw all the men away from the village to the fields below in Polacca Wash. Knowing that Sikyatki's demise would make available those same fields for his people, the Qöötsaptuvela *kikmongwi* agreed, and when the harvest was announced, he gathered his fighters and they lay in wait in the dark of night. When the Sikyatki men departed for harvest, "they rushed the village. In no time they were inside. Quickly they pulled the ladders from the rooftops of the houses where the women and children were . . . and set everything on fire. Some of the men had come with pitch they had gathered. This they smeared on the walls of the houses . . . which quickly caught fire." The men in the fields below saw the smoke and ran back, but Qöötsaptuvela's warriors "fell upon them. As soon as a man reached them, he was dispatched. Since the Sikyatki men had no weapons with which to resist, they died without being able to fight back."

A bare few Coyote Clan members survived by running away, and found succor in the village of Oraibi, far distant. They became the last arriving clan at Oraibi, and thus ranked at the bottom of the social order. "All the witches, those excrement people, perished." So, too, did the village *kikmongwi*, "who had hatched the plan." The fate of the maiden whose beauty had underlain the terror remains unremarked.

As in all Hopi narratives of destruction, variations exist, and in the case of Sikyatki some simply have the villagers, like those of Huk'ovi, abandoning their sorcery-ridden town and migrating elsewhere in order to bring an end to the *koyaanisqatsi*. But in each case the trigger for the rise of witchcraft and chaos lies with young men's contest over a maiden, by whose allure they are drawn away from the communitarian principles at the center of "good living." Their contest for the maiden's attention and services as wife highlights individual self-interest rather than the village's well-being. Sorcerers are looked upon as "excrement," yet their presence in village life seems almost necessary, the dark side of the mirror in an "Apollonian" society. Lust, jealousy, rage, and revenge all figure at the heart of a millennium of community conflict and violence. In each case—perhaps strange to Euroamerican sensibilities but consistent with the primacy of community in the Puebloan world—wholesale obliteration, rather than select individual persecution, is the storm that washes away the corruption and brings a fresh dawn for renewal.

With the end of Sikyatki and, in the distance, the long shadows of conquistadors and Franciscan friars working their way toward Tusayán, the "moment of the yellow dawn" drew near. At Awat'ovi Pueblo, whose "residents were wont to do many things," the nexus of prophecy, *koyaanisqatsi*, violence, and purification would link the ancient and recent past in ways that shaped the very heart of "Hopiness" today.

8

Liminal Men, Liminal Souls

———•◆•———

Time after time, contention within a village, or between
villages, or between clans caused people to leave, and in
the journeys that followed, they were looking for a place of
harmony where they could follow good teachings and a good
way of life . . . living together as people who were civilized
and worthy of being in the Fourth World.
I believe that when the destruction actually took place they
were mortally afraid of letting that Catholic thing grow and
spread. Some people regarded the padres as sorcerers.

—NUVAYOIYAVA, TEWA VILLAGE, 1978

Nuvayoiyava, "Big Falling Snow," was born in 1888, as the tensions
between the Hopis and the federal government over education,
economy, and culture were heading to a breaking point. As, too, were
tensions inside Oraibi. He lived through and beyond these crises, all
the while understanding them in the context of the Hopi past.

Born to Iechawe (Blue Smoke) of the Pehtowa (Wood, Stick,

Spruce) Clan, a woman of Tewa Village on First Mesa, and a Hopi father, Sitaiema, from Walpi, Nuvayoiyava's life proved as complicated as the wider Hopi world at the dawn of the twentieth century. His father left his mother while he was "still in the cradle," but later sponsored his initiation into the Kwakwanteu (One Horn) kiva society, which had its origins in the destruction of Palatkwapi many centuries earlier. His father was of the Water (Cloud, Mist) Clan, itself the principle clan of Palatkwapi. By Tewa and Hopi customs of matrilineal descent, he was Tewa, but by his induction into the One Horns he was also fully recognized as Hopi. Thus Nuvayoiyava's kinship and clan ties linked him to the Tanos of the Rio Grande Valley, their migration to Tusayán after 1696, and back to the "time," if not the place, of the very emergence of those migratory peoples who in time would become Hopis.

Nuvayoiyava's earliest years were those of a traditional Hopi youth. He and his friends protected precious seed corn from field rats by identifying their burrows and digging down to kill them with pointed sticks. Other times they crawled stealthily toward prairie dog colonies to shoot the sentries with arrows as they raised themselves to scan for predators. "If lucky enough to get one," they would gut it, singe off the hair and after salting, "wrap it in corn leaves and roast it in hot ashes," a cherished rustic meal. Sheep and "long-legged goats" needed tending as well, especially when pasturing overnight far from Tewa Village across Polacca Wash. Predators like coyotes were one concern, but sheep thievery between villages, and sometimes by Navajo neighbors, also required the boy's vigilance.

His Tewa stepfather Peki (Turned Over) of the Tewa Village Corn Clan taught Nuvayoiyava the secrets of Hopi corn cultivation, too. Since winter moisture was stored deep in the sands of the washes, seed corn had to be buried six to eight inches deep in order to find enough moisture to germinate. If the seasonal monsoons came on time, in late June and July, the rain would wash in sheets off the bedrock of the mesas above and provide floodwater irrigation just as the stalks were beginning to emerge through the sand into the sunlight. Now at their most vulnerable to rats and prairie dogs, Nuvayoiyava and other boys protected the cornfields day and night, as they did later when ripening ears drew crows and ravens. Once the ears matured and were harvested, the cornstalks were left standing in fields, "where the blowing sand would cover them up, and thus helped fertilize the ground." In addition to his Corn Clan knowledge, Peki was deeply respected by his fellow Tewa villagers, as someone with good judgement and a gentle, thoughtful manner in resolving conflicts. Nuvayoiyava, therefore, enjoyed an education in Tewa and Hopi culture unusually broad and deep, given that he "learned about rituals, ceremonies and traditions" of the Walpi One Horn fraternity from his father, and Corn Clan wisdom from his stepfather, toward growing corn in the sandy washes.

When about five or six years old, Nuvayoiyava's family sent him to the day school below First Mesa at Polacca. The Indian Agency at Keams Canyon had found the people of Tewa Village more receptive to the idea of children's education than the Hopis and often show-cased Tewa children as the hope for the future. Nuvayoiyava did not find school to his liking, however. "On the first day at school they gave us all new clothes, white man's style. We didn't like those clothes very much because they made us feel ridiculous. Altogether, we felt pretty strange, getting educated in a language we didn't understand." At recess the children shed their clothes, hid them nearby and "ran naked back up to the village up on the mesa." However, the truant officer at Walpi, Nuvayoiyava's uncle Chawkweina, chased the children "all through the village and over the roofs" and took them back down to Polacca, where they were forced to dress again. This happened several times before the Tewa kids surrendered to the inevitable. The school also changed his name, since the matrons had difficulty making sense of the lack of family names among the Hopi. Nuvayoiyava's name, they failed to understand, reflected his father's Water Clan lineage, a name chosen by his paternal aunts to make clear to others his "father's clan affiliations." Big Falling Snow signaled the Water Clan. But the teachers had difficulty with the prounciation and so shortened it to "Yava," which became his "family" name. He was given the English name "Albert" since one teacher who had taken a personal interest in the boy liked it over "Oliver." When initiated into the One Horn fraternity, however, he received a ceremonial name—Eutawisa (Close in the Antelope)—to indicate membership in that society. His life would always find him weaving between different cultural norms.

When Albert Yava turned eight he found himself transferred to the Boarding School at Keams Canyon, where his induction into white education intensified, since he no longer had the nightly respite of returning to his Tewa Village family. On his first day in Keams Canyon he was given a bath and had his hair cut "white man's style," which left him deeply distressed. "The long hair we boys wore on the sides symbolized rain, you might say fertility," and the short hair embarrassed him in front of his family when he returned for visits. His parents thought that the whites "were pretty high-handed and insensitive, as well as ignorant" of Hopi customs. He was well aware of struggles within Walpi, and even the villages on Second and Third Mesas, between "conservatives" and "progressives" around the government's education program, and was sympathetic to the fact that many parents were deeply suspicious of what the government programs might do to their children. Still, he and others found many of the teachers generally kind and they inclined "to learn white man's ways so that we'd know how to cope in later years."

When Yava reached eighth grade in the Keams Canyon school, the final year of instruction and when most of the teenagers would be returning to their home villages, with little to do but return, half-transformed, to traditional life, one teacher suggested he consider attending the Chilocco Indian School in Oklahoma to continue his education in the company of students from many different tribes throughout the West. His parents, however, strongly opposed his leaving Hopi society for a distant school, and none of his arguments—especially the fact that they "had no livestock to take care of, nothing"—could persuade them otherwise. He finally enlisted an uncle, Nelson Oyaping, who served as an agency policeman and who "in the Hopi-Tewa way" was responsible for his welfare, to sign the permission in lieu of his parents.

At Chilocco, Yava mixed with boys from dozens of western tribes. They attended classes for half the day and learned trades the other half—carpentry, blacksmithing, shoe- and harness-making. Each summer as many as three hundred of the boys were detailed to work in the beet fields of Colorado, backbreaking work that inspired him to look for a higher level of training. In the end, he earned a harness-maker's certificate and made harnesses for use in other reservations, as well as becoming an adept cobbler, making shoes for the Chilocco track team. By the time he graduated in 1910, he wasn't sure that he was "well educated," but had acquired skills that provided income throughout his life. He returned to the Hopi reservation to find tensions continuing, since the Oraibi split had not created a new world of *suyanisqatsi*. He returned to helping Peki with the corn and herding sheep, getting them to grass and always looking for water. Once, at Peki's urging, he explored a pueblo ruin east of First Mesa to find a water source, and after he and his stepbrother excavated around some sand-covered masonry, found a buried spring that came back to life once uncovered. He considered this a gift from Peki, who "had remembered something handed down from the past."

In time, however, Yava grew uneasy at what he found on the reservation. Few opportunities to earn money existed, raising sheep was a challenge, and he didn't find avenues to employ the trades he had acquired at Chilocco. He found some work on the new railroad down in Winslow, but when he learned that his mother back home in Tewa Village had fallen ill, he walked the sixty-five miles north to First Mesa. Fortunately, his livestock-handling and saddler skills proved useful to the Indian Agency at Keams Canyon, and once the agents understood his educational accomplishments and facility with English, he added the role of interpreter to his employment, which paid twenty dollars a month.

Yava's willingness to buck convention showed itself soon thereafter, when he began courting Ida Haupove of Tewa Village, who worked at the trading post at Keams Canyon. Her parents, however, disapproved of him as a son-in-law, so the two obtained a marriage license from the Indian Agency and were married in the First Baptist Church in Keams Canyon. Her mother's clan never accepted him, perhaps an echo of the curse that affected Hopi-Tewa relations. Albert and Yava had three daughters, but Ida died shortly after the last was born when her brakes failed on the steep road leading down off of First Mesa. Yava would marry again, this time a Hopi woman, Taiyomana, whom he met at a Niman (Home Dance) ceremony at Walpi—a dance to mark the departure of the *katsinam* as they return to their home in the San Francisco Peaks. Taiyomana had three children of her own, and after a complicated courtship that involved her own ex-husband summoning tribal police whenever Yava visited her, they, too, married in Keams Canyon. Yava now moved into her home, which had belonged once to his own biological father's mother; by customs of matrilocal residence, Yava's move into her home brought him closer to his father. Yet, this marriage, too, proved short-lived, since the tensions around her first husband and their children could not be resolved. Frustrated, Yava finally told her, "Okay, then, go back to your old man." They were formally divorced through the Tribal Court. Finally, Yava found a longer relationship with Virginia Scott, a Navajo woman whose husband had left her "Navajo style." They had two daughters and three sons together, but she, too, left him and the children, leaving him to parent alone in a hard land.

Albert Yava's memoir captures more than a lone man's transformation at the turn of the twentieth century at Flower Butte, however. In fact, he found it hard to imagine that outsiders would learn much from his personal details, when larger questions of history and culture fascinated him throughout his life. The Tewa migration to the Hopi Mesas figured far more prominently in his mind, as did the "curse" that defined their long-term relationship with their Hopi neighbors. So, too, did the history of clan migrations and the subtle rankings of power among them, which created the political terrain upon which Hopi history would be played out. His induction into the Kwakwanteu or "One Horn Lodge" provided him this deep background. Finally, the destruction of Awat'ovi occupies a startling amount of his narrative, at least insofar as his Tewa progenitors generally claimed no role and little knowledge of that formative event in Hopi history.

Yava's narrative emphasizes the martial experience of his Tewa ancestors in his rendering of their solicitation and relocation to Tusayán. Noting that "the people of the Hopi villages did not think of themselves as belonging to the same tribe," but rather, "Walpis, Mishongnovis, Shongopovis, Oraibis and so on," he saw the Snake and Bear clan emissaries to the Rio Grande in 1696 as driven by fear of attack from Utes, Apaches, and Comanches. These mounted raiders conducted harvest-time raids for Hopi corn. In addition to crops, these raiders also seized women and children, some of whom they retained as slaves, while others they sold to Spanish buyers at trade fairs. Many Hopi men died in the defense of their kinspeople. The population of Walpi, beset as well by "attacks from Oraibi . . . was down to seven families, and they were feeling pretty desperate."

The Walpi delegates undertook their four journeys across three hundred dangerous miles. Finally, after the presentation of three *pahos,* called *uudopeh* in Tewa, representing men, women, and land, bore the promise that if the Tanos would come to the defense of Walpi they would find reward in that town's sons and daughters as "husbands and wives," the people of Tsaewari accepted.

In Yava's telling, however, things took a strange turn once the Tewas reached the foot of First Mesa. Rather than welcoming them to settle as promised, the Walpis refused their guests the right to enter their town, stopping the Tanos somewhere near the ruins of Sikyatki Village. Perhaps, Yava wonders, "it was because there were so many Tewas in the group that they made the Walpis uneasy . . . there may have been as many as two hundred men, women and children in the group." The Walpis then, to the Tanos' dismay, "contacted the Utes and challenged them to make an attack on Walpi." "'We've got some real fighters here now. Why don't you come and try to drive them off?'" The Utes accepted the challenge.

Despite their arduous travels and lack of defensive location on the heights of the mesa, the Tewas, once scouts had warned them of the approaching Ute horsemen, prepared a battle plan. Agaitsay, the Tewa chief, divided his men into two parties, one to hold the Utes from the front while the other circled behind under the cover of the cliff-fall rocks. He ordered that his archers aim either for the warrior or his mount, knowing that a Ute unhorsed would be no match for his Tewa fighters. The Ute charge was fearsome, with their war bonnets waving and "little mirrors reflecting the sunlight." The Tewa warriors, however, stood strong, and an arrow brought down the Ute war captain. Once quarters had closed, the Utes changed to their lances, and the Tewa replied with war clubs, knocking some Utes off their horses. Each time the Tewas seemed to prevail, the Utes would regroup and charge, and yet were gradually forced back. Soon the Utes dismounted to face their attackers, shielding themselves at one moment behind the parfleches they had brought on the expedition, which would later give that place the Tewa name Tukyu'u, or Meat Point. Falling back even further, they sheltered behind several boulders, later called Kokwadeh, or Stone Wall. By day's end only three Utes remained able-bodied, and threw their bows out from behind the rocks and asked for a parley.

The Ute leader asked, "What people are you? We can see you're not Hopis." Agaitsay replied, "We are Tewatowa." The Ute apologized: "My cousin, we didn't know it was you. . . . I'm sorry, my brothers, that we fought against you. . . . we just came to get some corn and things like that."

Agaitsay said that the Tewas were in Hopi country to stay, and forbade the Utes from ever returning in war. The Utes collected their wounded men and departed, leaving their dead behind. The Tewas collected the weapons scattered across the battlefield, took scalps, and, locating the four bravest of the Ute warriors, removed their hearts and buried them at the precise place where battle was joined. A season later, seeing a tree had sprouted at that spot, they decided that they would defend that place forever. Today, Yava points out, the place is called Pingto'i in Tewa, "Place of Hearts," and a juniper tree grows inside the ring of stones they placed during the burial. A petroglyph on the cliff face at First Mesa commemorates this battle even today, showing a Tewa bison-hide shield and "a long row of marks indicating the number of Utes that were killed."

Yava's version recounts the decision by the Walpis to allow the victorious Tewas to establish their village on the northern heights of First Mesa, and the curse that prevented Hopis from ever learning the Tewa language. Tewas built their houses of stone "according to the clans they belonged to, with Bear clan, the leading phratry, assigned the most prominent," with houses arranged on the "four dies of the central court." Since Yava's Water Clan was affiliated with Bear, they too held a place of prominence. To Yava, had the Tanos failed the test of the Ute attack, they might never have been invited to settle on First Mesa.

Yava's version of the Tewa migration never mentions the second Pueblo Revolt of 1696 and the impetus it gave the Tanos/Tewas of Tsaewari to accept Walpi's invitation and leave the Spanish colony on the Rio Grande behind. He does mention later Tewa and Keres migrants who ventured west to escape the Catholic gaze and Spanish tributary demands, however. Some settled "down in the Wepo

Valley" (and the west side of First Mesa), another group on the south side "near what is now called Five Houses." Still another sojourned with the Zunis before following the Zuni Trail to Hopi, and a last group that "arrived here in a heavy mist, and because of the mist people didn't know the direction this group came from."

Variations in Tewa histories of migration and settlement in Tusayán may be a matter of differences in clan memory. But they signal something more: an anxiety about claiming a right to occupancy while simultaneously marking the distinct differences between Hopi and Tewa peoples and their histories. Tewas were clearly not the first "outsiders" to enter Flower Butte, nor to find a home there. But Tewa memory and history has worked hard to set them aside from the experience of other outsiders, perhaps because they knew well the fate of another "foreign" people, the residents of Awat'ovi, in the autumn of 1700.

Yava's concern about tensions between "natives" and "newcomers," insiders and outsiders, in the settlements of the Hopi mesas shapes his understanding of what transpired at Awat'ovi. His story of the Tewa migrations attends carefully to the sequence of arrivals, and insists that their presence was by invitation, rather than as refugees, as well as their temporal depth—"you can see that we aren't exactly newcomers in Hopi country . . . we were here when the first Anglos arrived from the East." Yet he insists as well that Tewa village continues to occupy a liminal place in what "Hopiness" really stands for, insisting that the Simpeng'i (Black Man) mask and dances—"to commemorate how we emerged into this world at Sibopay and began our long journey that eventually led us to Hopi country . . . were made on First Mesa to help the Tewas remember their old traditions and not get swallowed up by the Hopis."

Yava is also quick to mark the people of Awat'ovi as outsiders—"that big Laguna village on Antelope Mesa, Awatovi, had died just before we got here. It was destroyed in 1700, and we arrived according to our tradition, in 1702" (although his editor, Harold Courlander, notes that "the actual year of arrival is not certain"). Yava saw Antelope Mesa as a potpourri of linguistic identities—Kawaika'a was "Laguna" as well as Awatovi, as was Chakpahu. Akokavi was "a settlement of Hemis (Jemez) people." Recent ceramic analysis reinforces Yava's sense of the diversity of this easternmost mesa, as well. From 1325 forward, waves of diverse migrants entered the Hopi Mesas, some driven by drought, others by hunger, some by fear of Spanish oppression, while still others may have been drawn to the enduring ceremonial strength of the villages on the high mesas. The social map of Antelope Mesa shows a mosaic of peoples, each recalling distinct origins, resisting complete assimilation, yet also fully aware of the urgent need to find enduring cultural allies.

Yava's concerns about insider/outsider dynamics at First Mesa, and his extension of those to the settlements on Antelope Mesa, reflect a centuries-deep process at work in the "peopling" of Tusayán. Turmoil and travel were the watchwords of the fourteenth-century Southwest, and yet somehow balancing those forces was the "magnet" effect of a few "center-places"—the northern Rio Grande, the Zuni River Valley, and the Hopi Mesas, which appear "to have been a particularly popular destination, receiving thousands of immigrants during the A.D. 1300s and 1400s." Today, says archaeologist Kelly Hayes-Gilpin, "members of the Hopi Tribe . . . are explicit that contemporary Hopi identity is synonymous with social diversity . . . Hopi is explicitly an aggregation of different groups that maintain important aspects of their unique histories and traditions." These peoples spoke different languages, solicited permission to join existing villages, and, challenged to present their ceremonial powers, they were sometimes absorbed, and sometimes rejected. If denied, they would move on to another possible host. Finding a community to adopt them was essential. To remain outside one of the center-places would have been "isolating, undesirable, and perhaps even dangerous" in the unstable world of the times, according to archaeologist Patrick Duff.

And yet, this very embrace of distinct and different peoples under the umbrella of "Hopi" seems to have been forged out of endemic struggle and conflict. It is clear that intercommunal violence coursed across the Southwest between 1225 and 1300 as "Pax Chaco" disintegrated, with villages sacked and set ablaze and unburied bodies, often mutilated, strewn randomly across ancient sites. Indeed, village architecture that developed after 1300, high-mesa defensible locations with multistory terraced roomblocks, and narrow, controlled entrances into the central plazas, shows real attention to the presence of external enemies. These plazas may also have served to contain and control the pueblos' population and their internal terracing, in which the highest stories were reserved for the highest-ranking leadership and allowed those leaders to monitor relationships among their heterogeneous occupants. In the fourteenth century, the potential for conflict may have been more likely internal, among residents, and local, between nearby villages, than it ever was external. As Tessie Naranjo, of Santa Clara Pueblo, once commented to the author, "Plaza pueblos are as much about embracing people within, as they are about keeping people out."

Yava's narrative of Awat'ovi's demise reinforces this sense of internal conflict in dialogue with external tensions. Although its earliest founders, the Bow Clan, may have been "Hopis," by the early 1600s the town had absorbed migrating "Kawaikas, Payupkis and other Eastern Pueblos." Many of Awat'ovi ceremonies derived from these immigrants, since the songs that First Mesa "inherited from them" are "not in the Hopi language." When the Franciscans arrived "Awat'ovi was a big village. I think it had four rows of terraced houses, three plazas or courts, and five or six kivas." The Franciscans "were pretty successful at converting people at Awatovi . . . eventually more than half the population" accepted baptism. The converts abandoned their homes in the Western Pueblo and moved "to the north side to be near the church, you might say that Awat'ovi was broken into two halves." Although the majority of the people were adherents of the Catholic faith—perhaps only nominally so—"the padres gave the Awatovis a rough life. The people had to haul stones and timbers, construct the church buildings, and do everything they were told to do." The padres, it was said, "frequently took women and young girls into their quarters and seduced them," although the precise nature of the seduction is unnamed. In order to bring the women and girls into the convento, "the padres would send a young man to some distant place to get sacred water from a certain spring, and while he was gone they would take his wife. Some of these young men never returned home because they were killed by enemies."

According to Yava, Oraibi, Mishongnovi, and Awat'ovi all joined in the 1680 revolt in order to "get rid of the Castillas." The One Horn Society took a leading role in the rebellion, commemorating their victory by caching both the lances of the Spanish soldiers and the church bells themselves in secret crypts. At Awat'ovi, the church itself was destroyed, but the convento converted for residential use. "It began to look as if the Castillas weren't coming back."

And yet the Spanish did return in the year 1700. First to Awat'ovi, where Yava recalls that those who had been baptized as Catholics welcomed them, while others resented their return. When the padres began repairing and rebuilding the church and convento, the villagers at Walpi, Shongopovi, and Oraibi saw a new era of conversion coming upon them and grew restless. At Awat'ovi, according to Yava, "when the padres came back . . . they made the Catholic converts feel bold again. Ever since the uprising they had been kind of quiet, but now they were showing themselves and acting in a contentious way." Frictions long thought past, renewed themselves.

The form of the Catholic adherents' "contentious" acts provoked the *kikmongwi*, "a Bow Clan man," who felt his control of the town slipping away. Young people failed to attend to religious traditions and social norms. Constant trouble erupted between the traditionals and the Catholics, who were in the majority. People fought publicly. The Catholics were ridiculing and interfering with Hopi religious ceremonies. "The *kikmongwi* saw that everything was falling apart, but he couldn't stop it. He decided that the only thing that could be done was to destroy the village and wipe the slate clean." The stories that Yava had heard claimed, "The Awatovi chief was really responsible for everything that happened after that."

The *kikmongwi* of Awat'ovi first approached his counterpart at Walpi. Complaining that conditions had grown dire in his village, that it was "full of evil" and the "Castilla sorcerers" were contributing to rapes and killings and that ceremonies were being disrupted, he asked that Walpi detail some of its warriors to punish his people. It was, he suggested as in times before, the rupture that brought Hopi from the Third to this Fourth world. When the Walpi chief declined, saying his people wouldn't wage war on their own brothers and sisters, the *kikmongwi* shifted his focus to the leader of Oraibi. When asked why his men ought to wage war on kinsmen, he replied, "I only want you to kill the men. You can take the women and children as prisoners. They will help to keep your population flourishing." Again the Oraibi *kikmongwi* deferred, but when the Awat'ovi chief claimed he was already in negotiations with Walpi, and that they should go together, the former agreed. At Walpi they found the *kalatekmongwi*, or war chief, who seemed more willing. Explaining that the Oraibis would be entitled to all the women, the Awat'ovi *kikmongwi* promised that "you Walpi Reed Clan people, you can have all the land and the fields, because they're too far away from the Oraibis. The land is yours, the women are theirs."

The Walpi's war chief agreed, and although the Walpi *kikmongwi* told him that attacking a neighbor was "not the Hopi way," he gathered his Reed Clan warriors. Oraibi warriors suggested they gather for an attack in four days, position themselves beneath the walls of the pueblo, and the "Awat'ovi chief would stand on a high rooftop and give a signal when all the people were asleep in the kivas and houses." Just before the break of dawn the Awat'ovi chief waved a burning torch and the warriors stormed into the town, pulling the ladders from the kivas and trapping the men and boys who were resting after their all-night ceremonies. Throwing "burning cedar bark, firewood, and crushed chili peppers" into the kivas, those below died in their airless trap. Houses also caught fire, and the attackers slew any they met, old men and women and many of the boys. They herded the younger women and children out of the village and took them to Skull Ridge or Skull Mound. Dissension broke out between the Walpi and Oraibi warriors, since the Walpis had captured the younger women whom the Oraibis felt were their prizes. Anger exploded into violence, and many of the captives died, since after the Awat'ovi affair "people used to find a lot of skulls there." Exhausted by the carnage, they agreed to divide the surviving captives among Oraibi, Walpi, Mishongnovi, and Shungopovi. The women became the source of the Awat'ovi clans in the villages, including Tobacco, Rabbit, and Tansy Mustard.

Yava's narrative adds an unexpected wrinkle, however, that points to the role of clan membership in crosscutting intercommunal rivalries. It seems that some of those from Walpi and Oraibi had kinsmen in Awat'ovi, and betrayed the carnage yet to come. One story he heard from elders claimed that a Two Horn Society priest "dressed up in an Alosaka costume wandered through Awatovi chanting a song with hints of the tragedy to come." His song referred to the murder of three brothers—Sakieva, Momo'a, and Pakushkasha—by "Hopi converts to the Catholic Church" that had occurred some time in the past. "A gang of hooligans had built a big fire in a pit—and thrown the three brothers into it, killing them." The boys' bodies had been "rubbed with cornmeal" before being hurled alive into the flames, which symbolized that "whatever might be planted in Awatovi would never grow." The Two Horn priest sang a chant that warned his clansmen of imminent danger, urging them to flee the village for soon "everyone will be moaning and crying."

Only a few members of the Two Horn Society understood the oblique references, but a few managed to slip away and take refuge elsewhere, thereby preserving that fraternity in Hopi society. The *kikmongwi*, a Bow Clan member, also escaped, according to Yava, along with a few of his clan members. So, too, did the Tobacco Clan leader, identified in some accounts as Ta'polo himself, escape the coming destruction. He had "gathered the most important paraphernalia of the three big kiva societies in the village—the Two Horn, the Wuwuchim, and the Tataukyam—and carried it away in the dark and hid it in one of the canyons." Tobacco Clan survivors sought refuge among Navajos living below Antelope Mesa down in Jeddito Wash. Navajo Tobacco Clan, therefore, was born of at least one or more Awat'ovi women who escaped capture and distribution among the attackers. In time, those refugees' descendants would return and take up fields and gardens on lands that once belonged to their progenitors.

Once the destruction ended and the charred town lay deserted, the Tobacco Clan leader approached the Snake Clan at Walpi and offered his ceremonial rights and matériel to the Walpi leaders in exchange for safety and residence within the village. Tobacco Clan members told ethnographer Peter Whiteley in 1995 that Ta'polo himself had built the Tobacco Clan house and Takaukyam (Singers Society) kiva when "he moved into the newly established mesa-top town . . . following the massacre." He also arranged for at least some of his clan relatives to escape the destruction and live among the Navajos for some time, before rejoining him at Walpi. Further evidence of the mixed ethnic origins of Awat'ovi, according to Yava, lay in the fact that the most important traditional ceremonies from Awat'ovi, including the new fire ceremony, were performed in the "Laguna (Keres) language, not Hopi." Was Ta'polo, the author of Awat'ovi's annihilation, a descendant of Keresan migrants to Antelope mesa?

Not just a few Awat'ovi residents survived the massacre. Some family relatives, initiates of the Two Horn Society, and members of Tobacco Clan found escape. The survivors' ties to clans and ceremonies ancient and central to Hopi religion make it possible that the

annihilation of Awat'ovi was much more closely focused on eliminating a faction of Catholic converts than on wholesale elimination
of the entire community. This is consistent with the strategy of eliminating the threat of sorcery from within a given community, and yet
does little to explain just what form that sorcery took and why it so
threatened men like Ta'polo.

Albert Yava casts a brighter light on Awat'ovi than one might
expect. His intense interest in linking clan origin histories, migration pathways, and the heterogeneous nature of society on the Hopi
mesas to the destruction of Awat'ovi suggest his role as intercultural
envoy—not unlike those fugitive and captive survivors who crossed
villages and cultures in the aftermath of Awat'ovi's fall. His birth
in Tewa Village, his membership in both the Water and One Horn
clans, his initiation and education into One Horn history, which
afforded him "full-fledged" status as a Hopi, his time at Chilocco
Indian School and fluency in English, which in turn provided him
employment as agency interpreter, and a lifelong commitment to his
ritual and ceremonial duties all combined to place him in important
roles as multitalented cross-cultural mediator.

❧•❦

Two centuries earlier, the enigmatic Francisco de Espeleta performed
a role similar to Yava at the Hopi mesas. This Hopi man would serve
as a central, if ambiguous, leader and diplomat in the prelude to the
obliteration of Awat'ovi. His precise role remains confusing in Spanish documents, however, and no Hopi accounts exist for clarification.
He may have been the boy that Padre José de Espeleta rescued from
hanging in 1664 at Awat'ovi, "who had committed no offense other

than to attend to the father notary," and in doing so had run afoul of the lieutenant general of the province, Pedro Manso de Valdés, who in the constant infighting between secular government and the Church had prohibited "any Indians to go as escort" to the Franciscans. Apparently, a *doñado* (a youth "given to the Church and raised up") with the godparent sponsorship of the Padre Espeleta, he seems to have been born for the Badger Clan. Since Father Espeleta was stationed at Awat'ovi from 1663 to 1672, whence he passed along his enthusiasm for music and choral singing sufficiently that Navajos called that pueblo *Tallahogan*, the Singing House, he probably served as *padrino* to young Francisco during his early boyhood, under whose tutelage he learned to "read and write" and with whom he may have traveled to Mexico.

If Francisco de Espeleta were in his youth at Awat'ovi when Padre Espeleta arrived in 1663, he may have accepted baptism to gain the padre's protection and godparent sponsorship. He certainly would have received religious instruction along with the training in the Catholic liturgy. By the time of the 1680 revolt he would have been in young adulthood. He may have attended the padre when the latter was transferred to Oraibi in 1672, which would account for his later association with that village. José de Espeleta died at Oraibi, his throat cut and body hurled from the mesa, in an attack the Hopi sources claim was organized and executed by the Badger Clan. On the fragmentary evidence, Francisco de Espeleta's clan membership seems likely to have been Badger, and he may have turned on his Catholic faith in August 1680. At least one Spanish source accuses him of slaying his own *padrino*, describing Francisco as "a proverbial viper, cleverly implanted in [the padre's] household by the Devil."

Yet, when Francisco de Espeleta next appears in Spanish accounts some twenty years after the death of Father Espeleta, he seems ambivalent in his passion for the Pueblo rebellion and the revitalization of Hopi ceremonialism. As the reconquest solidified in the Rio Grande Valley after 1696, Spanish commanders and Franciscans alike turned their thoughts to the rebel strongholds to the west. Although Governor de Vargas had received the nominal submission to the Crown by the Zunis and Hopis in 1692, no Europeans had ventured toward the mesas since then. Yet "don Francisco," as Spanish accounts claim that his Hopi kinsmen termed him, had emerged as a prominent leader and spokesman during the hiatus. In early May of 1700, as "Cacique of Oraibi," he sent a message via envoys to Governor Pedro Rodríguez Cubero, "professing a readiness to rebuild churches and receive missionaries." At the same time, he sent word by runner to Padre Juan Garaicoechea at distant Zuni Pueblo. Garaicoechea had, in 1699, reopened the mission at Halona, the first step toward restoring the faith among the Western Pueblos. Espeleta invited him to "come and baptize children" in his town. Once Garaicoechea reached the Hopi Mesas on the twenty-eighth with his escort Alcalde José López Naranjo, however, "he was not permitted to visit Oraibi." It seems that an untrue rumor spread that the "messengers to Santa Fe had been killed," the anger at which prevented don Francisco's invitation from being realized. Espeleta promised "to notify him soon when they were ready for another visit." Padre Garaicoechea received a warmer welcome at Awat'ovi, finding that "the convent had been rebuilt or repaired by its Indians, who were glad to see their mission re-established." Garaicoechea baptized seventy-three "young Moquis" during his few days at Awat'ovi. "The other Moquis, while outwardly friendly, still dissuaded the missionary from visiting their homes."

Don Francisco's unexpected message to Padre Garaicoechea in May 1700 indicated a certain willingness to entertain a Catholic presence, if only ephemeral, in Oraibi. The ambiguity grows with the content of the message he carried to Santa Fe on October 11 of that year, as interpreted from the sources by the historian Hubert Howe Bancroft. In that month Espeleta led a delegation to Santa Fe to meet with Governor Pedro Rodríguez Cubero, "not as subjects and vassals of the crown, but as delegates of a foreign power to conclude a treaty of peace and amity." He is described at that conference as "one of the leading chiefs of the Oraybe," along with "twenty other delegates." He "proposed a simply treaty of peace" to Governor Cubero, "his nation, like Spain, to retain its own religion." Cubero countered that he "could offer peace only on the condition of conversion to Christianity." In reply, "the Moqui chief proposed as an ultimatum that the padres should visit one pueblo each year for six years to baptize, but postpone permanent residence till the end of that period. This scheme was likewise rejected, and Espeleta and his companion leaders went home for further deliberation."

Only one month later, devastation would be visited upon Awat'ovi. Badger Clan membership also provided Espeleta clansmen at Awat'ovi, Oraibi, and Mishongnovi. Since from 1680 forward he was living in Oraibi, he may not have witnessed the "all sorts of things" that the "residents of Awat'ovi were wont to do," but surely his clansmen in that town reported on those activities. Just what he made of those doings is unclear.

As "cacique of Orayvi," Francisco de Espeleta, in historian Charles Wilson Hackett's treatment of the documents, "came with more than one hundred of his people to the said pueblo [of Aguatubi], entered it, killed all the braves, and carried off the women, leaving the pueblo to this day desolate and unpeopled." The Hopis remained, according to Friar José Narváez Valverde, "in their heights in primitive freedom" under Espeleta's command, "because of his having been brought up and taught to read and write by one religious whose name was Espeleta. . . . since this uprising (1680) it has not been possible to reduce them."

❧·❧

Albert Yava and Francisco de Espeleta, as liminal men, straddled the complex forces of encounters between Hopis and outsiders. In their comprehension of multiple languages, cultures, and religious traditions, they worked in the perilous spaces in between, seeking, perhaps above all, to preserve Hopi ways while understanding those "ways" were themselves a matter of negotiation, confusion, compromise, and conflict. Despite a thorough education in the white man's ways and a lifetime exposure to Christian missionaries, Yava lived out his life as a defender of Hopi-Tewa traditional life and spiritual practices. "I myself have listened to these missionaries," he explained late in life. "They come to my house sometimes, and I invite them in and hear everything they have to say. Sometimes I have gone to one church or another on Sunday. Of course, a great deal of what they say is interesting. But I have not heard anything yet to persuade me that what they have is superior to what we Tewas and Hopis have." Of Francisco de Espeleta's feelings we know far less. On the one hand, he experienced baptism, adoption under compadrazgo (godparenthood), and training in the Catholic faith as a neophyte. On the other hand, he may have had a hand in the martyrdom of his own protector and padrino. By the year 1700 he seems to have been attempting to distance his Hopi kinspeople from Spanish imperial control, while proposing a limited Franciscan presence in Hopi country, allowing annual visits to individual Hopi villages in such a way as to mediate the impact of the conversion mission. If, indeed, he rallied warriors from Oraibi to participate in the devastation visited upon his natal village of Awat'ovi, he seems to have become alarmed at what he discovered was happening among his relatives on Antelope Mesa in the aftermath of Father Garaicoechea's brief visit in the spring of 1700, and increasingly so between his embassy to Governor Cubero in October of that year and the attack one month later.

Just what drew Espeleta's concern may lie in the story of another, even more ephemeral, character in the Awat'ovi story. The "young European man" discovered by the Peabody Expedition, intered in the makeshift altar in the church at Mission San Bernardo, provokes speculation. Canon law explicitly prohibited "the burial of a corpse or . . . body of a deceased person, not canonized or beatified, below or within the cubic content of a fixed or immoveable altar." Although the altar in which the "redeposited bundle burial" of the young man "about twenty-one years of age" seems not to have been constructed until after the burning of the church in the 1680 revolt, and thus perhaps beyond this proscription, "the legislation of the Church" stressed that even "altars of the intermediate or quasi-fixed type" maintained a "comparable dignity." It is unlikely, therefore, that Padre Garaicoechea conducted the burial during his time at Awat'ovi, even if he did engage in repair and rebuilding that showed archaeologically in a temporary place of worship fashioned within one of the standing rooms of the convento.

The burial, believed architectural historian Ross Gordon Montgomery, "could have been accomplished only between 1680 and the early summer of 1700," and conducted by one or more members of the community. As a secondary, or "redeposited" burial, the timing is suggestive, since the bones probably lay elsewhere while time or scavengers defleshed and disarticulated the skeleton. The body must have been that of a postulant or novitiate in the Franciscan order, whose name lies unrecorded in the scant records that survived the rebellion, or, less likely, that of a secular soldier assigned to the mission prior to August 1680. In either case, the young man may have died in the violence of that moment—perhaps his body lay exposed to the elements, and his bones gathered later—or he survived for some period of time only to pass away during the twenty-year hiatus, and his body defleshed by human hands. The latter seems less likely, for he would have been quite young in 1680 if he were twenty years old in say, 1690. If a postulant or novitiate in 1680, he must have held the respect of at least the "Catholic convert" faction, who so carefully bundled his bones in Hopi cotton cloth and laid them upon a woven Hopi tray basket in the makeshift altar as a sign of their, if not the formal Church's, veneration for him as a human being.

At first glance, this seems an unlikely scenario, that amid the passionate rejection of all things Spanish and Catholic during the Pueblo Revolt a young Franciscan-in-the-making would have been accorded such tender treatment, whether he survived the initial slaughter or died the same day as did the padres at Oraibi, Walpi, and Awat'ovi. But a case exists to suggest otherwise. During the days of rage that seized the Hopi Mesas, residents of the Pueblo of Halona at Zuñi allowed one of their padres—*kwan tatchui lok'yana* (Juan Greyrobe, Father-of-Us) to live, if he would adopt their manners and customs, grow out his hair, and marry a Zuni woman. As Frank Cushing would put it two hundred years later, Juan Greyrobe "had a Zuñi heart and cared for the sick and women and children, nor contended with the fathers of the people." In order that he be able to fulfill his new, indigenized mission, all "the ornaments of divine worship" in Halona's church of Nuestra Señora de La Candelaria were saved, and moved to a new fortified village atop Dowa Yalanne mesa, where Diego de Vargas, leading the forces of reconquest, would note their, but not the friar's, presence in 1692. Among those ornaments was the eighteen-inch-tall Santo Niño de Cíbu (Zuni), a statue of the infant Jesus, which today remains under the stewardship of the matrilineally descended Yatsattie family, whose progenitors preserved the figure in 1680. The Santo Niño embodies two attributes—both the male Christ Child and a female spirit representing the Zuni "Daughter of the Sun"—dual, symmetrical qualities once celebrated by an annual fiesta that drew many Hispano Catholics and Zunis together into the central plaza at Halona, yet now seldom observed.

The young man in the altar at Mission San Bernardo may have been held in similar esteem among the Catholic sympathizers. Perhaps he even lived beyond the day of judgment to care for the sick, and women and children, who likely were those whom the Franciscans attended most carefully, as vulnerable to the message of redemption in Christianity. His presence, however, to the anti-Catholic traditionalists, may well have provided the seed of anxiety that sorcerers inhabited the High Place of the Bow Clan, even after the purge of 1680. A Pahaana from distant lands, interred within the precinct of Awat'ovi, lying in wait for the return of Father Garaicoechea. With his imminent revival came the rebirth of the "doings" that the Hopi priesthood so feared.

9

At the Moment of the Yellow Dawn

Nowadays the Hopis want to forget that whole Awatovi affair. They're ashamed of what happened because they were supposed to be the Peaceful People.

—NUVAYOIYAVA, TEWA VILLAGE, 1978

The Pueblo of Awat'ovi—diverse, populous, creative, and quarrelsome—had become, during the critical two decades of 1680 to 1700, the focus of anxious attention among its Hopi kinsmen and clansmen. And yet precisely what activities and attitudes attracted looming violence remains unclear. The dominant explanation, at least in popular accounts today, lies with their embrace of Christianity between 1629 and 1680, and their willingness to entertain the Franciscans' return in May of 1700, even to the point of allowing their children to receive baptism. They had, according to Spanish accounts, "repaired and rebuilt the convento and church," in anticipation of the rebirth of the Holy Faith on Antelope Mesa. As this version goes, Catholic Awat'ovi died that Hopis might preserve the religion of their ancestors.

Yet this solution confronts several problems. First, each of the villages at Tuuwanasavi, or the "Earth-Center," was a mosaic of diverse clans who migrated from every direction across several centuries. First arrivals outranked later immigrants, clan rivalries were common, languages often incomprehensible, some rituals shared, some new and accepted, others rejected. Gaining entrance to the Hopi Mesas was not easy, as the Tanos discovered after their migration from Tsaewari. And even if accepted as neighbors, lines might be drawn around language and ceremony and clanship that harbored latent resentments. Many of these communities in the past had suffered punishment and desolation as the result of chaotic and corrupt behavior, or *koyaanisqatsi*. Those who survived carried those lessons forward, yet seem seldom to have been able to instantiate them in enduring ways. This pattern long predated the crisis at Awat'ovi, and would postdate it as well. One can hear premonitions and echoes of Awat'ovi in each of their histories.

Recall that the great earth/water serpent Balolokong destroyed Palatkwapi (the Red House) by earthquake and flood when the people there came to disregard Masauwu's teachings. Most offensive were the women who joined men in gambling games in the kivas, took part in lascivious Butterfly Dances, and enjoyed sex with "men who were not their husbands." Then the people of Hovi'itstuyqa perished when one of their own young men raped and absconded with the young bride from Tupats'ovi. Her poor, enraged husband recruited Yavapai warriors to revenge his shame—with the offer of captured women as their reward. Likewise, the residents of Huk'ovi abandoned their home when chased out by the ghostly flames of "Child-

Sticking-Out-Woman," a deity enraged that a Huk'ovi maiden might use *powa* (the power to change) toward selfish ends—in this case to avenge her rejection by a youth from neighboring Pivanhokyapi. The witch's ability to trigger the collapse of kiva roofs in Pivanhokyapi and kill the men trapped beneath prefigures in grim detail the events at Awat'ovi. Her supernatural powers and self-serving motives constituted the fundamental definition of "sorcery" in Hopi culture. Ironically, Pivanhokyapi itself would experience immolation as well, when women joined the gambling frenzy of *totolospi* and offered their own bodies as rewards. Finally, the legendary village of Sikyatki, whence the finest Hopi pottery would find its origins, was reduced to the shadow of rubble and ash one sees today on the winding road up to First Mesa. The cause? Sorcerers from the Swallow Clan meddled in two youths' competition over the affections for a Sikyatki maiden. The social chaos that followed spurred the village chief to invite warriors from "Old Walpi" (Qöötsaptuvela) to purify his people with fire and blood—and gain rights to Sikyatki's cornfields while doing so. These "tales of destruction" are central to Hopi historical patrimony today. Despite the creativity and precision of their details, they seem to convey one clear message: in the deep past, when women ventured beyond the edges of their culturally defined duties as maidens, wives, or mothers, *koyaanisqatsi* spread like a cancer through these communities.

In a different, apparently male-dominated register, between 1896 and 1906 intravillage tensions focused on the threat to Hopi religion posed by Protestant missions and "white man's" education, clan ranking, ceremonial status, and access to agricultural fields. The factional struggles suspended virtually all ceremonial activity at Oraibi; the clans responsible for important rituals in the ceremonial calendar

Hopi woman dressing the hair of an unmarried girl, 1900.

found their members split between the two factions. The attendant social chaos led to the fissure at Oraibi, brought about by leaders who hoped to restore *suyaanisqatsi* after a decade's turmoil. In this case, Hopis avoided overt violence by crafting a "push-of-war" between two factions, and allowing the creation of three new communities to relieve the social stress. Awat'ovi stands as only one among many community crises—yet the most traumatic and remembered—in the long history of Hopi people.

Second, like so many Pueblos in the seventeenth century, Awat'ovi cleaved into Catholic adherents or sympathizers versus those devoted to maintaining traditional religious observances and ceremonies. Yet, in the Spanish period, Oraibi (Mission San Francisco) and Shungopovi (Mission San Bartolome) also hosted—however much under coercion—Franciscan proselytizers. This begs the question of why Awat'ovi alone came to be the locus of "chaotic" practices. If only the Catholic converts were the cause of the chaos, why, then, ought "all the men and old women" of Awat'ovi die, when the evidence suggests that women and young people may have been the primary force behind the disruptive practices? Since the annihilation of his people was solicited by the *kikmongwi*, a regrettable but necessary cleansing of chaos and corruption, "just like at the end of the third world," why are the men and boys, as they wrap up the many days of the *wuwutcim* ceremony, the target of the massacre? Perhaps the most ancient of all Hopi ceremonials, the *wuwutcim* conferred elements of supernatural power on initiates, without which "the individual has not even the basis for a claim to political office . . . and eternally a *sukavungsino* (commoner) with no access to power." Although some Awat'ovinam would survive, the method of attack would suggest that the *wuwutcim* priesthood and young male initiates, trapped during their ceremonies in the kivas, were those most certain to die.

After all, these victims were performing the very form of piety that Ta'polo feared was vanishing from his community. Why were kivas the focus of the attack, if they represented the very deep memory of Hopi's movement from one world to another in their cycles of death and rebirth? How does the Pahaana prophecy underpin the events that unfolded at Awat'ovi? And how does the trauma of the event serve to shape the very essence of the Hopituh Shinumu (the Peaceful People) today?

One vein of understanding lies in the kivas themselves. During the Peabody Museum excavations of 1935–1939, Jo Brew's crews reopened Jesse Fewkes's "sorcerer's kiva," designated "Test 31" in the Peabody Expedition reports. It proved to be "the largest kiva" excavated at Awat'ovi, and "unusual in shape," in that the length was "almost exactly twice its width." It was located in the center of "what appeared to be a large plaza, occupying the area between the Spanish church and convento . . . and a house block of native dwellings . . . to the northwest." The kiva showed some of the longest duration of construction and use among those that the expedition investigated. Tree-ring cutting dates for its first construction extended to the middle years of the fourteenth century, and the latest timber samples yielded dates ranging from 1599 to 1628, just as the Franciscans arrived on the mesa. Thus it seems to have been somewhat isolated at the time of its first construction, some one hundred yards east of the Western Mound in an open plaza. Even then, the kiva may have held special prominence in Awat'ovi's ceremonial life. Only later, as the town grew and residential blocks were extended eastward, and especially after 1629, the kiva came to lie between the Franciscan mission and the residential houses of those Hopis who had relocated from the Western Mound to be closer to the Franciscans, which were constructed atop roomblocks of an earlier era. The "Catholic converts" probably dismantled portions of their homes in the Western Mound, at least so far as to salvage the precious roofing timbers, which in turn created some confusion for archaeologists looking at tree-ring data in the new homes that recorded cutting dates from times before the Franciscan mission. Whether they did so voluntarily, or under some form of coercion, is uncertain. The kiva, however, remained and seems to have hosted continuous use, however much its precise use may be confusing.

The rectangular kiva proved unusual in several other respects. An "unusually broad but low bench" some nine inches high extended from the rear end of the kiva one-third of its length, or about nine feet. Excavators found a "unique feature" in an embrasure from the floor level to the upper surface of the bench, lined with stone slabs, and in one corner a wooden post to steady the vertical slabs. A semicircular aperture or tunnel, some four inches in diameter, ran from the mouth of the embrasure to the rear of the kiva and connected there to the vertical ventilator shaft. The bench itself, and the aperture, was paved with "neatly fitted stone slabs." Nine "small circular holes" had been drilled through the paving stones of the bench, some in rows of three, others apparently isolated in their locations. The kiva floor was likewise paved with stone slabs, less carefully fitted than the bench, into which thirteen small circular holes had also been drilled, arranged in two parallel rows of four and five holes without a "definable pattern," although presumed to serve as loom anchors for men's traditional weaving activities, especially dance regalia. The slab-lined firebox "was filled with coal ash," and near the front end of the structure, excavators found a rectangular pit lined with "badly rotted" wooden boards. This may have served dual functions as a "foot-drum" and *sipapu*. The kiva walls "were of the usual flimsy construction" of later-period architecture at Awat'ovi, and although remnants of plaster survived, the plaster showed "no evidence of paint," as had the earlier kivas of the Western Mound. These later walls may reflect modification in the shape of the kiva, especially its extension to a rectangular shape.

The kiva's contents proved similarly striking to Watson Smith, the specialist who developed techniques for recording the famous murals found at Awat'ovi. Six "restorable" post-Sikyatki jars lay near the front, as did "three pottery objects that resembled what had elsewhere been identified as candlesticks, certainly of Spanish inspiration." In addition to five fairly common loom blocks, used by Hopi

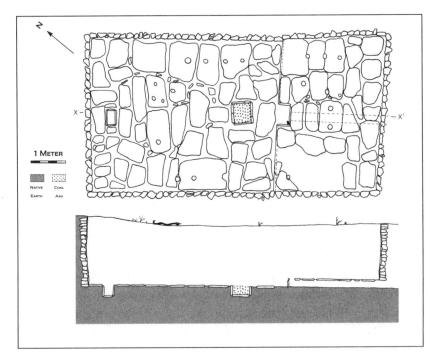

Peabody excavation floor plan of T31, or "the Sorcerer's Kiva."

men for the weavings they created in the kivas, a "metal arrow point" and "several disarticulated human bones" were found, apparently "thrown into the kiva after it had burned." On the bench itself lay a "fractured human skull," facedown. Remains of charred beams lay on the bench, and "fragments of charred grass and reeds were scattered" on the floor. Many of the floor stones and the remnants of plaster "showed discoloration by fire."

The Peabody excavators explored only one other kiva in the vicinity of Mission San Bernardo, one located within the eastern roomblock itself, termed "Test 22, Room 10" in their report. Of the sixteen kivas excavated by Brew's crews at Awat'ovi, Test 22 was second only to Test 31 (the Sorcerer's Kiva) in size. Unlike T31, however, it was situated within a block of residential rooms about 100 feet from the Mission. Test 22 also formed an unusual rectangle, measuring some 20 feet in length and 16 feet in width. Like T31, it featured a substantial one-foot-high bench that extended some one-third of the length of the room, as well as an extension around two sides of the kiva that provided sitting space for kiva participants, uncommon among Awat'ovi's kivas. A rectangular slab-lined firepit was filled with coal ash, like T31. It, too, had numerous small circular holes drilled in the paving stones of the floor, although none in the bench itself. Most striking, however, was an absence—"no evidence of a sipapu or footdrum was discovered in the floor."

Watson Smith was again surprised. Like T31, the walls of this kiva showed a light plastering, but "no evidence of paint," so common in the murals of the kivas excavated in the Western Mound. It, too, harbored extensive evidence of burning and violence, and abundant charred viga and latilla timbers scattered throughout the lower levels of fill. A "human mandible, human ilium," fragments of a human skull and a "human scapula" lay somewhat deeper. The walls were blackened and burned, and atop the slab-paved bench lay charred piles of cornhusks. Four loom blocks lay on the side-benches, discolored and cracked by fire. Nearby, a basalt object that suggests an ax, or maul. A "skeleton of a dog lay on the floor," while "scattered profusely over the floor and tops of the benches were quantities of charcoal, ashes, charred logs, plants, twigs and grass, all suggesting remnants of roofing materials." The logs offered three quite reliable cutting dates of 1422, 1657, and 1696, suggesting that the kiva—if its builders had reused the earliest pieces from preceding versions—may have been remodeled as late as 1696, during the period in which the people of Awat'ovi had been wont to do all sorts of things.

Both kivas lay in close association with the residences of the Catholic converts and Mission San Bernardo, and exhibited distinctive differences in size (larger), shape (rectangular), decoration (lacking painted wall murals), floor features (aperture ventilator in T31, *sipapu* absent in T22), and fill features (ceramic replicas of Spanish candlesticks), plus clear evidence of violent ends—burned fuels and roofing materials, weapons, and disarticulated human remains—and data suggesting construction and use during or immediately after the Franciscan period. Only one other kiva at Awat'ovi, Kiva A, which lay in between the Western Mound and the eastern village/mission complex, showed any evidence of the European presence, in its case, "the bones of a domestic sheep" that lay on the floor. Kiva A was clearly in use during the 1629–1680 period, but displayed no signs of violent destruction.

Were these "sorcerers' kivas"? According to numerous Puebloan accounts, successful witch- or sorcerer-slaying required extreme measures. The slain witch's body must be butchered, scattered, bones ground to meal, and burned, lest the malevolent spirit be able to reconstitute itself. The remains were either tossed to the winds, or ritually sealed in the place of their death, never to be exhumed. Whole artifacts might be sealed within as well, like the ceramic jars the Peabody excavators discovered. Yet nothing points to such a conclusion so much as the skeleton of the dog found on the floor of T22. Throughout the Puebloan world, coyotes, dogs, and witches are found in association with one another in stories about emergence, conflict, chaos, and renewal. They also converge in association around the symbol of the *sipapu*, the aperture through which people have migrated from a world riven by corruption to a new life in which they might practice being "people who were civilized and worthy of being in the

Fourth World." Coyotes were (and are) thought of as "a witch's pet," and are the preferred form into which sorcerers transform themselves "in order to travel more stealthily at night." Dogs, especially black dogs, are likewise suspected, especially if they "bark or whine for no apparent reason or they dig up the ground around the house which is usually interpreted as a bad omen." Yet domesticated dogs also play a liminal role in Pueblo thought, for they have long served humans as scouts, camp guards, nighttime village sentries, and household pets. Dogs, therefore, stand midway between the generally negative associations of coyotes and their own, more positive aspects, even to the point of receiving reverential treatment after being sacrificed in the Niman (Going Home) ceremonies in July, their skulls adorned with "corn wafers, corn mush, meat, prayer meal, and tobacco" before being ritually deposited in crevices in the mesa cliffs.

Of the 72 cases of dog remains recovered by archaeologists in the Southwest, spanning more than a thousand years of Puebloan history, 46 (63 percent) feature dogs in either pit-houses or kivas, with the next most frequent context those scattered on surfaces. According to archaeologist William Walker, pit-houses (in their early manifestations) and kivas are associated with ceremonial activities in which passage from "underworlds" to the current world are prominent. Likewise, anomalous human remains (those associated with violent ends) are predominantly found in pithouses or kivas—127 of 253, or 50 percent—with the next highest percentage (27 percent) found in surface structures with evidence of destruction. Clearly, humans who suffered death in subterranean spaces (or who had their bodies thrown in after their death) and dogs share an association with death. The frequency of dogs in those spaces leads in two, obliquely similar directions—dogs died either as partners of the humans or as guardians of the passageways between the underworld and this world. Dogs were slain as a "witch's pet," or sacrificed to assure that the executed humans, thrown into the depths of the underworld, might never again emerge through the *sipapu*. According to Walker, a dog in a kiva could either be "a witch executed at the threshold of the underworld" or "a faithful dog protector sacrificed to stand spiritual watch and prevent witches from crawling up from below."

Kiva T31 was certainly that same kiva that J. W. Fewkes had excavated in the early 1890s, and which his Hopi workmen had termed the "sorcerer's kiva" upon their disturbing discovery of the bodies that lay therein. But the T22 kiva suggests that there may well have been more than one "sorcerer's kiva" at Awat'ovi. The Brew expedition excavated only three kivas in the eastern village, including the spectacularly preserved example that lay beneath the altar of Mission San Bernardo, the uncovering of which had led to the revelation of the altar burial. Since that kiva, designated 788, had been carefully filled with sand prior to the construction of the church, it held no clues to activities during the mission period. Surely other kivas existed at the site, and, given the consistencies found in the random (if very small) sample chosen by Brew, seem likely to have contained a similarly confusing set of traits as do T31 and T22. Each show deviations from what might have been considered orthodox usage, and yet each hewed to standard elements as well. Each found its end in fire and blood.

In other words, in at least two of the kivas in which the attackers trapped their victims, people had combined traditional Hopi architectural styles with later modifications in shape and furniture—the elongated "altars"—and Spanish paraphernalia—candlestick holders. The absence of wall paintings, so prominent throughout Antelope Mesa, and in one case, a *sipapu* (although the rectangular pit in T31 may have served as such) suggests that specific Katsina ceremonies might not have been included in the form of worship therein, although the white plastering may have simply been in preparation for the painting of murals, whatever their features. These two kivas also hint at an extension of the Franciscan pedagogical architecture found at Awat'ovi and several other pre-Revolt missions, the "convento kivas" located in mission courtyards that the padres constructed during the 1630s and 1660s as "familiar places" for the religious instruction of Pueblo youth, perhaps both boys and girls. One such was located beneath the "cloister garth" at San Bernardo de Aguatubi, according to Ross Montgomery. These "theaters of conversion" had fallen into disuse by the time of the Revolt, but they may have lingered on in the minds of the "Catholic converts" at Awat'ovi as places of contemplation and worship once their churches lay burned and ruined. And yet these "Catholic converts" seem not to have rejected all traditional ceremonial duties, either, as those who died were trapped in kivas during the *wuwutcim* initiation rituals.

Other evidence points to the residents of Awat'ovi experimenting with new forms of piety during the post-Revolt decades. Excavating the ruined church's nave, Brew's Hopi workmen removed 118 burials (including the young European man interred in the altar). Although interring the dead in that location was forbidden under canon law, in practice it seems common throughout the Spanish colonial world. Since Hopi rebels during the Pueblo Revolt had burned and destroyed the church at San Bernardo de Awat'ovi, excavators had a layer of melted adobe and burned timbers that clearly delineated between pre-Revolt and post-Revolt burials. Sixty-nine of the 118 bodies had been interred *after* the destruction of the church. All had been laid out in extended, Christian fashion, rather than the flexed-and-bundled fashion of traditional Hopi burials. Fifty-nine of these "Christian" interments featured burial offerings—an eclectic mix of Catholic saint's medallions, rosary beads, Hopi ceramics, and wooden *pahos* (prayer sticks). This mixed assemblage of burial goods also drew Ross Montgomery's Catholic (and deeply prejudiced) interpretation. "This is a significant commentary," he wrote, "on the transitional type of Christianity often found among primitive peoples subjected to the persuasive influence of zealous and apostolic missionaries who converted them to an incipient but nevertheless efficacious form of Catholicism. These primitive Christian Moqui had faith and rendered good works within their varied but limited capacities." He could only conclude "the unflexed Indian burials beneath the church floor were of Christians, and some interments were occasioned by the friars' permission, while others were made after their departure."

"Limited capacities," Montgomery thought. Alternatively, we might see the forms of devotion that developed at Awat'ovi in the aftermath of the Revolt as expressions of a very human effort to create spiritual security during troublous times. The rage against the Spanish presence that swept the Puebloan world in August 1680 enveloped the Western Pueblos as well, and even those with Catholic sympathies proved unable, except perhaps in the case of Father Juan Greyrobe at Zuni, to prevent the deaths and destruction visited upon the missions and their personnel. And yet one member of Mission San Bernardo—the nameless young man in the altar burial—seems to have retained special standing among at least one faction at Awat'ovi. He, too, may have died in the Revolt, his body thrown onto the middens or from the escarpment, only to have his bones later collected and bundled for reburial. Or he may have been protected somehow, like Father Greyrobe, and given the chance to survive in a new role—that of a liminal man and liminal soul, residing among the people of the pueblo in return for "becoming Hopi" in some manner. In either case, the presence of his bones in the makeshift altar of the ruined church signals a form of heterodoxy that is more fully realized in the interments in the church nave and fragmentary evidence in the two kivas most closely associated with the mission.

⇝∙⇜

During the period of independence from Spanish colonial rule and Franciscan indoctrination, some residents of post-Revolt Awat'ovi continued to bury their loved ones in the ruined mission church, accompanied by cherished symbols of both Hopi and Catholic spiritual life. The lens of rubble and ash in the nave was sufficiently thick and visible to preclude that those sixty-nine burials were those of "Catholic converts" who died in the rebellion itself, evidence that the interments occurred over some period of time during the two decades leading up to the return of the Franciscans in the spring of 1700. That Fray Garaicoechea did not remark upon their presence to affirm the continuing fealty of the "converted Indians" to Catholic ways—even if in violation of canon law—implies their graves had been covered with a further strata of melted adobe and windblown soil by the time of his arrival that year. The symbolic mixing of Hopi and Franciscan burial goods seems a part of practice in life, as well, if the unusual elements present in the kivas represents how the people of Awat'ovi sought to shape their religious life during the same period. Gathering in those kivas in conjunction with the traditional ceremonial calendar, men and women, if we can infer from the anxiety expressed by their neighbors, undertook to craft new expressions of devotion and to call upon numinous forces both traditional and intrusive during a painful period of uncertainty about their own future and that of the world. An emergent community of worship offered some solace.

Their neighbors grew increasingly worried, perhaps in part because Francisco de Espeleta, now *cacique* at the staunchly conservative village of Oraibi, heard of the doings on Antelope Mesa. Given his training and depth of knowledge of Catholic ritual gained under the tutelage of Fray José de Espeleta, he might, more than many, have seen the unraveling of traditional Hopi religious life as imminent. The decades of the interregnum were not quiet times on the Hopi mesas, however much they may have thought the elimination of the Franciscan missions might have distanced them from the outer and threatening world. Shortly after 1682, some or all of the southern Tiwa peoples of Sandia Pueblo on the Rio Grande sought refuge and shelter on Second Mesa, founding the village of Payupki, where they would reside until conflict with the neighboring Hopi village of Chukubi stimulated them to return to their Rio Grande home in 1748. In the summer of 1696, survivors of de Vargas's punishment of the Jemez Pueblo participants in the short-lived "second" Pueblo Revolt also headed west and made residence among the Hopi at the unknown site of Akokavi (Jemez oral history suggests Sikyatki or Walpi, as well), although they would return in the early 1700s, finding their presence unwelcome. Perhaps most significant, the Tanos of Tsaewari were on the move that same summer, on the journey that would result in the founding of Tewa Village on First Mesa, at the behest of the Walpi Snake Clan leadership. Each of these refugee peoples had experienced the worst of Spanish colonization and brought with them powerful opposition to the Catholic Church. And yet they also brought their own unique forms of Pueblo ceremonial life, which even in the centuries before 1540 had presented stresses that the formative communities on Flower Butte had experienced as volatile.

The Hopi mesas, some three hundred miles distant from the bloody Spanish reconquest and resettlement of the Rio Grande, were anything but insulated from that trauma. Overwhelmed by refugees fleeing that conflict, assaulted in their fields and villages by raiding Utes, Apaches, and Navajos, so militarily weak that Walpi, at least, was driven to the indignity of soliciting aid from experienced Tano fighters, and witnessing at Awat'ovi the emergence of a heterodox experimental piety that posed an alternative to the practice of orthodox Hopi religion, the entrenched spiritual and political leadership sensed the end of their world fast approaching. The arrival of the Franciscan friars Garaicoechea and his fellow Franciscan Antonio Miranda in May of 1700, probably timed to overlap with the former mission's patron saint feast day of May 28, intensified this anxiety.

The Hopi delegation that visited Governor Pedro Rodríguez Cubero in Santa Fe in October of that year, led by Francisco de Espeleta, doubtless knew that the Tanos were on the move toward Hopi. Those seasoned fighters would soon strengthen Hopi's ability to resist Indian raiders and Spanish forces alike. Spanish accounts suggest outrage at the proposal Espeleta laid out, positioning himself as a delegate "of a foreign power to conclude a treaty of peace and amity" threefold in its aims. Suspecting that Espeleta and his twenty-six fellow leaders sought to buy time for the incorporation of the "apostate Tanos" into Hopi defenses, Governor Cubero scoffed at Espeleta's terms. To fashion a process of annual visitation by Franciscans to individual Hopi villages would delay the Hopis' return to the faith for years, as would the provision to establish the right of those Hopis who wished to do so to "retain their own religion."

From the Hopis' perspective, however, the delegation's proposal sought to fold relationships with Spanish Franciscans into a process similar to that of preceding centuries, when new arrivals would call at the gates of established towns to display and demonstrate the efficacy of their ceremonial practices. If those ceremonies enhanced Hopi life, especially in summoning life-giving rains, the newcomers would find welcome. If the petitioner's ceremonies promised little, their admission to the village was rejected—a reasonable, if disheartening, outcome for the wanderers. Espeleta's proposal offered a practical, political solution that would allow Hopi culture to adopt, adapt, and evolve, as it had always done, and as was unfolding in the kivas of Awat'ovi. Governor Cubero's arch and arrogant rejection of their offer and his insistence on Hopi "conversion to Christianity" as the only road to peace, in fact, destroyed the possibility of peace.

As Espeleta's delegation returned disheartened to the Hopi Mesas in mid-October, surely the future lay heavily in their minds. They were working within their understanding of the cyclical nature of history, as they understood through the Pahaana prophecy. When chaos and crisis threatened the harmony of Hopi life, as it had in cycles of corruption, crises, and renewal in their passages between the preceding three worlds, Pahaana, the "white elder Brother," might be expected to "adjudicate between those who had sincerely adhered to the Hopi way and those who had departed from it," according to ethnographer Peter Whiteley. Those who had strayed—sorcerers— would suffer beheading. The October delegation's offer had provided, at least from Francisco de Espeleta's liminal experience, a "Hopi Way" that, had the governor agreed, would have placed Cubero in the role of Pahaana and brought the Spanish into alignment with the Hopi understanding of history.

When the delegation resettled in their respective villages, they may have heard another unsettling report from Awat'ovi. During Fray Garaicoechea and Miranda's time on Antelope Mesa—a length of residency indiscernible from the scanty documents—the friars had created a new church in one wing of the convento, removing several Hopi alterations and building a long, narrow nave and apse and a baptismal font that employed a pot "of 17th century Hopi type, except for the size and shape, which were not native." A mere fraction in size to the church destroyed in the rebellion, still it stood as evidence of the Franciscans' intent to return the "converted Indians of Aguatubi" fully to the faith. Garaicoechea and Miranda may have been as equally dismayed as many of the established Hopi priests, if for very different reason, when they saw how the people of Awat'ovi had experimented with the Holy Faith.

A second piece of construction proved even more alarming. During the Peabody's 1938 and 1939 field seasons, another structure came to light in the far northeastern corner of the site. This turned out to be an unfinished, even hastily abandoned, effort by the Franciscans to build a military barracks/stable where a detachment of Spanish cavalry soldiers could be stationed. Measuring some 150 feet wide and 120 feet deep, with stalls for a dozen horses and barracks for an equal or greater number of soldiers, it was clearly intended to be a substantial, permanent statement of the Crown's martial presence. No adobe walls had been raised atop the stone foundations, and even those foundations were not entirely laid into their trenches. The excavators realized that the project had been suddenly suspended. It seems likely that the Franciscans had become aware of the imminent arrival of the Tano migrants, perhaps only by rumor, and knew that once they combined with the hostile parties from the mesa villages to the west that their project would be in real danger.

As word of Governor Cubero's rejection of the Hopi delegation's proposal circulated across the mesas, and evidence of the Spanish intent to restore a pure version of the Catholic faith—by force of arms if necessary—became evident, *koyaanisqatsi* rose from latent to evident. Although the experimental religious practices at Awat'ovi seem to have been indulged by neighbors for two decades, the perfect storm of refugees pouring into the Hopi country, the arrival of the Tanos and other refugees packing a fierce anti-Spanish stance, the expectation that Spanish soldiers would soon accompany the next foray of Franciscans to Antelope Mesa, and resentment around Awat'ovi's power and privilege provoked a maelstrom of fear and anger.

As would their counterparts two centuries later when confronted with *koyaanisqatsi* at Oraibi, Espeleta and his fellow leaders in the mesas to the west saw only one solution. The corruption at Awat'ovi—a symptom of the widespread disorder throughout Hopi lands—must end so balance could be restored. In keeping with the long history of leaders summoning devastation upon their own people, Ta'polo, whose status at Awat'ovi must have been compromised by the alternative forms of worship there, called upon allies in distant villages for aid. They laid plans for the fulfillment of the Pahaana prophecy, with or without the aid of "elder brother." Espeleta and his one hundred warriors from Oraibi may have formed the core, but many other kinsmen and clansmen joined in, perhaps not fully realizing their role in making history, yet attracted by the promises of women and maidens and a chance to gain the rich planting fields and orchards associated with Awat'ovi. At the moment of the yellow dawn a blanket snapped in the fading darkness, a fortress gate swung wide, and the purifying slaughter began.

❧·❦

The present troubles the ghosts of the past. One can hear it in the voices of the tourists who visit the ruins of Troy each year to discern the truth of its destruction in *The Iliad* and *The Aeneid* as they reflect on the currency of the ancient tales. Or in the American Southwest, where visitors wonder at the profound silences that now blanket places like Chaco Canyon, Mesa Verde, and the wind-swept Salinas Pueblos and missions of the Estancia Basin in New Mexico. Public interest in the annihilation of Awat'ovi has waxed and waned with its shadowy presence in the popular imagination. Even Hopis themselves, who on the one hand may "want to forget the whole Awat'ovi affair," find it a source of continuing conversation among tribal members. One hears that the town's demise stemmed from "the Catholic orgies" conducted in some of the kivas, and thus a case of corruption purified. On the other hand, a Hopi sobriety activist once explained that Hopis kept Awat'ovi in their minds as an equivalent of the fourth and fifth steps of Alcoholics Anonymous ("a fearless and searching moral inventory, followed by admission to God, to ourselves, and another human being the exact nature of our wrongs").

Rejection and embrace of the story take other forms as well. In a recent history of the Peabody Museum's Awatovi Expedition, Eric Polingyouma, from Shungopovi Village, cautions that Awat'ovi, like neighboring Antelope Mesa villages, "was not a Hopi village. It was settled by Keresans." Later, Hopis from Homol'ovi did join the founders of Awat'ovi, and "relationships with nearby Hopi villages were good, some Keresans married into Hopi, and religious ceremonies were adopted that are still practiced today." In the years following the Pueblo Revolt, he explains, "attempts to rebuild Hopi life were interrupted again by the arrival of Catholic fathers at Awat'ovi in 1700. Their arrival brought the Hopi villages together, and Hopis destroyed Awat'ovi. . . . no one has ever claimed the village."

On the other hand, Leigh J. Kuwanwisiwma, of the Greasewood Clan of Bacavi Village and director of the Hopi Cultural Preservation Office, draws a direct line from Bow Clan claims from Chaco Canyon to Aztec Ruins National Monument and finally to the founding of Awat'ovi in the thirteenth century. Emphasizing clan lineages over Polingyouma's linguistic associations, Kuwanwisiwma sees Awat'ovi as solidly within the broad affinity group of Hisat'sinom (people from long ago) who over time came to subscribe to the "Hopi way of life . . . cooperation, sharing, respect, compassion, earth stewardship, and, most of all, humility." Like Albert Yava, he also notes deep tensions that predated the Franciscan Catholic intrusion, especially in the rivalry between Awat'ovi and Oraibi for predominance in ceremonial life. Awat'ovi, he explains, was the only Hopi town with a full compliment of eighteen ceremonial societies; Oriabi had seventeen. The latter only joined in the ruination of their rival once they were promised that Two Horn priests and Antelope Clan women would be given them as captives, who would complete their ceremonial ranks. As director of the Hopi Cultural Preservation Office, Kuwanwisiwma occasionally guides tours of the restricted Awat'ovi ruins, to tell of its founding and demise.

Awat'ovi resides in a liminal zone. Physically on Antelope Mesa, which long stood as a borderland between the Rio Grande Puebloan world and that of the Hopis, and in memory, an event that runs counter to every idea of "the Hopi way." The lack of fixity persists in other aspects, too. The Peabody Expedition left another potent and unresolved legacy. One hundred and eighteen bodies were excavated from the church itself, not the "sorcerer's kiva" that Fewkes discovered. They cannot speak, but they give rise to a swirl of voices. Disinterred during the 1930s excavations, more than half are from burials in the mission church nave that postdate the rebellion of 1680, and may involve some victims of the massacre itself. At least some are among the nearly one hundred sets of human remains from Awat'ovi neatly arranged in archival cardboard boxes along one wall of stainless-steel rolling storage in Harvard's Peabody Museum. Their disposition under the Native American Graves Protection and Repatriation Act of 1990 is uncertain. Since the site of Awat'ovi lay outside Hopi Reservation lands in the 1930s (rather, on lands assigned the Hopis by executive order), the vast collection of the Peabody Expedition is not, ironically, the responsibility of the Peabody Museum, but of the Bureau of Indian Affairs. That, too, remains unsolved.

Standard protocol would require repatriation of bodies and associated ritual artifacts to the Hopi Tribe, but that resolution is clouded by phantoms of the past. If the people of Awat'ovi were indeed transgressors of tradition who deserved their fate, they might well continue to be considered disturbing to Hopi society, whose reburial might reintroduce their trauma into the mesas. The Hopi Tribe is reluctant to reclaim these bodies. Yet neither are they willing to disclaim them, since their descendants still number among the citizens of the Hopi nation. To complicate matters, since many of these burials seem to have been conducted in Christian or pseudo-Christian fashion, and interred during the two decades of experimentation at Awat'ovi, it is possible that the Catholic Church could claim to have a right in their disposition. Without ceremonial precedent, it might be dangerous to everyone, Hopi and non-Hopi alike, were their disposition mishandled. So the bodies remain at Harvard under lock and key, while the politics of the present wrestle with the legacy of the past.

Ruins provoke an ache in our historical imagination. Whether the remnants of our direct ancestors, or the broader human family, they invite us to reflect on the fragility of our lives. We know full well that our own homes and towns and cities are destined to lie in rubble at some point in the future, and that our remains may someday be carried as ash on the wind or as bones, gnawed by rats under a decaying city's moon. In light of the events of the preceding millennium, we see Hopis grappling with the very issues that absorb our days—how to define our own communities in relation to others, especially those "outsiders" who wish to take shelter under our eaves, and to create humble and humane avenues for intercultural understanding. The twin forces of absorbing new neighbors and excluding aliens seem intensely central to the catastrophe at Awat'ovi Pueblo in the autumn of 1700, and to the survival of its remnant peoples. In the Awat'ovi case, new forms of pious practice apparently involved both women and men, and born of those peoples' religious experience in this heterodox community, comprised the "transgression" that caused senior leadership among the

Hopis to summon its destruction. And even then, Awat'ovi did not die. Surviving Awat'ovi women brought the Mamzrau ritual to the village of Walpi and the Sand, Rabbit, Coyote, and Butterfly clans to Oraibi. Others found shelter among Navajo bands in the nearby Jeddito Wash, for in 1882 members of the Tobacco People subclan of the Tachii'nii (Red Running into Water Clan) "felt so strongly about their rights to land about Awat'ovi" that the area now called the Jeddito Island of Navajo Partitioned Land (NPL) was set aside for them, "totally surrounded by Hopi Partitioned Land (HPL)," according to ethnohistorian David Brugge. Navajo traditions also indicate that Deer, Rabbit, Tansy Mustard, and Ye'ii (Hopi Katsina) subclans descended from clan mothers who escaped death at Awat'ovi. Not unlike the children born of undocumented mothers who are afforded citizenship in our nation today.

Neither, too, would Christianity be forever excluded from the mesas. Hopi peoples now embrace an array of denominations: from Mennonites to Mormons to Protestants to Pentecostals. Even Sáliko, *"Maumzrau'mongwi,"* or chief of the Mamzrau Society, whose narrative guided Jesse Fewkes to the sorcerer's kiva, had "become Christian" by 1920. Many do so while continuing to honor and perform the traditional ceremonials that assure rainfall, abundant harvests, and the Hopi Way. Catholicism would not return to the Hopi mesas until 1928, in the Saint Joseph Mission in Keams Canyon, and even then the Church came to minister to local Navajos, not the Hopis. Yet in June 2000, Hopi tribal chairman Wayne Taylor invited Bishop Donald Pelotte to meet with a small group of thirty Hopi Catholics. Pelotte "in meaningful dialogue ... expressed to them his sincere sorrow for any contribution the Catholic Church or any of its members may have had to the painful history shared by the Catholic Church and the Hopi."

Today, the relentless winds that shredded the tents of the Peabody Expedition blow across wire fencing that protects the ruins of the High Place of the Bow Clan. Each gust elicits a tone from the wires, fitting for the town's Navajo name—Tallahogan—The Singing House. With one note a piece of the past is covered by sand, with another the sand blows clear of the past. This is the nature of history on the mesa of sorrows.

ACKNOWLEDGMENTS

This book found its origins in a conversation with archaeologist Ruth Van Dyke in 2001, when we each held resident scholar appointments at the (then) School of American Research. I was in the final stages of completing *Captives and Cousins*, a book on intercultural captivity and slavery in the Southwest Borderlands, and Ruth wondered if I knew a variant of that theme in the distribution of the women who survived the massacre at Awat'ovi Pueblo among the villages of the assailants—were they victims or redeemed from bondage? The following years found me at SAR (which became the School for Advanced Research in 2007) as research faculty, administrator, and executive. *Mesa of Sorrows* reflects the "peculiar alchemy" of the many diverse humanists, social scientists, Native scholars and artists that exemplified SAR's community. For more than a decade's dwelling within that energy and eclecticism, I am grateful. Of special note are resident and visiting colleagues Rebecca A. Allahyari, the late David M. Brugge, Catherine Cameron, Cynthia Chavez Lamar, Catherine Cocks, the late Linda S. Cordell, Sarah Croucher,

Armand Fritz, Severin Fowles, George Gumerman, Laura Holt, the late Michael Kabotie (Lomawywesa), John Kantner, Doug Kiel, Stephen H. Lekson, Nancy Owen Lewis, Ramson Lomatewama, the late Hartman Lomawaima, Tsianina Lomawaima, Tiya Miles, Melissa Nelson, Timothy R. Pauketat, Douglas W. Schwartz, Thomas E. Sheridan, David H. Snow, Phillip Tuwaletstiwa, and the late David J. Weber.

St. John's College president Michael Peters and dean J. Walter Sterling paid me the honor of a visiting scholar invitation in the college's Liberal Arts Program in 2013–2014, during which I completed a first draft of the manuscript and heard echoes of "windy Ilium" in Awat'ovi's story. Alison Colborne at the Laboratory of Anthropology at the Museum of Indian Arts & Cultures in Santa Fe and Patricia Kervick at the Peabody Museum of Archaeology and Ethnology at Harvard University endured my research requests for years. Elizabeth DePalma Digeser and Stuart Smith at the University of California, Santa Barbara, recruited me back to the shores of the Pacific, and each contributed to my thinking about the violence of orthodoxy, heterodoxy, and heresy in cultures ancient and modern, as did friends and colleagues Ryan Abrecht, Liza Black, Debra Blumenthal, Hal Drake, Paige Digeser, Greg Goalwin, Jeff Hoelle, John I. W. Lee, Ann Marie Plane, Adam Sabra, Amber Vanderwarker, Sarah Watkins, and Greg Wilson. Special thanks to Hopi Cultural Preservation officer Leigh J. Kuwanwisiwma, author, musician, interpreter, and guide. All helped me to understand the trauma and promise encompassed in the deep history of the Southwest; none bear responsibility for errors in my interpretations thereof.

Don Lamm kept this book alive against high odds, as did Lynne Withey, who provided enthusiasm when my morale flagged. Its completion may have surprised my agent, Lisa Adams of the Garamond Agency, but she gracefully never let that show. At W. W. Norton, Alexa Pugh's voice remained gentle and encouraging no matter what strains I imposed upon her. My editor, John Glusman, gave me the single best writing instruction I have ever received: "It is your job to make your reader feel smart, not how smart you are."

Lila and Jeremy helped me to understand the essence of this story: let us try not to make strangers of our kinfolk and neighbors.

NOTES

CHAPTER ONE: THE GATE UNGUARDED

1 **"The women and maidens":** Henry R. Voth, *The Traditions of the Hopi*, Field Columbian Museum 96, Anthropological Papers 8 (1905), quote 249–250.

2 **For them it remained:** Author's site visit with Hopi Cultural Preservation officer Leigh J. Kuwanwisiwma, September 11, 2014. C. L. Redman, S. James, and D. Notarianni, *Awatovi Ruins of Antelope Mesa: Preservation and Development Plans*, OCRM Report No. 78, Arizona State University (1990).

5 **The crisis at Awat'ovi:** Ruth Benedict, *Patterns of Culture* (Boston: Mariner Books 2006 [1934]), 78–79.

5 **Honor between men:** Stephen Mitchell, "Introduction" to Homer, *The Iliad* (New York: Free Press, 2012), quote xxiii.

5 *Tuhu'osti,* **autumn:** The following is drawn from Fewkes, "A-Wa'-To-Bi: An Archaeological Verification of a Tusayán Legend," *American Anthropologist* 6 (October 1893): 363–376, based on narrative of Saliko given to A. M. Stephen, 1892—Saliko, descendant of survivor of massacre, in 1892 "Mamzrau'mongwi," or chief of the Mamzrau Society (women's initiation ceremony based on knowledge preserved by her ancestor); note that by 1920 Saliko had "become a Christian" and moved off the mesa; the Mamzrau ceremony was extinct at Walpi from E. C. Parsons, "The Hopi Wöwöchim Ceremony in 1920," *American Anthropologist* 25, no. 2 (1923): 156–187, esp. 171–72; more narrative details from Michael Lomatumay'ma, Lorena Lomatumay'ma, and

Sidney Namingha, Jr., "The Destruction of Awat'ovi," in *Hopi Ruin Legends: Kiqotutuwutsi*, collected, translated, and edited by Ekkehart Malotki (Lincoln: University of Nebraska Press, 1993), 298–409.

6 **Once, six other villages:** The seven villages on Antelope Mesa were Awat'ovi, Kawaika'a, Chakpahu, Pink Arrow, Nesuftonga, Koko-pnyama, and Lululongturque; John Otis Brew, "Hopi Prehistory and History to 1850," in Alfonso Ortiz, ed., *Handbook of North American Indians*, vol. 9, *Southwest*, 514–523, quote 514 (Washington, DC: Smith-sonian Institution, 1979); for Hopi view on Chaco-to-Tuuwanasavi, see Leigh J. Kuwanwisiwma in David Grant Noble, *In Search of Chaco: New Approaches to an Archaeological Enigma* (Santa Fe, NM: SAR Press, 2004), 41–47; for post-Chaco migrations and "gathering of the clans" motifs, see Patrick D. Lyons, *Ancestral Hopi Migrations*, Anthropological Papers of the University of Arizona, No. 68 (2003); Wesley Bernardini, *Hopi Oral Tradition and the Archaeology of Identity* (Tucson: University of Arizona Press, 2005).

6 **Wuwutcim societies initiated:** E. C. Parsons, "The Hopi Wöwöchim Ceremony in 1920," *American Anthropologist* 25 no. 2 (1923): 156–187.

7 *totokya*, **the climax of the ritual:** Ibid., 166–173.

8 **"moment of the yellow dawn":** Michael Lomatumay'ma, "The Destruction of Awatovi," in *Hopi Ruin Legends*, quotes, 399.

8 **"There was crying":** Ibid., quote 399–401.

8 **"Wherever they came":** Ibid., quote 403.

9 **"These are ours":** Ibid., quote 405.

9 **"In that case no one":** Ibid.

10 **"has been considered":** Ibid., quote 407; Eric Polingyouma, "Awat'ovi, A Hopi History," in Hester A. Davis, *Remembering Awatovi: The Story of an Archaeological Expedition in Northern Arizona, 1935–1939* (Cambridge, MA: Peabody Museum Monographs, no. 10, copyright 2008 by the President and Fellows of Harvard College), xv–xviii, quote xvii.

10 **Alexander McGregor Stephen:** Don D. Fowler, *A Laboratory for Anthropology: Science and Romanticism in the American Southwest, 1846–1930* (Albuquerque: University of New Mexico Press, 2000), 138–139.

12 **"whether she would be willing":** Fewkes, "A-Wa'-To-Bi," 363–376, quote 365–366.

14 **"the other villages got together":** Byron Adams, as quoted in type-script report of April 1939 Hopi delegation address at Office of Indian Affairs, Washington, DC, in "Press Notice and Reviews, 1937–1977," folder, 995-11, 5-16, Awatovi Collections, Peabody Museum, Cambridge, MA.

CHAPTER 2: THE SORCERER'S KIVA

15 **"there has been"**: Eric Polingyouma, "Awat'ovi, A Hopi History," in Davis, *Remembering Awatovi*, quote xvii.

15 **"Observing the anxiety"**: Fewkes, A-Wa'-To-Bi," quote 375.

16 **witchcraft outbreak at Salem**: For Salem, the classic works include Paul Boyer and Stephen Nissenbaum, *Salem Possessed: The Social Origins of Witchcraft* (Cambridge, MA: Harvard University Press, 1974); John Demos, *Entertaining Satan: Witchcraft and the Culture of Early New England* (Oxford: Oxford University Press, 2004 [updated ed.]); for recent anthropological approaches, see Pamela J. Stewart and Andrew Strathern, *Witchcraft, Sorcery, Rumors, and Gossip* (Cambridge: Cambridge University Press, 2003); Peter Geschiere, *The Modernity of Witchcraft* (Charlottesville: University of Virginia Press, 1997).

17 **"the first professional anthropologist"**: Fowler, *A Laboratory for Anthropology*, 117–125.

18 **"find out all you can"**: Ibid., quote 118–119.

19 **"Many Buttons"**: Ibid., quote 119.

21 **Cushing-led Hemenway Expedition**: Ibid., 148–171.

22 **their massive masonry walls**: Martha A. Sandweiss, "The Necessity for Ruins: Photography and Archaeology in the American Southwest," in May Castleberry, ed., *The New World's Old World: Photographic Views of Ancient America* (Albuquerque: University of New Mexico Press, 2003), 62–85.

23 **"Not only does Dr. Fewkes"**: Cushing to Baxter, June 16, 1891; Matthews to Cushing, January 7, 1891; quoted in Fowler, *A Laboratory for Anthropology*, 162.

23 **Zuni and Hopi**: In time, anthropologists would see that the differences between each tribe outweighed in many respects the similarities. Zuni prehistory seemed oriented more toward cycles of eastern (Mogollon) in-and-out migration that swelled and shrunk villages, whereas the Hopi mesas had been almost constantly absorbing new clans since the late thirteenth century, primarily from the Four Corners region. Social psychological differences were identified as well by ethnographers like Ruth Benedict, who saw Zunis as less beset by internal divisions and less subject to fissioning, since they had maintained Halona as a single community across the three centuries since Spanish contact. See Stephen Plog, *Ancient Peoples of the American Southwest* (London and New York: Thames & Hudson, 2008), 156–160.

24 **"Stephen's intimate knowledge"**: Fowler, *A Laboratory for Anthropology*, quote 163.

25 **Fewkes's essay**: Fewkes, "A-Wa'-To-Bi," 363–376, based on narrative of Saliko

given to A. M. Stephen, 1892. Fewkes later says that Ta'polo himself brought the phallic society of Tataukyamu from Awat'ovi to Walpi, strong evidence that he survived the massacre. See also J. W. Fewkes, "Preliminary Account of an Expedition to the Cliff Villages of the Red Rock Country and the Tusayan Ruins of Sikyatki and Awatobi, Arizona, in 1895," in *Smithsonian Institution Annual Report*, 557–588, and Fewkes, "The Alosaka Cult of the Hopi Indians," *American Anthropologist* 1, no. 3 (1899): 527n; on the "defection" of Hopis during Fewkes's 1895 excavations, see J. O. Brew to D. Scott, March 1, 1935, 995-11, Box 1, F2, Awat'ovi Archives, Peabody Museum.

29 **white women from New York:** Margaret Jacobs, *Engendered Encounters: Feminism and Pueblo Cultures, 1879–1934* (Albuquerque: University of New Mexico Press, 1999).

29 **widespread and terrifying warfare:** Jonathan Hass and Winifred Creamer, *Stress and Warfare Among the Kayenta Anasazi in the Thirteenth Century* (Chicago: Field Museum of Natural History, 1993); Christy G. Turner and Jacqueline Turner, *Man Corn: Cannibalism and Violence in the Prehistoric American Southwest* (Salt Lake City: University of Utah Press, 1998); Stephen H. Lekson, *Chaco Meridian: Centers of Political Power in the Ancient Southwest* (Lanham, MD: Rowman AltaMira, 1999); Steven A. LeBlanc, *Prehistoric Warfare in the American Southwest* (Salt Lake City: University of Utah Press, 1999); James F. Brooks, "Violence and Renewal in the American Southwest," *Ethnohistory* 49, no. 1 (Spring 2002): 205–218.

30 **the Chacoan cultural system:** Stephen H. Lekson, ed., *The Archaeology of Chaco Canyon: An Eleventh-Century Pueblo Regional Center* (Santa Fe, NM: SAR Press, 2006).

32 **Chaco Canyon unraveled:** Ibid.

32 **"in our history":** John Kantner, *Ancient Puebloan Southwest* (Cambridge: Cambridge University Press, 2004), quote 99–100; Paul Pino quoted in Ana Sofaer, *The Mystery of Chaco Canyon* (film, 1999).

33 **the two faces of sorcery:** For the dual nature of the status of *powaaqti* (pl., "witches or sorcerers"), see Peter M. Whiteley, *Deliberate Acts: Changing Hopi Culture Through the Oraibi Split* (Tucson: University of Arizona Press, 1988), quote 214–215.

34 **the Four Corners region:** Brian R. Billman, Patricia M. Lambert, and Banks L. Leonard, "Cannibalism, Warfare, and Drought in the Mesa Verde Region During the Twelfth Century A.D." in *American Antiquity* 65, no. 1 (2000): 145–178, summary, 167–169; recent identitification of trachybasalt temper sources in the Four Corners region, however, suggests the ceramics could have been locally produced, therefore indicating internecine, rather than xenophobic, violence. See David Gonzales, Fumi Arakawa, and Alan

Koenig, "Petrographic and Geochemical Constraints on the Provenance of Sanadine-bearing Temper in Ceramic Potsherds, Four Corners Region, Southwest USA," *Geoarchaeology: An International Journal* 30 (2015): 59–73.

36 **"the remains of few men":** Kristen A. Kuckelman, "Bioarchaeological Signatures of Strife in Terminal Pueblo III Settlements in the Northern San Juan," AAPA paper, 2010; Crow Canyon Research Reports, http://www.crowcanyon.org/ResearchReports/CastleRock/Text/crpw_contentsvolume.asp; for comparison of Cowboy Wash with Sacred Ridge (an earlier case of massacre) as an example of "ethnic cleansing" in the ancient Southwest, see James A. Potter and Jason P. Chuipka, "Perimortem Mutilation of Human Remains in an Early Village in the American Southwest: A Case of Ethnic Violence," *Journal of Anthropological Archaeology* 29 (2010): 507–523; for a survey of witchcraft cases in Southwest prehistory and ethnography, see J. Andrew Darling, "Mass Inhumation and the Execution of Witches in the American Southwest," *American Anthropologist* 100, no. 3 (1998), 732–752.

37 **Homol'ovi II:** William H. Walker, "Where Are the Witches of Prehistory?" *Journal of Archaeological Method and Theory*, 5, no. 3 (1998): 245–308, case discussed 287–293, quote 293.

38 **The arrival of the Katsina religion:** E. Charles Adams, *The Origin and Development of the Pueblo Katsina Cult* (Tucson: University of Arizona Press, 1991).

39 **Thus was the fate of sorcerers, wizards:** J. Andrew Darling, "Mass Inhumation and the Execution of Witches in the American Southwest," *American Anthropologist* 100, no. 3 (1998): 732–752, quote 741.

41 **Cushing's public statements:** "Killing Sorcerers: Remarkable Customs of the Zuni Indians in New Mexico," reprinted in Jesse Green, ed., *Cushing at Zuni: The Correspondence and Journals of Frank Hamilton Cushing, 1879–1884* (Albuquerque: University of New Mexico Press, 1990), 340–342.

42 **"first witnessed the trial":** Ibid., 342.

42 **The Oraibi crisis of 1906:** Whiteley, *Deliberate Acts*, 214–215; Jerrold Levy, *Orayvi Revisited: Social Stratification in an "Egalitarian" Society* (Santa Fe, NM: SAR Press, 1992).

CHAPTER 3: THE SINGING HOUSE

44 **"I wonder if":** Stoner to Brew, June 20, 1938, letter in Correspondence File, #995-11, Awatovi Records, Peabody Museum of Archaeology and Ethnology, Cambridge, MA.

44 **The people of Antelope Mesa:** Pedro de Tovar, in George Parker Winship, *The Coronado Expedition, 1540–1542*, Smithsonian Institution, Fourteenth

Annual Report of the Bureau of American Ethnology, Part II (Washington, DC: Government Printing Office, 1896), 489.

45 **"received the submission"**: Tovar, in Winship, *Coronado Expedition*, quotes 488–489.

46 **"about one thousand Indians"**: George Peter Hammond and Agapito Rey, *Expedition into New Mexico Made by Antonio de Espejo, 1582–1583, as Revealed in the Journal of Diego Pérez de Luján, a Member of the Party* (Los Angeles: The Quivira Society Publications, 1929), quote 95.

46 **disappointment after disappointment**: Ibid., quote 96.

47 **"They harvest much cotton"**: Fray Estévan de Perea, in Fray Alonso de Benavides, *Revised Memorial of 1634, with Numerous Supplementary Documents Annotated by F. W. Hodge, G. P. Hammond, and Agapito Rey* (Albuquerque: University of New Mexico Press, 1945), quotes 76–77.

47 **the friars' message of doom**: Daniel T. Reff, "Contextualizing Missionary Discourse: The Benavides Memorials of 1630 and 1634," *Journal of Anthropological Research* 50 (1994): 51–67.

48 **For example, Friar Alonso**: Frederick Web Hodge, George Hammond, and Agapito Rey, eds. and trans., *Fray Alonso de Benavides' Revised Memorial of 1634* (Albuquerque: University of New Mexico Press, 1945), quotes 7, 76–77, 93–95; Reff, "Contextualizing Missionary Discourse"; Jane Tar, "The Fame and Trials of Luisa de la Ascensión, the Nun of Carrión (1565–1636)," paper presented at the Midwest Modern Language Association Meetings, 2008; for a sweeping treatment of Marianist themes in peace and war, see Amy G. Remensnyder, *La Conquistadora: The Virgin Mary at War and Peace in the Old and New Worlds* (Oxford and New York: Oxford University Press, 2014).

49 **However much conversions**: J. O. Brew, Part 2, "The Excavation of Franciscan Awatovi," in Ross Gordon Montgomery, Watson Smith, and John Otis Brew, *Franciscan Awatovi* (Cambridge, MA: Reports of the Awatovi Expedition, Peabody Museum, Harvard University, Report No. 3, 1949), 53–54 (hereafter *Franciscan Awat'ovi*); Montgomery, "San Bernardo de Aguatubi, an Analytical Restoration," ibid., 132–135.

49 **Alas, Porras's church**: Ross Gordon Montgomery, Part 3, "San Bernardo de Aguatubi, an Analytical Reconstruction," in *Franciscan Awat'ovi*, 186.

50 **Friars were enjoined**: William L. Merrill, "Indigenous Societies, Missions, and the Colonial System in Northern New Spain," in Clara Bargellini and Michael K. Komanecky, eds., *The Arts of the Missions of Northern New Spain* (Mexico City: Colegio de San Ildefonso, 2009), 123–153.

50 **Coercion and studied violence**: Ibid., esp. 135.

52 **"For four years"**: Wíkvaya as quoted in Voth, *Traditions of the Hopi*, 268–269.

52 **According to friars**: Matthiew Liebmann, "At the Mouth of the Wolf:

the Archaeology of Seventeenth-Century Franciscans in the Jemez Valley of New Mexico," in Timothy J. Johnson and Gert Melville, eds., *Franciscan Evangelization in the Spanish Borderlands II* (Oceanside, CA: American Academy of Franciscan History, 2015), 1–18, quote 9.

53 **"the old men":** Benavides (1630), quoting Vetancurt, in *Franciscan Awat'ovi*, 11.

53 **Redesigning and repositioning the church:** Samuel Y. Edgerton, *Theaters of Conversion Religious Architecture and Indian Artisans in Colonial Mexico* (Albuquerque: University of New Mexico Press, 2001); Barbara J. Mills and William H. Walker, *Memory Work: Achaeologies of Material Practices* (Santa Fe, NM: SAR Press, 2008), quote 36.

54 **"where there were nothing":** Montgomery, "Superposition," in *Franciscan Awatovi*, 134–137, quotes 134, 135.

54 **Indeed, nearly two meters:** Brew, *Franciscan Awatovi*, 65–67; James E. Ivey doubts that the altar treatment was anything more than construction preparation. See Ivey, "Convento Kivas in the Missions of New Mexico, *New Mexico Historical Review* (April 1998): 121–152.

55 **Before the discovery:** J. O. Brew, Part 1, "The History of Awatovi," in *Franciscan Awatovi*, 99.

57 **the Mission Nuestra Señora:** James E. Ivey, *The Spanish Colonial Architecture of Pecos Pueblo, New Mexico: Archaeological Excavations and Architectural History of the Spanish Colonial Churches and Related Buildings at Pecos National Historical Park, 1617–1995* (Intermountain Region, NPS: Professional Paper No. 59, 2005), 39–73.

57 **the arrival of Padre Alonso:** France V. Scholes, "Troublous Times in New Mexico," *Historical Society of New Mexico, Publications in History*, vol. II (Albuquerque, 1942), 13–14.

58 **a rather more "grave" incident:** Charles W. Hackett, *Historical Documents Relating to New Mexico, Nueva Vizcaya, and Approaches Thereto, to 1773*, vol. 3 (Washington, DC: Carnegie Institution, 1937), 259–260; Anton Daughters, "'Grave Offenses Worthy of Great Punishment': The Enslavement of Juan Suñi, 1659," *Journal of the Southwest* 54, no. 3 (Autumn 2012): 437–452. For Posada and the Inquisition trial of Governor López de Mendizábal, see http://newmexicohistory.org/people/lopez-de-mendizabal-bernardo.

59 **Espeleta, a "highly spiritual man":** Brew, "Spaniards at Awatovi," in *Franciscan Awatovi*, 17–18; Andrew O. Wiget, "Truth and the Hopi: An Historiographic Study of the Documented Oral Tradition Concerning the Coming of the Spanish," *Ethnohistory* 29, no. 3 (1982): 181–199.

60 **Espeleta also began:** Fray José Narváez Valverde, "Notes upon Moqui and

Other Recent Ones upon New Mexico (Written at Senecú, Oct. 7, 1732),"
in Hackett, *Historical Documents*, 1937, vol. 3, 385–387.

60 **Perhaps the most famous:** Frederick Wright Gleach, *Powhatan's World and Colonial Virginia: A Conflict of Cultures* (Lincoln: University of Nebraska Press, 1997); Frances Leon Swadesh, "Structure of Spanish-Indian Relations in New Mexico," in Paul M. Kutsche, ed., *The Survival of Spanish American Villages* (Colorado Springs: Center for Southwestern Studies, 1979), 53–61.

62 **"consented and gave permission":** Wiget, "Truth and the Hopi," quote 189–190; Hackett, *Historical Documents*, 1937, vol.3, quote 147.

62 **the local Inquisition:** David Weber, *The Spanish Frontier in North America* (New Haven, CT: Yale University Press, 1992), 133–137; Brew, *Franciscan Awatovi*, quote 18.

64 **The Hopis' Navajo neighbors:** Letter from David M. Brugge to author, February 25, 2005.

65 **Nuestra Señora de la Macana:** Fray Angélico Chávez, "Nuestra Señora de la Macana," *New Mexico Historical Review* 34 (1959): 81–100. "Nuestra Señora de la Macana" or "Our Lady of the War Club." As the story goes, in 1598 the Oñate colony brought with them to New Mexico a religious statue of Our Lady of the Toledo Sacristy, which later transformed into "Nuestra Señora de la Macana" through a miracle. The apparition occurred in the early 1670s to the ten-year-old gravely ill, paralyzed daughter of the Spanish colonial governor Juan de Durán de Miranda (1671–1675). The statue told the child the province would be destroyed in six years by the Pueblo Indians. As the statue predicted, the revolt occurred. During the battle, a warrior hit the statue in the head with a sharp macana (Aztec or Nahuatl for a double-sided obsidian war club). Miraculously, only a small scar appeared on the back of the figure's head. Fray Buenaventura de los Carros carried the statue back to Mexico City, where her name was changed. He placed the sculpture in the Convento Grande de Francisco, where it remains today. The young girl lived and returned to Mexico City with the survivors of the Pueblo Revolt.

There are only four known paintings dating to the eighteenth century that tell the story of this phenomenon, Diaz said. Each tells the story of the Pueblo Revolt. They are the only known visual interpretations of the battle that were created close to the time of the event, most likely by either a witness or someone who was told about the revolt. Franciscan priest, historian, and author Fray Angélico Chávez wrote about the image in the "New Mexico Historical Review" in 1959: "A most colorful and intriguing tidbit of New Mexican history is the image of Nuestra Señora de la Macana . . . with its own peculiar story. For this story is a most curious mixture of legend and history. Although both the statue and the story are intimately connected with seventeenth-century New Mexico, particularly with the great Indian Rebellion of 1680, neither was remembered by New Mexicans since those eventful times." https://www.trinitystores.com/store /read-more/virgin-macana.

66 **nativistic purification:** Colin G. Calloway, *One Vast Winter Count: The Native American West Before Lewis and Clark* (Norman: University of Oklahoma Press, 2003), 165–188, quote 186; James F. Brooks, *Captives & Cousins: Slavery, Kinship, and Community in the Southwest Borderlands* (Chapel Hill: University of North Carolina Press, 2002), 51–55.

66 **mythology of a "bloodless reconquest":** For the last days of Pueblo independence, see Matthew Liebmann, *Revolt: An Archaeological History of Pueblo Resistance and Revitalization in 17th Century New Mexico* (Tucson: University of Arizona Press, 2012); for the best treatment of Pueblo-Spanish relations in postreconquest New Mexico, which details continuing struggles for religious and spiritual authority between Franciscans and Pueblo religious leaders, see Tracy L. Brown, *Pueblo Indians and Spanish Colonial Authority in Eighteenth-Century New Mexico* (Tucson: University of Arizona Press, 2013).

CHAPTER 4: WOLVES FROM THE EAST

68 **"And when all":** Lucy Lippard, *Down Country: The Tano of the Galisteo Basin, 1250–1782* (Santa Fe: Museum of New Mexico Press, 2010), quote 245, quoting Carbonel, from John L. Kessell, Rick Hendricks, and Meredith Dodge, eds., *Blood on the Boulders: The Journals of Don Diego de Vargas, 1694–1697* (Albuquerque: University of New Mexico Press, 1998), 688.

68 **Ogap'oge:** On toponym for Santa Fe, see J. P. Harrington, "Old Indian Geographic Names Around Santa Fe, New Mexico," *American Anthropologist* 22, no. 4 (October–December 1920); for the confrontation at Awat'ovi, see Brew, "The History of Awat'ovi," in *Franciscan Awatovi*, 19; Remensnyder, *La Conquistadora*, 351–353.

69 **Galisteo Basin:** http://galisteo.nmarchaeology.org/history/spanish-colonial -period.html, accessed August 15, 2013.

71 **Once the rebellion erupted:** John Kessell, *Pueblos, Spaniards, and the Kingdom of New Mexico* (Norman: University of Oklahoma Press, 2008), 119–175.

73 **New San Lazaro, or Tewige:** Lucy Lippard, *Down Country*, 217–218, n. 4. Courlander says he confirmed the location of Tsewageh as on the *south* side of Rio Santa Cruz near La Puebla, and there is a likely-looking patch on the bench above the river there. Lippard says Tewige was on the current site of

Santa Cruz de la Cañada, which would be north of the river. Yava features a photo of what he believed to be Tsewageh, a white clay band evident in the distant ridge, 74.

73 **Far to the west, the "Moquis":** Brooks, *Captives and Cousins*, 85–87.

74 **"sometimes other Hopi villages":** Albert Yava, *Big Falling Snow: A Tewa-Hopi Indian's Life and Times and the History and Traditions of His People*, edited and annotated by Harold Courlander (Albuquerque: University of New Mexico Press, 1978), quote 26, reprinted by permission of the Emma Courlander Trust.

75 **Popular notions of timeless Indian:** Kelley Hays-Gilpin, "All Roads Lead to Hopi," *Las vías del noroeste, II: Propuesta para una perspectiva sistèmica e interdisciplinaria* (Mexico City: UNAM, Instituto de Investigaciones Antropológicas, 2008), 65–82.

75 **"When a clan arrived":** Yukíoma of Oraibi, "The Wanderings of the Hopi," in H. R. Voth, *The Traditions of the Hopi* (Chicago, 1905), quote 24.

76 **"although the Hopi *region*":** Bernardini, *Hopi Oral Tradition and the Archaeology of Identity*, quote 166.

76 **After the revolt of 1680:** Kessell, *Pueblos, Spaniards, and the Kingdom of New Mexico*, 125, quotes 133–135; Yava, *Big Falling Snow*, quote 88; E. C. Parsons, "Early Relations between Hopi and Keres," *American Anthropologist* 38, no. 4 (1936), for Eastern Pueblo influences at Antelope Mesa.

78 **"because they are traveling about":** Lippard, *Down Country*, quotes 240–241, 242; citing Espinosa, 174.

78 **"where they had":** Lippard, *Down Country*, quote 242.

79 **"to make a home in our country":** Ibid., 245.

79 **Rebellion flamed elsewhere:** Espinosa, *Crusaders of the Rio Grande*, quotes 243–244.

80 **Vargas recovered quickly:** Lippard, *Down Country*, 246; Don Diego de Vargas, July 3–4, 1696, in Kessel, Hendricks, and Dodge, eds., *Blood on the Boulders*, quote 793.

81 **"a bundle of prayer feathers":** Yava, *Big Falling Snow*, 27–28.

82 **After departing Tsaewari:** Stewart Peckham, "Postulated Movements of the Tano or Southern Tewa, A.D. 1300–1700," *Archaeological Society of New Mexico Papers*, no. 16 (1990).

82 **Some 400 people:** Yava, *Big Falling Snow*, 28.

83 **"How pitifully ignorant":** Edward Dozier, "The Role of the Hopi-Tewa Migration Legend in Reinforcing Cultural Patterns and Prescribing Social Behavior," *Journal of American Folklore* 69, no. 272 (April–June 1956): 176–180, quotes 176–177.

83 **"when our ancestors":** Yava, *Big Falling Snow*, 32–33.

84 **"chew it up but do not"**: Ibid., 34–35.

85 **"few Hopis have even"**: Paul V. Kroskrity, *Language, History, and Identity: Ethnolinguistic Studies of the Arizona Tewa* (Tucson: University of Arizona Press, 1993), 8–16. Memories differ as to whether the Tanos participated in the destruction of Awat'ovi. The majority of published accounts say that the migrants arrived shortly after the violence, but certainly within a few months, since all agree the Tanos were critical in the summer 1701 defeat of a Spanish punitive expedition under orders from Governor Cubero. Edward P. Dozier, however, a Tewa ethnographer from Santa Clara Pueblo, states definitively that Awat'ovi fell to attackers "under the leadership of Espeleta, the Chief of Oraibi, warriors from all the villages, *including those from Hano* [emphasis added]. . . ." See Edward P. Dozier, *Hano: A Tewa Indian Community in Arizona* (New York: Holt, Rinehart & Winston, 1966), quotes 13–14.

CHAPTER 5: AT PLAY IN THE FIELDS OF THE LORD

87 **"an unprecedented opportunity"**: Davis, *Remembering Awatovi*, quotes 22–26.

90 **"without applying to the Hopis"**: Awatovi Historical Material, Brew to Scott original memo, March 1, 1935, 995-11, Box 1, F 2, Peabody Museum Archives, Cambridge, MA.

91 **Antiquities Act of 1906**: http://www.nps.gov/archeology/tools/Laws/antact.htm (accessed February 15, 2014).

92 **Indian Reorganization Act**: Francis Paul Prucha, *The Great Father: The United States Government and American Indians* (Lincoln: University of Nebraska Press, 1986), 311–389.

92 **the Hopi constitution**: Robert Hecht, "Oliver Lafarge, John Collier, and the Hopi Constitution of 1936," *Journal of Arizona History* 26, no. 2 (Summer 1985): 145–162.

95 **"familiar with the materials"**: Davis, *Remembering Awatovi*, quotes 28–29.

95 **"We are quite comfortable"**: Davis, *Remembering Awatovi*, 35, 77; J. O. Brew, "The First Two Seasons at Awatovi," *American Antiquity* 3, no. 1 (1937): 122–137, quote 128.

96 **Brew's plan of work**: Davis, *Remembering Awatovi*, 39; Brew "The Excavation of Awatovi," in Marnie Gaede, ed., *Camera, Spade and Pen: Inside View of Southwestern Archaeology* (Tucson 1980), 103–109, quote, 109.

98 **"in this mound"**: Brew, "The First Two Seasons," 129.

98 **The Western Mound proved**: Brew, "The First Two Seasons," 129–133; on Kayenta district, see Linda S. Cordell and Maxine E. McBrinn, *Archaeology of the Southwest*, 3rd ed. (Walnut Creek, CA: Left Coast Press, 2012), 212–214.

99 **80,000 potsherds**: Cordell and McBrinn, *Archaeology of the Southwest*, 277.

101 **As the 1936 season:** Brew, "The First Two Seasons," quotes 134–136.

102 **The 1937 excavation season:** J. O. Brew, "Preliminary Report of the Peabody Museum Awatovi Expedition of 1937," *American Antiquity* 5, no. 2 (1939): 103–114.

103 **It had become clear to Brew:** Brew, "Part II: The Excavation of Franciscan Awatovi," in *Franciscan Awat'ovi*, Fig. 4, 54–55, 75, 86–88; for a counterexample of total convento destruction in the Revolt, see James E. Ivey, *The Spanish Colonial Architecture of Pecos Pueblo*, although he notes that the Hawikuh (Zuni) and San Marcos (Keres) conventos show "clear evidence of Indian occupation," 348.

105 **"points with calculable sureness":** Montgomery, "Part III: San Bernardo de Aguatubi, in *Franciscan Awat'ovi*, quote 179.

106 **In late August of 1937:** Davis, *Remembering Awatovi*, 131–132; T. E. Raynor, "Tucson Priest Says First Mass Since 1700 in Ruins of Old Spanish Mission," *Tucson Daily Citizen*, September 9, 1937, p. 12, #995-11, Awatovi Records, Box 5, F.2, Peabody Museum.

106 **"recently been elected president":** Father Stoner Folder, Stoner to Brew, June 20, 1938, letter in correspondence file, #995-11, Awatovi Records, Box 5, F.2, Awatovi Records, Peabody Museum.

107 **"the first European settlement":** Hayden to Cammerer, director of National Park Service, June 22, 1938, quoting Stoner, #995-11, Awatovi Records, Box 4, F.4, Peabody Museum.

108 **"very glad to talk":** Brew to Stoner, July 11, 1938; Brew to Wilson, November 17, 1938; Brew to Nussbaum, November 22, 1938, #995-11, Awatovi Records, Box 4, F.4, Peabody Museum.

109 **"its youth":** Brew to Stauble, February 3, 1939; Brew to Heinzmann, February 2, 1939, #995-11, Awatovi Records, Box 4, F.4, Peabody Museum.

109 **"the box containing":** Heinzmann to Brew, February 15, 1939; Stauble to Brew, January 27, 1939, #995-11, Awatovi Records, Box 4, F.4, Peabody Museum.

109 **"a good many years":** Watson Smith, *One Man's Archaeology*, a self-published 1984 typescript in the archives of the Catherine McElvaine Library, School for Advanced Research, Santa Fe, 123–124.

110 **"chief of the badger clan":** Brew in Camp Journal, May 26, June 20, June 22, 1939, in #995-11, Box 7, F.5, Awatovi Collections, Peabody Museum.

111 **"Indians Ask Science to Leave":** Byron Adams, undated and un-sourced newspaper clipping, #995-11, Awatovi Collection, Box 5, F.16, Peabody Museum.

111 **"with the fieldwork finished":** Davis, *Remembering Awatovi*, 188–189; Brew, "Preliminary Report of the Peabody Museum Awatovi Expedition of 1939," *Plateau* 13, no. 3 (1941): 39–48, 48.

CHAPTER 6: YOU WILL FIND ME POOR, WHILE YOU RETURN
IN THE GRANDEUR OF PLENTY

113 **"It is not hard to see":** Jerrold E. Levy, *Orayvi Revisited: Social Stratification in an "Egalitarian" Society* (Santa Fe, NM: SAR Press, 1992), quote 29.

114 **"exploring the site thoroughly":** "Reunion," in Smith, *One Man's Archaeology,* 341-5 to 341-7; "Watson Smith: Oral History," conducted by Constance Silver, July 31, 1978," typescript, #995-11, Awatovi Historical Materials, Box 24, F.1, Peabody Museum.

117 **"Many men's ages shall pass":** "The Pahanna Myth and Prophecy," quoted in Richard O. Clemmer, "'Then Will You Rise and Strike my Head from My Neck': Hopi Prophecy and the Discourse of Empowerment," in *American Indian Quarterly* 19, no. 1 (1995): 31–73, quotes 31–32.

118 **"assigns order":** Clemmer, "Then Will You Rise," quotes 67, 32.

118 **The Pahanna prophecy:** Matthew Restall, *Seven Myths of the Spanish Conquest* (Oxford: Oxford University Press 2004).

119 **An "Edenic" world:** William M. Clements, "'A Continual Beginning, and Then an Ending, and Then a Beginning Again': Hopi Apocalypticism in the New Age," *Journal of the Southwest* 46, no. 4 (2004): 643–660, commentator *PZ, 658, 645.

120 **"grafted on to":** Clements, "'A Continual Beginning,'" quote 645; Whiteley, *Deliberate Acts,* quote 270.

120 **The people of Tusayán:** For debates and archaeological case studies, see E. Charles Adams, *The Origin and Development of the Pueblo Katsina Cult* (Tucson: University of Arizona Press, 1991); Polly Schaafsma, *Kachinas in the Pueblo World* (Albuquerque: University of New Mexico Press, 1994); Peabody Museum/Hopi Tribe Website on Katsinas, see http://140.247.102.177/katsina/; for violence associated with the period of Katsina origins, see Florence Hawley Ellis, "Patterns of Aggression and the War Cult in the Southwestern Pueblos," *Southwestern Journal of Anthropology* 7, no. 2 (Summer 1951), 177–201; John Ware and Eric Blinman, "The Origin and Spread of Pueblo Ritual Sodalities," in Michele Hegmon, ed., *The Archaeology of Regional Interaction: Religion, Warfare, and Exchange Across the American Southwest & Beyond* (Boulder: University Press of Colorado, 2000): 381–410; Alison R. Freese, "Send in the Clowns: An Ethnohistorical Analysis of the Sacred Clowns' Role in Cultural Boundary Maintenance Among the Pueblo Indians," Ph.D. diss., American Studies Department, University of New Mexico, 1991).

121 **"masks" of classical *katsinam* figures:** The earliest datable Katsina image

in the Rio Grande region comes, ironically, from the northern Tiwa Pot Creek Pueblo, ancestral to both today's Taos and Picurís pueblos, long assumed to have *not* adopted the Katsina religion. See Kelly Ann Hays (Hays-Gilpin), "Kachina Depictions on Prehistoric Pueblo Pottery," in Schaafsma, *Kachinas in the Pueblo World*, 47–62, image, 57, Fig. 6.8; Polly Schaafsma, *Warrior, Star, and Shield: Imagery and Ideology of Pueblo Warfare* (Santa Fe, NM: Western Edge Press, 2000); Severin Fowles, Chapter Six, "Katsina and Other Matters of Concern," in *An Archaeology of Doings: Secularism and the Study of Pueblo Religion* (Santa Fe, NM: SAR Press, 2013).

122 **"tales of destruction":** Michael Lomatuway'ma, Lorena Lomatuway'ma, and Sidney Namingha, Jr., *Hopi Ruin Legends*, collected and translated by Ekkhart Malotki (Lincoln: University of Nebraska Press, 1993), 75–116.

123 **That women in the Eastern Pueblos:** Michelle Hegmon, Scott G. Ortman, and Jeanette L. Mobley-Tanaka, "Women, Men, and the Organization of Space," in Patricia L. Crown, ed., *Women & Men in the Prehispanic Southwest* (Santa Fe, NM: SAR Press, 2001), 43–90, quote 77, see esp. Table 2.3, Dimensions of Women's Status in the Pueblo Sequence, 86–87; Edward P. Dozier, "Rio Grande Pueblos," in Edward H. Spicer, ed., *Perspectives in American Indian Culture Change* (Chicago: University of Chicago Press, 1961), 116–117.

124 **"cycles of evangelism":** Brew, "The History of Awatovi, the Conversion," in *Franciscan Awatovi*, quotes 9, 10.

125 **Like Pahaana, the friars' methods:** Wiget, "Truth and the Hopi," 184–186; Anton Daughters, "'Grace Offenses Worthy of Great Punishment': the Enslavement of Juan Suñi, 1659," *Journal of the Southwest* 54, no. 3 (Autumn 2012): 437–452.

125 **"believed themselves":** Delno C. West, "Medieval Ideas of Apocalyptic Mission and the Early Franciscans in Mexico," *The Americas*, 45, no. 3 (January 1989): 293–313, quote 294, 296; see also E. Randolph Daniel, *The Franciscan Concept of Mission in the High Middle Ages* (Lexington: University Press of Kentucky, 1975), esp. 26–36; Brett Edward Whalen, *Dominion of God: Christendom and Apocalypse in the Middle Ages* (Cambridge, MA: Harvard University Press, 2009).

126 **"split," or fissioning:** Levy, *Orayvi Revisited*, quote 162.

126 **"very good church":** Brew, "The History of Awatovi, The Conversion," in *Franciscan Awatovi*, quotes 18, 24; John P. Wilson, "Awatovi—More Light on a Legend," *Plateau* 44, no. 2 (Winter 1972): 125–130; Clemmer, "Then Will You Rise," citing Edmund Nequatewa, "Truth of a Hopi and Other Clan Stories of Shungopovi," *Museum of Northern Arizona Bulletin* 8 (1936): 70–94, quote 41.

127 **Oraibi would retain its prominence:** Whiteley, *Deliberate Acts*, 31–37;

Calhoun quoted in Thomas Donaldson, *Moqui Pueblo Indians of Arizona and Pueblo Indians of New Mexico: Extra Census Bulletin* (Washington, DC: United States Census Printing Office, 1893), 25.

129 **An invitation:** Agent William Mateer, quoted in Whiteley, *Deliberate Acts*, 40.

130 **David L. Shipley:** Agent D. L. Shipley, quoted in Whiteley, *Deliberate Acts*, 74–75.

131 **In June 1890:** Whiteley, *Deliberate Acts*, 75.

132 **Ralph P. Collins:** Collins, quoted in Whiteley, *Deliberate Acts*, 77.

132 **the land allotment program:** Whiteley, *Deliberate Acts*, 79–81.

133 **"a restricted and tenuous":** Levy, *Oraivi Revisited*, quotes 3.

134 **a series of drought years:** Whiteley, *Deliberate Acts*, 98.

134 **Powerful ceremonial clans:** Levy, *Orayvi Revisited*, 8, map of clan lands, Fig. 2, 37; Table of Clan Ranking by Ceremonial Status and Land Holdings, as Well as Membership, Table 3.1, 41; Clemmer, "Then Will You Rise," quotes 56.

135 **When it came in 1906:** Whiteley, *Deliberate Acts*, 107.

136 **Finally, on September 6:** Ibid., 109.

136 **The women and children:** Ibid., 108–109.

137 **An anxious stalemate:** Ibid., 110–111.

137 **Perry declined:** Ibid., 113–114.

138 **Yet this version:** Ibid., 264–265.

139 **Of course, internal politics:** Ibid., 269.

140 **"A corollary of *Pahaana*'s return":** Whiteley, *Deliberate Acts*, 269–272.

140 **tool of religious leaders:** Clemmer, "Then Will You Rise," 58.

CHAPTER 7: ACROSS THIS DEEP AND TROUBLED LAND

142 **"Aliksa'i. They say":** Malotki, *Hopi Tales of Destruction*, quote 143.

142 **"laden with actors":** Ekkehart Malotki, *Hopi Ruins Legends*, x, quoting Christopher Vecsey, from *Imagine Ourselves Richly: Mythic Narratives of North American Indians* (New York: Crossroad Publishing Co., 1988), quote 24.

143 **Palatkwapi (Red-Walled City . . .):** Patrick D. Lyons, *Ancestral Hopi Migrations* (Tucson: University of Arizona Press, 2003), 89–90, quote from T. J. Ferguson, and Micah Lomaomvaya, *Hoopoq'yaqam niqw Wukoskyai (Those Who Went to the Northeast and Tonto Basin): Hopi-Salado Cultural Affiliation Study* (Kykotsmovi, AZ: Hopi Cultural Preservation Office, 1999), 78; Bernardini, *Hopi Oral Tradition*, 74–80.

144 **Founded by a coalition:** Courlander, "The Destruction of Palatkwapi," in *The Fourth World of the Hopis: The Epic Story of the Hopi Indians as Pre-*

served in their Legends and Traditions (New York: Crown Publishers, 1971), quote 57; Edmund Nequatewa, "The Legend of Palotquopi," in Edmund Nequatewa, "Truth of a Hopi," quote 77.

147   **The destruction of Palatkwapi:** Bernardini, *Hopi Oral Tradition*, quotes 75–76; on Balolokong, see David A. Phillips, Jr., Christine S. Vanpool, and Todd L. Vanpool, "The Horned Serpent in the North American Southwest," in David A. Phillips, Jr., Christine S. Vanpool, and Todd L. Vanpool, eds., *Religion in the Puebloan Southwest* (Lanham, MD: AltaMira Press, 2006), 17–30.

148   **One of those villages:** This narrative is created from two accounts that conform closely to one another in the broad details of the destruction of Hovi'itstuyqa. The author has blended each for the richest details and conformation with later ethnographic accounts. See Edmund Nequatewa, "The Destruction of Elden Pueblo, A Hopi Story," *Plateau* 28, no. 2 (1955): 37–45; Malotki, "The End of Hovi'itstuyqa," in *Hopi Tales of Destruction*, 97–123. I have not followed Nequatewa's association of Hovi'itstuyqa with Elden Pueblo, near Flagstaff, AZ, since its dating and distance from the likely setting on Anderson Mesa/Chavez Pass make it an unlikely candidate, and since Hopis have a different name for Elden today (Pasiwvi), and in the clear identification that the region in which this drama unfolded was Nuvakwewtaqa, the Hopi term for the Chavez Pass (see ibid., 97).

154   **The biological necessity:** Southwestern archaeologists estimate, through computer modeling, that Ancestral Puebloan communities of interaction required at least 475 participants to ensure "enough potential mates to constitute a demographically stable social unit." Few villages in the fourteenth century had populations this large, thus requiring the interaction with neighbors to create new families. See Nancy M. Mahoney, "Redefining the Scale of Chacoan Communities," in John Kantner and Nancy M. Mahoney, eds., *Great House Communities Across the Chacoan Landscape* (Tucson: Anthropological Papers of the University of Arizona, no. 64, 2000), 19–27.

155   **The people of Tupats'ovi:** Harold Colton and Edmund Nequatewa, "The Ladder Dance: Two Traditions of an Extinct Hopi Ceremonial," *Museum of Northern Arizona Notes* 5, no. 2 (1932): 5–12; Malotki, *Hopi Ruin Legends*, 87, n. 1

155   **courtships and marriage:** See Edmund Nequatewa, "Hopi Courtship and Marriage: Second Mesa," *Museum Notes, Museum of Northern Arizona* 9, no. 3 (1933), esp. 3, where is discussed the fact that parents are always alert for the use of witchcraft by maidens to attract husbands.

157   **famous Ladder Dance:** Edmund Nequatewa, "The Ladder Dance at Pivanhokyapi," in *Truth of a Hopi*, 107–112, reference to California Indians, 112; Malotki, "The Abandonment of Huk'ovi," in *Hopi Tales of Destruction*, 90–96.

161 **the story of Huk'ovi's abandonment:** Malotki, "The Abandonment of Huk'ovi," Introduction, 69–90, quotes 70, 77.

163 **"no one belonged to anyone":** Bernardini, *Hopi Oral Tradition*, 44–48, quotes 47, 48.

164 **Sityatki was no longer occupied:** Steven A. LeBlanc, "Regional Interaction and Warfare in the Late Prehistoric Southwest," in Michelle Hegmon, ed., *The Archaeology of Regional Interaction: Religion, Warfare and Exchange Across the American Southwest and Beyond* (Boulder: University Press of Colorado 2000), 41–70, quotes 58–59; Malotki, "Introduction: The Demise of Sikyatki," in *Hopi Tales of Destruction*, 55–58.

164 **"was so enchanted":** Malotki, "The Demise of Sityatki," in *Hopi Tales of Destruction*, 57.

166 **material tensions were second:** Malotki, "The Demise of Sikyatki," 59–68; for the Hopi footracing tradition, see Matthew Sakiestewa Gilbert, "Hopi Footraces and American Marathons, 1912–1930," *American Quarterly* 62, no. 1 (March 2010): 77–101.

170 **an end to the *koyaanisqatsi*:** Malokti, on *koyaanisqatsi*, 55–58.

CHAPTER 8: LIMINAL MEN, LIMINAL SOULS

171 **"Time after time":** Yava, *Big Falling Snow*, quotes 37, 95.

172 **"If lucky enough":** Ibid., quotes 6–7.

173 **"On the first day":** Ibid., quote 10.

174 **"white man's style":** Ibid., quotes 11, 12.

175 **Chilocco Indian School:** Ibid., quotes 15–16. For a history of the Chilocco Indian School, see K. Tsianina Lomawaima, *They Called it Prairie Light: The Story of the Chilocco Indian School* (Lincoln: University of Nebraska Press, 1995).

175 **"well educated":** Yava, *Big Falling Snow*, quotes 18–19.

177 **"Okay, then, go back":** Ibid., quotes 24–25.

178 **"the people of the Hopi villages":** Ibid., quote 26.

178 **"husbands and wives":** Ibid., quote 27.

178 **"it was because there were so many":** Ibid., quotes 28–29.

179 **"little mirrors reflecting":** Ibid., quotes 29–31.

180 **"according to the clans":** Ibid., quotes 33–34.

181 **"you can see that we aren't":** Ibid., quotes 34–35.

182 **"the actual year":** Courlander in ibid., 144, n. 6. See also Irving Panabale, *Big Standing Flower: The Life of Irving Panabale, an Arizona Tewa Indian* (Salt Lake City: University of Utah Press, 2001), ed. Robert A. Black, who notes that "The Tanos/Tewas were reported to be at First Mesa in 1701 and most likely were involved in the attack on Awatovi," xxiv.

Yava's reference to Awat'ovi being a "Laguna" village seems to mean that its founding clan, at least (Bow Clan) may have been Keresan speakers, since Laguna Pueblo itself, on the San Jose River just east of Grants, New Mexico, was not founded until 1697, by a mixed group of Cochiti, Santo Domingo, Cieneguilla, and Jemez (Towa) refugees from the punishments visited upon the 1696 rebels, who first took shelter with Acoma Keresans, then hived off (along with some Acomas) to found the new village of Laguna, or *Kawaik'a* (named for the old lake behind a beaver dam) in 1697. The Spanish established a small church as a *visita* of the Acoma Mission in 1707, when the population was 330 souls. The village grew rapidly, thanks to its location on the main east-west trail from the Spanish colony to Zuni and Hopi, and by 1782 exceeded Acoma in population. At that point Acoma was converted to a *visita* of the Laguna Mission. Florence Hawley Ellis, "Laguna Pueblo," in Alfonso Ortiz, ed., *Handbook of North American Indians: Southwest* (Washington, DC: Smithsonian Institution, 1979), 438–449; for the challenges to understanding the social mosaic at Hopi in the fourteenth century, see Bernardini, *Hopi Oral Tradition*, 160–178, quotes 161–162; Kelly Hayes-Gilpin, "All Roads Lead to Hopi," in C. Bonfiglioli et al., eds., *Las vías del noroeste, II: Propuesta para una perspectiva sistèmica e interdisciplinaria* (Mexico City: UNAM, Instituto de Investigaciones Antropológicas, 2008), 65–82; Andrew Duff, *Western Pueblo Identities: Regional Interaction, Migration, and Transformation* (Tucson: University of Arizona Press, 2002), 159–192, esp. 184.

183 **"Pax Chaco"**: Bernardini, *Hopi Oral Tradition*, quotes 173–175.

184 **"Kawaikas, Payupkis"**: Yava, *Big Falling Snow*, quotes 88–89.

184 **"get rid of the Castillas"**: Ibid., quotes 90–91.

185 **a bow Clan man"**: Ibid.

185 **"full of evil"**: Ibid., quotes 92–93.

187 **the Tobacco Clan leader:** The Tobacco Clan leader is identified as Ta'polo by Whiteley (drawing upon Lomatuway'ma et al., *Hopi Ruin Legends*, 406–409), and, although these accounts claim Ta'polo died as an act of self-sacrifice at Awat'ovi, Whiteley was taken into the Tobacco Clan house and shown the Taatawkyam (Kwan, or Singers Society) kiva at Walpi in 1995. Whiteley doesn't believe that Ta'polo could have held the office of *kikmongwi*, since that would have been reserved for Bow Clan (founding) members, nor the *kalatekmongwi* (War Chief), as that office more likely would be held by a member of the Badger, Reed/Eagle, or Coyote Clan. Thus he sees Ta'polo as probably the *tsa'kmongwi*, "advisor and formal

announcer for the Kikmongwi (also called Crier Chief)"; see also Harold Courlander, *Hopi Voices: Recollections, Traditions, and Naratives of the Hopi Indians* (Albuquerque: University of New Mexico Press, 1982), 57–60. Whiteley, "Re-imagining Awat'ovi," quote 154.

188 **"he moved into the newly established":** Yava, *Big Falling Snow,* quotes 93–95.

190 **"the Badger Clan":** For Francisco's clan identity, see Whiteley, "Re-imagining Awat'ovi," 154–155.

190 **If Francisco de Espeleta:** Ibid., 147–166; for Francisco de Espeleta as executioner of Padre Espeleta, see Espinosa, *Crusaders of the Rio Grande,* 348, n. 11.

191 **"professing a readiness":** Whiteley, *Deliberate Acts,* 19–20, quoting Bandelier 1889: 221–222; Brew, "Spaniards at Awatovi," *Franciscan Awatovi* (Declaration of Enríquez), May 1664, quotes 16, 17–18, 21.

192 **"not as subjects and vassals":** Hubert Howe Bancroft, *History of Arizona and New Mexico, 1530–1888,* vol. 17 (San Francisco: The History Co., 1889), quote 222.

192 **"all sorts of things":** Charles Wilson Hackett, *Historical Documents Relating to New Mexico, Nueva Vizcaya, and Approaches Thereto, to 1773* (Washington, DC: Carnegie Institution, 1937), 385–386; Ralph Emerson Twitchell, *The Spanish Archives of New Mexico* (Cedar Rapids, IA: Torch Press, 1914), 419, n. 422.

193 **"I myself have listened":** Yava quote from Courlander, *Hopi Voices,* in "Hopi Religion and the Missionaries," Southwest Crossroads website: http://southwestcrossroads.org/record.php?num=574 (accessed July 7, 2014).

194 **"young European man":** Montgomery, "Functional Analysis of the Franciscan Buildings," in *Franciscan Awatovi,* 178–179.

194 **"could have been accomplished":** Ibid., quotes 179–180. The author's notion that this could be the body of a "pious comrade" reburied by Spanish soldiers "on one of the several occasions when they were in the vicinity of Aguatubi during the *Reconquista*" seems far-fetched, given the clear presence of Hopi material culture with the body, and the bundled nature of the interment.

195 **rejection of all things Spanish:** Andrew Wiget, "Father Juan Greyrobe: Reconstructing Traditional Histories, and the Reliability and Validity of Uncorroborated Oral Tradition," *Ethnohistory* 43, no. 3 (1996): 459–482; *Franciscan Missions of the Southwest,* Issue 1 (Society for the Preservation of the Faith Among Indian Children, Franciscan Fathers at St. Michael's, Arizona, 1913), quotes 20–21; author's visit with the Yatsattie family, Halona Village, New Mexico, October 16, 2010.

CHAPTER 9: AT THE MOMENT OF THE YELLOW DAWN

197 **"Nowadays the Hopis":** Yava, *Big Falling Snow*, 95.

201 **the *wuwutcim* ceremony:** For the primacy and power of the *wuwutcim* (Wuwutsim), see Whiteley, *Deliberate Acts*, 235–236.

201 **"Test 31":** Watson Smith, *Prehistoric Kivas of Antelope Mesa, Northeastern Arizona* (Cambridge, MA: Papers of the Peabody Museum of Archaeology and Ethnology, Harvard University, 1972), vol. 39, no. 1, 70–75; note on deviation of T31 bench from norm, 115–116.

204 **"Test 22, Room 10":** Ibid., 67–70.

206 **Both kivas lay:** Ibid., 41–46.

206 **Were those "sorcerers' kivas"?:** William H. Walker, "Practice and Non-human Social Actors: The Afterlife Histories of Witches and Dogs in the American Southwest," in Barbara Mills and William H. Walker, *Memory Work: Archaeologies of Material Practices* (Santa Fe, NM: SAR Press, 2008), 137–157, quotes 142, 152.

207 **Of the 72 cases:** Walker, "Practice and Nonhuman Social Actors," 139.

208 **Kiva T31 was certainly:** For convento kivas, see James E. Ivey, "Convento Kivas in the Missions of New Mexico," *New Mexico Historical Review* 73, no. 2 (April 1998): 121–152; David M. Holtcamp, "When Is a Convento Kiva? A Post-Colonial-Critical Indigenous Critique of the Convento Kiva at Pecos National Historical Park" (M.A. thesis, University of New Mexico, 2013); Brew, *Franciscan Awatovi*, 95–99. Peter Whiteley also sees spiritual experimentation at the root of the Awat'ovi massacre, in his case, the use of peyote. See "Re-imagining Awat'ovi," 147–166.

209 **Other evidence points:** John Otis Brew, "The First Two Seasons at Awatovi," *American Antiquity* 3, no. 2 (1937): 122–137; Brew, Camp Journal, Awatovi, 1939, Manuscript, Peabody Museum, Harvard University; Brew, "Preliminary Report of the Peabody Museum Awatovi Expedition of 1937," *American Antiquity* 5, no. 2 (1939): 103–114; Brew, "Preliminary Report of the Peabody Museum Awatovi Expedition of 1939," *Plateau* 13, no. 3 (1941): 37–48; *Franciscan Awatovi*, 95–99, 178–181.

212 **Tiwa peoples of Sandia Pueblo:** Elizabeth A. Brandt, "Sandia Pueblo," in Alfonso Ortiz, ed., *Smithsonian Handbook of North American Indians: The Southwest* (Washington, DC: Smithsonian Institution, 1979), 345; and Joe S. Sando, "Jemez Pueblo," ibid., 422; for the dispute between Payupki and Chukubi, see Edward S. Curtis, "Why Payupki Was Abandoned," in *The North American Indian*, vol. 12, *The Hopi* (1922), 203–206.

214 **"adjudicate between those":** Whiteley, *Deliberate Acts*, 270.

215 **"of 17th century Hopi type"**: Brew, "The Excavations at Franciscan Awa-tovi," 88–91, 89.

215 **A second piece of construction:** Ibid., 91–92; Montgomery, "A Functional Analysis of the Franciscan Buildings," in *Franciscan Awatovi*, 229–238.

217 **"want to forget"**: Eric Polingyouma, "Awat'ovi, a Hopi History," in Davis, *Remembering Awatovi*, xv–xviii, quotes xv, xviii.

218 **Leigh J. Kuwanwisiwma:** Kuwanwisiwma, "Yupköyvi: The Hopi Story of Chaco Canyon," in David Grant Noble, *In Search of Chaco*, 41–47; Kuwan-wisiwma, Stewart B. Koyiyumptewa, and Anita Poleahla, "Pasiwvi: Place of Deliberations," in Christian E. Downum, ed., *Hisat'sinom: Ancient Peoples in a Land Without Water* (Santa Fe, NM: SAR Press, 2012), 7–9, quote 9.

219 **more than half are from burials:** Brew, *Franciscan Awatovi*, 95–99, esp. 97.

219 **Standard protocol would require:** Kuwanwisiwma, site visit, September 11, 2014; Davis, *Remembering Awatovi*, 189.

220 **we see Hopis grappling:** David M. Brugge, *The Navajo-Hopi Land Dispute*, (Albuquerque: University of New Mexico Press, 1999), 8; Brugge, letter to author, February 25, 2005, quote 2. Members of the Ye'ii clan, according to Brugge, told the trader William Beaver at the Sacred Mountain Trading Post that their Hopi "ancestors were so mad at the other villages that they no longer wanted to be Hopis," presumably after the fall of Awat'ovi. The late Maxwell Yazzie told Brugge that some of Awat'ovi's survivors fled "first to the south, then returned north past Antelope Mesa to Tachii' Spring on the southeastern portion of Black Mesa and finally went on to Canyon de Chelly," where they joined their new Navajo kinspeople.

221 **"become Christian"**: E. C. Parsons, "The Hopi Wöwöchim Ceremony in 1920," *American Anthropologist* v. 25 n. 2 (1923), 156–187, 171–172; History of the Saint Joseph Mission, http://www.stjosephmission.com/HISTORY.html.

BIBLIOGRAPHY

Adams, E. Charles. *The Origin and Development of the Pueblo Katsina Cult.* Tucson: University of Arizona Press, 1991.

Bancroft, Hubert Howe. *History of Arizona and New Mexico, 1530–1888.* Vol. 17. San Francisco: The History Co., 1889.

Benavides, Fray Alonso de. *Revised Memorial of 1634, with Numerous Supplementary Documents Annotated by F. W. Hodge, G. P. Hammond, and Agapito Rey.* Albuquerque: University of New Mexico Press, 1945.

Benedict, Ruth. *Patterns of Culture.* New York: Mariner Books, 2006 [1934].

Bernardini, Wesley. *Hopi Oral Tradition and the Archaeology of Identity.* Tucson: University of Arizona Press, 2005.

Billman, Brian R., Patricia M. Lambert, and Banks L. Leonard. "Cannibalism, Warfare, and Drought in the Mesa Verde Region During the Twelfth Century A.D." *American Antiquity* 65, no. 1 (2000): 145–178.

Black, Robert, trans. and ed. *Standing Flower: The Life of Irving Pabanale, the Arizona Tewa Indian.* Salt Lake City: University of Utah Press, 2001.

Boyer, Paul, and Stephen Nissenbaum. *Salem Possessed: The Social Origins of Witchcraft.* Cambridge: Harvard University Press, 1974.

Brandt, Elizabeth A. "Sandia Pueblo." In Alfonso Ortiz, ed., *Smithsonian Handbook of North American Indians: The Southwest.* Washington, DC: Smithsonian Institution, 1979.

Brew, John Otis. "The Excavation of Awatovi." In Marnie Gaede, ed., *Camera, Spade, and Pen: Inside View of Southwestern Archaeology.* Tucson: University of Arizona Press, 1980.

Brew, John Otis. "The First Two Seasons at Awatovi." In *American Antiquity* 3, no. 2 (1937): 122–137.

Brew, John Otis. "The History of Awatovi." In Ross Gordon Montgomery, Watson Smith, and John Otis Brew, *Franciscan Awatovi*. Cambridge: Reports of the Awatovi Expedition Peabody Museum, Harvard University, Report #3, 1949.

Brew, John Otis. "Hopi Prehistory and History to 1850." In Alfonso Ortiz, ed., *Handbook of North American Indians*. Vol. 9, *Southwest*, 103–109. Washington, DC: Smithsonian Institution, 1979.

Brew, John Otis. "Preliminary Report of the Peabody Museum Awatovi Expedition of 1939." *Plateau* 13, no. 3 (1941): 37–48.

Brooks, James F. *Captives & Cousins: Slavery, Kinship, and Community in the Southwest Borderlands*. Chapel Hill: University of North Carolina Press, 2002.

Brooks, James F. "Violence and Renewal in the American Southwest." *Ethnohistory* 49, no. 1 (Spring 2002): 205–218.

Brown, Tracy L. *Pueblo Indians and Spanish Colonial Authority in Eighteenth-Century New Mexico*. Tucson: University of Arizona Press, 2013.

Brugge, David M. *The Navajo-Hopi Land Dispute*. Albuquerque: University of New Mexico Press, 1999.

Calloway, Colin G. *One Vast Winter Count: The Native American West Before Lewis and Clark*. Norman: University of Oklahoma Press, 2003.

Chávez, Fray Angélico. "Nuestra Señora de la Macana." *New Mexico Historical Review* 34 (1959): 81–100.

Clements, William M. "'A Continual Beginning, and Then an Ending, and Then a Beginning Again': Hopi Apocalypticism in the New Age." *Journal of the Southwest* 46, no. 4 (2004): 643–660.

Clemmer, Richard O. "'Then Will You Rise and Strike My Head from My Neck': Hopi Prophecy and the Discourse of Empowerment." *American Indian Quarterly* 19, no. 1 (1995): 31–73.

Colton, Harold, and Edmund Nequatewa. "The Ladder Dance: Two Traditions of an Extinct Hopi Ceremonial." *Museum of Northern Arizona Notes* 5, no. 2 (1932): 5–12.

Cordell, Linda S., and Maxine E. McBrinn. *Archaeology of the Southwest*, 3rd ed. Walnut Creek, CA: Left Coast Press, 2012.

Courlander, Harold. *The Fourth World of the Hopis: The Epic Story of the Hopi Indians as Preserved in their Legends and Traditions*. New York: Crown Publishers, 1971.

Courlander, Harold. *Hopi Voices: Recollections, Traditions, and Narratives of the Hopi Indians*. Albuquerque: University of New Mexico Press, 1982.

Cushing, Frank Hamilton. "Killing Sorcerers: Remarkable Customs of the Zuni Indians in New Mexico." Reprinted in Jesse Green, ed., *Cushing at Zuni: The*

Correspondence and Journals of Frank Hamilton Cushing, 1879–1884. Albuquerque: University of New Mexico Press, 1990.

Darling, J. Andrew. "Mass Inhumation and the Execution of Witches in the American Southwest." *American Anthropologist* 100, no. 3 (1998): 732–752.

Daughters, Anton. "'Grace Offenses Worthy of Great Punishment': The Enslavement of Juan Suñi, 1659." *Journal of the Southwest* 54, no. 3 (Autumn 2012): 437–452.

Davis, Hester A. *Remembering Awatovi: The Story of an Archaeological Expedition in Northern Arizona, 1935–1939.* Cambridge, MA: Peabody Museum Monographs, no. 10. Copyright 2008 by the President and Fellows of Harvard College.

Demos, John. *Entertaining Satan: Witchcraft and the Culture of Early New England.* Oxford: Oxford University Press, updated edition 2004).

Dozier, Edward P. "Rio Grande Pueblos." In Edward H. Spicer, ed., *Perspectives in American Indian Culture Change,* 116–117. Chicago: University of Chicago Press, 1961.

Dozier, Edward. "The Role of the Hopi-Tewa Migration Legend in Reinforcing Cultural Patterns and Prescribing Social Behavior." *Journal of American Folklore* 69, no. 272 (April–June 1956): 176–180.

Duff, Andrew. *Western Pueblo Identities: Regional Interaction, Migration, and Transformation.* Tucson: University of Arizona Press, 2002.

Dungoske, Kurt E., and Cindy Dungoske. "History in Stone: Evaluating Spanish Conversion Efforts Through Hopi Rock Art," in Robert Preucel, ed., *Archaeologies of the Pueblo Revolt: Identity, Meaning, and Renewal in the Pueblo World,* 114–131. Albuquerque: University of New Mexico Press, 2007.

Edgerton, Samuel Y. *Theaters of Conversion: Religious Architecture and Indian Artisans in Colonial Mexico.* Albuquerque: University of New Mexico Press, 2001.

Ellis, Florence Hawley. "Laguna Pueblo." In Alfonso Ortiz, ed., *Handbook of North American Indians: Southwest,* 438–449. Washington, DC: Smithsonian Institution, 1979.

Ellis, Florence Hawley. "Patterns of Aggression and the War Cult in the Southwestern Pueblos," *Southwestern Journal of Anthropology* 7, no. 2 (Summer 1951): 177–201.

Espinosa, J. Manuel, ed. and trans. *Crusaders of the Rio Grande: The Story of Don Diego de Vargas and the Reconquest and Refounding of New Mexico.* Chicago: Institute of Jesuit History, 1942.

Ferguson, T. J., and Micah Lomaomvaya. *Hoopoq'yaqam niqw Wukoskyai (Those Who Went to the Northeast and Tonto Basin): Hopi-Salado Cultural Affiliation Study.* Kykotsmovi, AZ: Hopi Cultural Preservation Office, 1999.

Ferguson, T. J., Kurt E. Dongoske, and Leigh J. Kuwanwisiwma. "Hopi Perspectives on Southwest Mortuary Studies." In Douglas R. Mitchell and Judy

L. Brunson-Hadley, eds., *Ancient Burial Practices in the American Southwest: Physical Anthropology and Native American Perspectives*, 9–26. Albuquerque: University of New Mexico Press, 2001.

Fewkes, Jesse Walter. "A-Wa'-To-Bi: An Archaeological Verification of a Tusayan Legend." *American Anthropologist* 6 (October 1893).

Fewkes, Jesse Walter. "The Alosaka Cult of the Hopi Indians." *American Anthropologist* 1, no. 3 (1899).

Flint, Lawrence Lloyd. "The Western Tewa Transformation: A Theory in Development." M.A. thesis, American University, 1975.

Fowler, Don D. *A Laboratory for Anthropology: Science and Romanticism in the American Southwest, 1846–1930.* Salt Lake City: University of Utah Press, 2000.

Fowles, Severin. *An Archaeology of Doings: Secularism and the Study of Pueblo Religion.* Santa Fe, NM: SAR Press, 2013.

Franciscan Fathers. *Franciscan Missions of the Southwest*, Issue 1. Society for the Preservation of the Faith Among Indian Children, Franciscan Fathers at St. Michael's, Arizona, 1913.

Freese, Alison R. "Send in the Clowns: An Ethnohistorical Analysis of the Sacred Clowns' Role in Cultural Boundary Maintenance Among the Pueblo Indians." Ph.D. diss., American Studies Department, University of New Mexico, 1991.

Geschiere, Peter. *The Modernity of Witchcraft.* Charlottesville: University of Virginia Press, 1997.

Gilbert, Matthew Sakiestewa. "Hopi Footraces and American Marathon, 1912–1930." *American Quarterly* 62, no. 1 (March 2010): 77–101.

Gleach, Frederick Wright. *Powhatan's World and Colonial Virginia: A Conflict of Cultures.* Lincoln: University of Nebraska Press, 1997.

Glenn, Edna, John R. Wunder, Willard Hughes, and C. L. Martin. *Hopi Nation: Essays on Indigenous Art, Culture, History, and Law.* Zea E-Books. Book 11. http://digitalcommons.unl.edu/zeabook/11.

Hackett, Charles W. *Historical Documents Relating to New Mexico, Nueva Vizcaya, and Approaches Thereto, to 1773.* Washington DC: Carnegie Institution, 1937.

Hammond, George Peter, and Agapito Rey. *Expedition into New Mexico by Antonio de Espejo, 1582–1583, as Revealed in the Journals of Diego Pérez de Luján, a Member of the Party.* Los Angeles: The Quivira Society Publications, 1929.

Harrington, J. P. "Old Indian Geographic Names Around Santa Fe, New Mexico." *American Anthropologist* 22, no. 4 (October–December 1920).

Hass, Jonathan, and Winifred Creamer. *Stress and Warfare Among the Kayenta Anasazi in the Thirteenth Century.* Chicago: Field Museum of Natural History, 1993.

Hays, Kelly Ann. "Kachina Depictions on Prehistoric Pueblo Pottery." In Schaafsma, ed., *Kachinas in the Pueblo World*, 47–62.

Hays-Gilpin, Kelley. "All Roads Lead to Hopi." In *Las vías del noroeste. II: Propuesta para una perspectiva sistémica e interdisciplinaria*. Mexico City: UNAM, Instituto de Investigaciones Antropológicas, 2008.

Hecht, Robert. "Oliver Lafarge, John Collier, and the Hopi Constitution of 1936." *Journal of Arizona History* 26, no. 2 (Summer 1985): 145–162.

Hegmon, Michelle, Scott G. Ortman, and Jeanette L. Mobley-Tanaka. "Women, Men, and the Organization of Space." In Patricia L. Crown, ed., *Women & Men in the Prehispanic Southwest*, 43–90. Santa Fe, NM: SAR Press, 2001.

Hodge, Frederick Web, George Hammond, and Agapito Rey, eds. and trans. *Fray Alonso de Benavides' Revised Memorial of 1634*. Albuquerque: University of New Mexico Press, 1945.

Holtcamp, David M. "When Is a Convento Kiva? A Postcolonial-Critical Indigenous Critique of the Convento Kiva at Pecos National Historical Park." M.A. thesis, University of New Mexico, 2013.

Ivey, James E. "Convento Kivas in the Missions of New Mexico." *New Mexico Historical Review* (April 1998): 121–152.

Ivey, James E. *The Spanish Colonial Architecture of Pecos Pueblo, New Mexico: Archaeological Excavations and Architectural History of the Spanish Colonial Churches and Related Buildings at Pecos National Historical Park, 1617–1995*. Intermountain Region, NPS: Professional Paper No. 59, 2005.

Jacobs, Margaret. *Engendered Encounters: Feminism and Pueblo Cultures, 1879–1934*. Albuquerque: University of New Mexico Press, 1999.

Kabotie, Michael (Lomawywesa). *Migration Tears: Poems About Transitions*. Los Angeles: American Indian Studies Center, UCLA, 1987.

Kantner, John. *Ancient Puebloan Southwest*. Cambridge: Cambridge University Press, 2004.

Kessell, John. *Blood on the Boulders: The Journals of don Diego de Vargas, 1694–1697*. Edited by John L. Kessell, Rick Hendricks, and Meredith Dodge. Albuquerque: University of New Mexico Press, 1998.

Kessell, John. *Pueblos, Spaniards, and the Kingdom of New Mexico*. Norman: University of Oklahoma Press, 2008.

Kroskrity, Paul V. *Language, History, and Identity: Ethnolinguistic Studies of the Arizona Tewa*. Tucson: University of Arizona Press, 1993.

Kuckelman, Kristen A. "Bioarchaeological Signatures of Strife in Terminal Pueblo III Settlements in the Northern San Juan." AAPA paper, 2010. Crow Canyon Research Reports. http://www.crowcanyon.org/ResearchReports/CastleRock/Text/crpw_contentsvolume.asp.

Kuwanwisiwma, Leigh J., Stewart B. Koyiyumptewa, and Anita Poleahla. "Pasi-wvi: Place of Deliberations." In Christian E. Downum, ed., *Hisat'sinom: Ancient Peoples in a Land Without Water*, 7–9. Santa Fe, NM: SAR Press, 2012.

LeBlanc, Steven A. *Prehistoric Warfare in the American Southwest*. Salt Lake City: University of Utah Press, 1999.

LeBlanc, Steven A. "Regional Interaction and Warfare in the Late Prehistoric Southwest." In Michelle Hegmon, ed., *The Archaeology of Regional Interaction: Religion, Warfare, and Exchange Across the American Southwest and Beyond*, 41–70. Boulder: University Press of Colorado, 2000.

Lekson, Stephen H. ed., *The Archaeology of Chaco Canyon: An Eleventh-Century Pueblo Regional Center*. Santa Fe, NM: SAR Press, 2006.

Lekson, Stephen H. *Chaco Meridian: Centers of Political Power in the Ancient Southwest*. Lanham, MD: Rowman AltaMira, 1999.

Lekson, Stephen H. *A History of the Ancient Southwest*. Santa Fe, NM: SAR Press, 2009.

Levy, Jerrold E. *Orayvi Revisited: Social Stratification in an "Egalitarian" Society*. Santa Fe, NM: SAR Press, 1992.

Liebmann, Matthew. "At the Mouth of the Wolf: The Archaeology of Seventeenth-Century Franciscans in the Jemez Valley of New Mexico." In Timothy J. Johnson and Gert Melville, eds., *Franciscan Evangelization in the Spanish Borderlands II*. Oceanside, CA: American Academy of Franciscan History, 2015.

Liebmann, Matthew. *Revolt: An Archaeological History of Pueblo Resistance and Revitalization in 17th Century New Mexico*. Tucson: University of Arizona Press, 2012.

Lippard, Lucy. *Down Country: The Tano of the Galisteo Basin, 1250–1782*. Santa Fe: Museum of New Mexico Press, 2010.

Lomatumay'ma, Michael, Lorena Lomatumay'ma, and Sidney Namingha, Jr. *Hopi Ruin Legends: Kiqotutuwutsi*. Collected, translated, and edited by Ekkehart Malotki. Lincoln: University of Nebraska Press, 1993

Lomatumay'ma, Michael, Lorena Lomatumay'ma, and Sidney Namingha, Jr. *Hopi Tales of Destruction*. Collected, translated, and edited by Ekkehart Malotki. Lincoln: University of Nebraska Press, 2002.

Lomawaima, K. Tsianina. *They Called It Prairie Light: The Story of the Chilocco Indian School*. Lincoln: University of Nebraska Press, 1995.

Lyons, Patrick D. *Ancestral Hopi Migrations*. Anthropological Papers of the University of Arizona, no. 68. Tucson: University of Arizona Press, 2003.

Mahoney, Nancy M. "Redefining the Scale of Chacoan Communities." In John Kantner and Nancy M. Mahoney, eds., *Great House Communities Across the Chacoan Landscape*, 19–27. Anthropological Papers of the University of Arizona, no. 64. Tucson: University of Arizona Press, 2000.

Martin, Debra. "Ripped Flesh and Torn Souls." In Catherine Cameron, ed.,

Invisible Citizens: Captives and Their Consequences. Salt Lake City: University of Utah Press, 2008.

Merrill, William L. "Indigenous Societies, Missions, and the Colonial System in Northern New Spain." In Clara Bargellini and Michael K. Komanecky, eds., *The Arts of the Missions of Northern New Spain,* 122–153. Mexico City: Colegio de San Ildefonso, 2009.

Mills, Barbara J., and William H. Walker. *Memory Work: Archaeologies of Material Practices.* Santa Fe, NM: SAR Press, 2008.

Mitchell, Stephen. "Introduction," *The Iliad/Homer.* New York: Free Press, 2012.

Montgomery, Ross Gordon, Watson Smith, and John Otis Brew. *Franciscan Awatovi: The Excavation and Conjectural Reconstruction of a 17th-Century Spanish Mission Establishment at a Hopi Indian Town in Northeastern Arizona.* Papers of the Peabody Museum of American Archaeology and Ethnology. Vol. XXXVI. Copyright 1949 by the President and Fellows of Harvard College.

Nequatewa, Edmund. "Truth of a Hopi and Other Clan Stories of Shungopovi," *Museum of Northern Arizona Bulletin* 8 (1936): 70–94. Edited by Mary-Russell Ferrel Colton. Flagstaff: Northern Arizona Society of Science and Art.

Noble, David Grant. *In Search of Chaco: New Approaches to an Archaeological Enigma.* Santa Fe, NM: SAR Press, 2004.

Panabale, Irving. *Big Standing Flower: The Life of Irving Panabale, an Arizona Tewa Indian.* Salt Lake City: University of Utah Press, 2001.

Parsons, E. C. "Early Relations Between Hopi and Keres." *American Anthropologist* 38, no. 4 (1936): 554–560.

Parsons, Elsie Clews. "The Hopi Wöwöchim Ceremony in 1920." *American Anthropologist* 25, no. 2 (1923): 156–187.

Peckham, Stewart, "Postulated Movements of the Tano or Southern Tewa, A.D. 1300–1700." *Archaeological Society of New Mexico Papers,* no. 16 (1990).

Phillips, David A., Jr., Christine S. Vanpool, and Todd L. Vanpool. "The Horned Serpent in the North American Southwest." In David A. Phillips, Jr., Christine S. Vanpool, and Todd L. Vanpool, eds., *Religion in the Puebloan Southwest,* 17–30. Lanham, MD: AltaMira Press, 2006.

Polingyouma, Eric. "Awat'ovi, A Hopi History." In Hester A. Davis, *Remembering Awatovi: The Story of an Archaeological Expedition in Northern Arizona, 1935–1939,* xv–xviii. Cambridge, MA: Peabody Museum Monographs, no. 10. Copyright 2008 by the President and Fellows of Harvard College.

Potter, James A., and Jason P. Chuipka. "Perimortem Mutilation of Human Remains in an Early Village in the American Southwest: A Case of Ethnic Violence." *Journal of Anthropological Archaeology* 29 (2010): 507–523.

Prucha, Francis Paul. *The Great Father: The United States Government and American Indians.* Lincoln: University of Nebraska Press, 1986.

Raynor, T. E. "Tucson Priest Says First Mass Since 1700 in Ruins of Old Spanish Mission." *Tucson Daily Citizen,* September 9, 1937.

Reff, Daniel T. "Contextualizing Missionary Discourse: The Benavides Memorials of 1630 and 1634." *Journal of Anthropological Research* 50 (1994): 51–67.

Remensnyder, Amy G. *La Conquistadora: The Virgin Mary at War and Peace in the Old and New Worlds.* Oxford and New York: Oxford University Press, 2014.

Restall, Matthew. *Seven Myths of the Spanish Conquest.* Oxford: Oxford University Press, 2004.

Sando, Joe S. "Jemez Pueblo." In Alfonso Ortiz, ed., *Smithsonian Handbook of North American Indians: The Southwest,* 418–429. Washington, DC: Smithsonian Institution, 1979.

Sandweiss, Martha A. "The Necessity for Ruins: Photography and Archaeology in the American Southwest." In May Castleberry, ed., *The New World's Old World: Photographic Views of Ancient America.* Albuquerque: University of New Mexico Press, 2003.

Schaafsma, Polly. *Kachinas in the Pueblo World.* Albuquerque: University of New Mexico Press, 1994.

Schaafsma, Polly. *Warrior, Star, and Shield: Imagery and Ideology of Pueblo Warfare.* Santa Fe, NM: Western Edge Press, 2000.

Sheridan, Thomas E., Stewart B. Koyiyumptewa, Anton Daughters, Dale S. Brenneman, T. J. Ferguson, Leigh Kuwanwisiwma, and LeeWayne Lomayestewa, eds., *Moquis and Kastiilam: Hopis, Spaniards, and the Trauma of History.* Tucson: University of Arizona Press, 2015.

Smith, Watson. *Prehistoric Kivas of Antelope Mesa, Northeastern Arizona.* Papers of the Peabody Museum of Archaeology and Ethnology, vol. 39, no. 1. Cambridge, MA: Harvard University, 1972.

Stewart, Pamela J., and Andrew Strathern. *Witchcraft, Sorcery, Rumors, and Gossip.* Cambridge: Cambridge University Press, 2003.

Swadesh, Frances Leon. "Structure of Spanish-Indian Relations in New Mexico." In Paul M. Kutsche, ed., *The Survival of Spanish American Villages,* 53–61. Colorado Springs: Center for Southwestern Studies, 1979.

Talayesva, Don C. *Sun Chief: The Autobiography of a Hopi Indian.* 2nd ed. Edited by Leo W. Simmons, forewords by Matthew Sakiestewa Gilbert and Robert V. Hine. New Haven, CT: Yale University Press, 2013.

Tar, Jane. "The Fame and Trials of Luisa de la Ascensión, the Nun of Carrión (1565–1636)." Paper presented at the Midwest Modern Language Association Convention, Minneapolis, 2008.

Titiev, Mischa. *Old Oraibi: A Study of the Hopi Indians of Third Mesa.* Papers of the Peabody Museum of American Archaeology and Ethnology, vol. 1, no. 2. Cambridge, MA: Harvard University, 1944.

Turner, Christy G., and Jacqueline Turner. *Man Corn: Cannibalism and Violence in the Prehistoric American Southwest.* Salt Lake City: University of Utah Press, 1998.

Twitchell, Ralph Emerson. *The Spanish Archives of New Mexico.* Cedar Rapids, IA: Torch Press, 1914.

Voth, Henry R. *The Traditions of the Hopi.* Field Columbian Museum 96, Anthropological Papers 8 (1905).

Walker, William H. "Where are the Witches of Prehistory?" *Journal of Archaeological Method and Theory* 5, no. 3 (1998): 245–308.

Ware, John, and Eric Blinman. "The Origin and Spread of Pueblo Ritual Sodalities." In Michele Hegmon, ed., *The Archaeology of Regional Interaction: Religion, Warfare, and Exchange Across the American Southwest and Beyond,* 381–410. Boulder: University Press of Colorado, 2000.

Weber, David. *The Spanish Frontier in North America.* New Haven, CT: Yale University Press, 1992.

West, M. L. *The Making of the "Iliad": Disquisition and Analytical Commentary.* Oxford: Oxford University Press, 2011.

Whalen, Brett Edward. *Dominion of God: Christendom and Apocalypse in the Middle Ages.* Cambridge, MA: Harvard University Press, 2009.

Whiteley, Peter. *Deliberate Acts: Changing Hopi Culture Through the Oraibi Split.* Tucson: University of Arizona Press 1988.

Whiteley, Peter. "Re-Imagining Awat'ovi." In Robert Preucel, ed., *Archaeologies of the Pueblo Revolt: Identity, Meaning, and Renewal in the Pueblo World,* 147–166. Albuquerque: University of New Mexico Press, 2007.

Wiget, Andrew O. "Truth and the Hopi: An Historiographic Study of the Documented Oral Tradition Concerning the Coming of the Spanish." *Ethnohistory* 29, no. 3 (1982): 181–199.

Wilson, John P. "Awatovi—More Light on a Legend." *Plateau* 44, no. 2 (Winter 1972): 125–130.

Winship, George Parker. *The Coronado Expedition, 1540–1542.* Smithsonian Institution, Fourteenth Annual Report of the Bureau of American Ethnology, Part II. Washington, DC: Government Printing Office, 1896.

Yava, Albert. *Big Falling Snow: A Tewa-Hopi Indian's Life and Times and the History and Traditions of His People.* Edited and annotated by Harold Courlander. Albuquerque: University of New Mexico Press, 1978.

IMAGE CREDITS

Page 3:   Courtesy of James F. Brooks.
Page 13:   Map by Ezra Zeitler.
Page 18:   LC-USZ62-69640. Courtesy of Library of Congress, Washington, DC.
Page 20:   NAA INV 10057500. Courtesy of National Portrait Gallery, Smithsonian Institution, Washington, DC.
Page 21:   Ref. # NPG.95.23, Albumen silver print. Black, James Wallace (1825–1896). Courtesy of National Portrait Gallery, Smithsonian Institution, Washington, DC.
Page 26:   Jesse W. Fewkes, "A-WA'-TO-BI: An Archeological Verification of a Tusayan Legend," *American Anthropologist* 6, no. 4 (October 1893): 370.
Page 31:   Courtesy of National Anthropological Archives, Smithsonian Institution, Washington, DC.
Page 33:   Courtesy of John Kantner.
Page 36:   Courtesy of Bureau of Land Management, Department of the Interior.
Page 40:   Original in "My Adventures in Zuni" by Frank Hamilton Cushing, in *The Century* 26 (1882): 44.
Page 63:   © President and Fellows of Harvard College, Peabody Museum of Archaeology and Ethnology, PM# 39-97-10/77546 (digital file #98520121).
Page 65:   Courtesy of Palace of the Governors, Santa Fe, NM.
Page 72:   Courtesy of Fray Angelico Chavez History Library, Museum of New Mexico, Santa Fe.

Page 85: Photo by James Mooney. Courtesy of National Anthropological Archives, Smithsonian Institution, Washington, DC.

Page 86: Map by Ezra Zeitler.

Page 89: Map by Ezra Zeitler.

Page 95: © President and Fellows of Harvard College, Peabody Museum of Archaeology and Ethnology, PM# 2014.1.11.5.1 (digital file #96630014).

Page 97: © President and Fellows of Harvard College, Peabody Museum of Archaeology and Ethnology, PM# 2014.1.11.13.2 (digital file #99090080).

Page 99: © President and Fellows of Harvard College, Peabody Museum of Archaeology and Ethnology, PM# 2014.1.11.12.1 (digital file #96630016).

Page 102: © President and Fellows of Harvard College, Peabody Museum of Archaeology and Ethnology, PM# 2004.1.123.1.20 (digital file # 98500061).

Page 122: Courtesy of Jason S. Ordaz.

Page 129: ART21688, Smithsonian American Art Museum, Washington, DC/Art Resource, Inc.

Page 156: Map by Ezra Zeitler.

Page 165: © President and Fellows of Harvard College, Peabody Museum of Archaeology and Ethnology, PM# 39-97-10/21738 (digital file #60740778).

Page 200: © President and Fellows of Harvard College, Peabody Museum of Archaeology and Ethnology, PM# 2004.1.301.1 (digital file #98350013).

Page 204: Adapted from Figure 44 in Watson Smith, "Prehistoric Kivas of Antelope Mesa, Northeastern Arizona," *Papers of the Peabody Museum of Archaeology and Ethnology*, vol. 39, no. 1. Copyright 1972 by the President and Fellows of Harvard College.

INDEX

Page numbers in *italics* refer to illustrations.